WALT WHITMAN AND THE MAKING
OF JEWISH AMERICAN POETRY

IOWA WHITMAN SERIES

Ed Folsom, series editor

WALT WHITMAN AND THE MAKING OF JEWISH AMERICAN POETRY

Dara Barnat

University of Iowa Press, Iowa City

University of Iowa Press, Iowa City 52242
Copyright © 2023 by the University of Iowa Press
uipress.uiowa.edu
Printed in the United States of America

Design by Ashley Muehlbauer

No part of this book may be reproduced or used in any form or by
any means without permission in writing from the publisher. All
reasonable steps have been taken to contact copyright holders of
material used in this book. The publisher would be pleased to make
suitable arrangements with any whom it has not been possible to reach.

Printed on acid-free paper

Charles Reznikoff, excerpts from *The Poems of Charles
Reznikoff: 1918–1975*, edited by Seamus Cooney. Copyright ©
2005 by The Estate of Charles Reznikoff. Reprinted with the
permission of The Permissions Company, LLC on behalf of Black
Sparrow / David R. Godine, Publisher, Inc., godine.com.

A version of chapter 3 appears in *Insane Devotion:
On the Writing of Gerald Stern*, edited by Mihaela
Moscaliuc (Trinity University Press, 2016).

Library of Congress Cataloging-in-Publication Data
Names: Barnat, Dara, author.
Title: Walt Whitman and the Making of Jewish American Poetry /
Dara Barnat.
Identifiers: LCCN 2022045059 (print) | LCCN 2022045060 (ebook) |
ISBN 9781609389079 (paperback; acid-free paper) |
ISBN 9781609389086 (ebook)
Subjects: LCSH: Whitman, Walt, 1819–1892—Criticism and interpre-
tation. | Whitman, Walt, 1819–1892—Influence. | American poetry—
Jewish authors—History and criticism. | LCGFT: Literary criticism.
Classification: LCC PS3238.B33 2023 (print) | LCC PS3238 (ebook) |
DDC 811/.3—dc23/eng/20230103
LC record available at https://lccn.loc.gov/2022045059
LC ebook record available at https://lccn.loc.gov/2022045060

CONTENTS

INTRODUCTION Walt Whitman and American
Jewry: A Holy Exchange 1

ONE Charles Reznikoff, the Jewish Objectivist Poets,
and Walt Whitman 32

TWO Whitman versus High Modernists: On Karl
Shapiro and Kenneth Koch. 53

THREE Whitman's Poetics of Witness: Muriel
Rukeyser, Allen Ginsberg, and Gerald Stern 77

FOUR Jewish American Women Poets Respond
to Walt Whitman: Adrienne Rich, Alicia Ostriker, and
Marge Piercy. 108

CONCLUSION The Enduring Jewish American
Walt Whitman 139

ACKNOWLEDGMENTS 145

NOTES 149

WORKS CITED 175

INDEX 193

But in Israel, great interest was aroused by the poetry of Walt Whitman who, a century ago, sang "the song of America" out of a feeling of the absolute holiness of the completely secular. Whitman is an outstanding figure in a movement which has been accumulating spokesmen in the past three generations. These visionaries have claimed that mystical experience may well continue to flourish among men, since it is a basic human experience, rooted in the very nature of mankind.

—GERSHOM G. SCHOLEM, "Reflections on the Possibility of Jewish Mysticism in Our Time"

WALT WHITMAN AND THE MAKING OF JEWISH AMERICAN POETRY

INTRODUCTION

Walt Whitman and American Jewry: A Holy Exchange

In an early section of "Song of Myself," Walt Whitman declares and delights in an American selfhood—having been born "here" in America, with a lineage stretching back many generations: "My tongue, every atom of my blood, form'd from this soil, this air / Born here of parents born here from parents the same, and their parents the same" (29).[1] How does Whitman, a non-Jewish, American-born poet, become so instrumental in the tradition of Jewish American poetry, especially for poets whose parents, and often they themselves, were not "born here" on "this soil"?[2] References to Jewish people in *Leaves of Grass* do not reveal much about Whitman's ideas of nineteenth-century practices of Jewry in America or elsewhere. There are two relatively minor references to Jewish figures in the 1891–1892 last (so-called deathbed) edition of *Leaves of Grass*, in the poems "Salut au Monde!" and "Song of the Answerer." In the former, Whitman celebrates Jewish people around the world, "waiting in all lands for your Messiah!" (119). In the latter, a Jewish figure is one of the personas that the "Answerer" meets: "A Jew to the Jew he seems, a Russ to the Russ" (136).[3] These instances depict Jewish people mostly as a far-off, distant Other, waiting "in all lands" but not necessarily in Whitman's own America.

"Doings at the Synagogue," from March 29, 1842, a journalistic account by Whitman of "the Jews' synagogue in Crosby Street,"[4] is another source that articulates perceptions by Whitman of Jewish immigrants in New York. The beginning of this account, by and large, echoes the sentiments found in

2 INTRODUCTION

the poems from "Song of Myself," where Jewish people holding a service in a synagogue are depicted as practicing unfamiliar rituals and speaking in an odd tongue. One finds Whitman as a journalist rather perplexed by the "scene" of these traditions being enacted, with prayers in Hebrew; Whitman observes, "It may perhaps be well to say here, that as we had no one to explain to us what we saw, and as the whole scene from beginning to end resembled nothing that we had ever seen before, our relation professes to give merely the scene as it appears to the eyes of an utter stranger." In Whitman's piece, the services are described as contrived, almost staged, like a type of theatre: "After the performance had continued for some time . . . some of the Jews went up to the semicircular panel work before mentioned, unlocked it, and opened the doors." When the rabbi (or "priest," as Whitman writes) opens the ark to display the Torah, "utter[ing] a kind of chant," Whitman employs the image of "large sugar loaves" to describe the sacred scrolls (83). Thus, Jewish people in America end up being portrayed mostly as foreign and Other by Whitman. In such instances in Whitman's poetry and prose, Jewish people are depicted as stereotypes, and a marginal group at that, within the majority culture of America.[5]

However, in a passage toward the end of "Doings at the Synagogue," Whitman presents a more nuanced depiction of the service, where he writes of an appreciation of the history of these Jewish rituals, with the experience resonating as "holy":

> Of course, to our perceptions, the whole affair had much the aspect of an unintelligible mummery. Still, we could not divest ourselves of the thought that we were amid the people of ancient Jewry; the people who had kept themselves apart from the contagion of the world, and adhered strictly to the customs, and observances, and laws of their forefathers. . . . We were in a holy city. (83–84)

Together with Whitman's confusion, one detects a sense of respect and awe, a glimpse of spiritual connectedness. The word "holy" that Whitman uses to define the synagogue (the "holy city"), and the overall mood of holiness, evokes language that Gershom Scholem, the eminent Jewish philosopher, would use, around one hundred years later, to describe Whitman himself: "A century ago [Whitman] sang 'the song of America' out of a feeling of the absolute holiness of the completely secular . . . [offering] the possibility of mysticism in [a] non-traditional form" (52). In Scholem's essay "Reflections on the Possibility of Jewish

Mysticism in Our Time," a text that also serves as the epigraph for this book, he locates Whitman as a bridge between the sacred and the secular for Jewish people, gesturing to Whitman's later reception among Jewish philosophers, critics, poets, and writers. At this point of exploring the foundations of the Whitman–Jewish relationship, the juxtaposition of Whitman's and Scholem's "holiness" shows an early mutuality between Whitman and Jewish people in America. It is Whitman who writes of discovering a sense of holiness in the Jewish American experience, not only Jewish Americans who would come to find holiness in the writing of Whitman. Such a traversing of cultural, religious, and social boundaries in America is precisely what engenders the intersections of Jewish American poets and the non-Jewish poet Whitman.

In the preface to the first edition of *Leaves of Grass*, Whitman claimed that "the greatest poet" was a prophet or "seer" (*Whitman: Poetry and Prose* 9–10), though whether Whitman could have predicted that his poetry would become such an instrumental foundation for English-language and Yiddish-language Jewish American poetry in America, or the nuanced ways in which his poetics would be enfolded into this tradition, is an impossibility. This phenomenon includes, but goes beyond, the most famous case of a Jewish American poet appropriating Whitman: that of the American Beat poet Allen Ginsberg. Part of what this project seeks to illustrate is that far from Ginsberg alone, numerous Jewish poets in America, well beyond the ones discussed in this book, upon encountering Whitman, have responded to Whitman and even adopted his poetics and ethos into their own.

With Whitman such a crucial precursor for so many Jewish American poets, selecting the poets to feature in this study, who are thus presented as emblematic of how Whitman has been received for more than two centuries, is no simple task. The process of selecting poets to include, and by extension to exclude, has been somewhat vexed. From the outset, I wish to state that the objective of this book is not to provide an encyclopedic account of every poet whose work displays engagement with Whitman—an endeavor whose results would likely be partial and reductive. What I am offering is one poetic and cultural narrative, which I would argue is important for a fuller understanding of how Whitman's paradigmatic poetic legacy has been integrated into the tradition of Jewish American poetry, often around the milieu of High Modernism and Ezra Pound, a sense of exclusion from the majority, non-Jewish culture of America, and a desire to endorse a more democratic poetics. There is a Whitmanian

4 INTRODUCTION

multitude of alternate methods, approaches, frameworks, and lenses through which to analyze Whitman in a Jewish American poetic context.

By focusing on representative case studies of mostly twentieth- and twenty-first-century poets, in whose writing Whitman is an evident intertext, this study invites readers to consider these and many other adoptions of Whitman by Jewish poets, which exist in innumerable variations in Jewish American poetry, literature, and criticism. Fundamentally, this project hopes to contribute to this arena of investigation rather than offer a set delineation of Whitman's critical reception within the multifaceted, complex, constantly evolving tradition of Jewish poetry in America. In the poet Yehoshua November's foreword to *101 Jewish Poems for the Third Millennium*, writing about the complexities of defining what in fact constitutes a Jewish poem, November aptly observes, "Jews have been adhering to and rebelling against Jewish texts and traditions for thousands of years" (xiv). Not only am I in agreement with November's notion about the nature of Jewish poetry, but I would claim that this contradictory act of "adhering to" and "rebelling against" Jewish texts precisely applies to attitudes of Jewish American poets toward Whitman—oftentimes both for and against, and everything in between.[6]

Some of the English-language Jewish American poets of the twentieth century whose responses to Whitman may fall outside the scope of my study, but whose writing would be compelling to explore, are Delmore Schwartz, Aaron Kramer, Carl Rakosi, George Oppen, Louis Zukofsky, Carl Sandburg, Edgar Lee Masters, Vachel Lindsay, Allen Grossman, Anthony Hecht, Louis Untermeyer, Jean Starr Untermeyer, John Hollander, and Irving Feldman. But a few examples of poems by these poets in which Whitman's themes and forms resonate, are Schwartz's "America, America!," Oppen's "Of Being Numerous," Zukofsky's "A," Hollander's "Humming," and Feldman's "The Pripet Marshes." Also, Rakosi, Oppen, and Zukofsky, being of the Jewish Objectivist group with Charles Reznikoff, are included as part of the discussion in chapter 1; however, the potential work on these poets, together and separately, is far from complete.

Other twentieth-century poets whose work would enrich studies of Whitman and Jewish American poetry include Gertrude Stein,[7] David Lehman, David Antin, Harvey Shapiro, Philip Levine, Jorie Graham, Hal Sirowitz, Howard Nemerov, Howard Schwartz, Rodger Kamenetz, Philip Schultz, Jerome Rothenberg, C. K. Williams, and Charles Bernstein. Graham, for instance, in a 2018 interview with Peter Mishler, stated, "'Do I contradict myself, very well, then I contradict myself, I am large, I contain multitudes,' says Whitman—a line I always quote because of how succinctly and brilliantly it marries the sensation of our body/mind/soul/inner complexity to the original, great, naïve, dream of democracy" (Literary Hub). It would certainly be valid to interpret Graham's statement, referencing linkages between Whitman, the corporeal, and the political, vis-à-vis this wider genealogy and the group of Jewish American women poets explored in chapters 3 and 4. Also, in the conclusion, I touch on Rothenberg's description of Whitman in the introduction to *New Selected Poems* (1970–1985), Williams's book of critical essays titled *On Whitman*, and Bernstein's repetitious, Whitman-style poem, "Solidarity Is the Name We Give to What We Cannot Hold." My remarks about these poets' perceptions of Whitman are but starting points for studies of the endlessly varied ways in which Whitman is alluded to and imagined in Jewish American writing.

Yet other examples of Jewish American poets from the twentieth and twenty-first century, whose responses to Whitman would be potentially revealing, are Gary Pacernick,[8] Norman Finkelstein, Edward Hirsch,[9] Bob Perelman, Herbert Levine, Alan Shapiro, Denise Levertov, Lynn Melnik, Jacqueline Osherow, Maxine Kumin, Stanley Kunitz, Robert Pinsky, Ben Lerner, and Michael Heller. Levine, for example, in a 2019 article titled "The Voice We Need Now: Whitman at 200," writes that "Whitman's democratic wisdom is as relevant today as when it was written." Heller's poetry is a site of extensive engagement with Whitman, as exemplified by the poem "Sag Harbor, Whitman, As If an Ode," in which the speaker, together with Whitman, describes "thoughts of Sagaponack, of Paumanok, 'its shore gray and / rustling'" (148–149). In Lerner's 2015 novel titled *10:04*, too, Whitman appears as one of the main characters. Lerner intimates, in an interview about Whitman's role in the book, "the embarrassment of Whitman that has been obsessing me" and describes Whitman as "a figure that to me mediates between prose and poetry" (Clune).[10] Such a statement is indicative of the more contradictory interpretations of Whitman found in this study more broadly.

Alongside Heller and Lerner, there are other contemporary poets, from distinct backgrounds, regions, and religious and cultural identifications, whose work would be likewise deserving of a study of the responses (or the lack thereof) to Whitman. The writing by poets such as Joy Ladin,[11] Eugene Ostashevsky, Alicia Jo Rabins, Rosebud Ben-Oni,[12] Hadara Bar-Nadav, Ariel Resnikoff, Yehoshua November, Erika Meitner, Joy Katz, Adam Kirsch, Stephanie Burt, Ilya Kaminsky, Rachel Zucker, Jason Schneiderman, Rob Halpern, and Nomi Stone would be fascinating to survey since these poets engage with Jewish (and American)

6 INTRODUCTION

concerns from such radically different aesthetic, cultural, religious, and political points of view. Scholar Yosefa Raz has explored some of Halpern's more negative readings of Whitman.[13] Additionally, in a critical essay titled "Song," Burt mentions Whitman's musicality, stating, "Nobody does it like Whitman" (343). With these nuanced and often deeply conflicting viewpoints, it would be salient to consider these poets in the context of those poets spotlighted in this book (not to mention other literary and cultural frameworks outside of Jewishness). While it seems perhaps premature to make overarching claims about Whitman's role for these poets (individually or collectively), I believe that with regard to different expressions of Jewish culture, gender identity, sexual identification, and politics, any study of responses to Whitman (both for and against) would be worthwhile.

One additional site I will mention as potentially fruitful for interpretations of Whitman in a Jewish context, is that of English-language Jewish poets, translators, and essayists who reside in Jerusalem or Tel Aviv, Haifa, or elsewhere, and with strong literary and cultural connections to other mainly English-speaking countries, such as Rachel Tzvia Back, Karen Alkalay-Gut, Linda Zisquith, Bill Freedman, Lisa Katz, Harold Schimmel, Shirley Kaufman, Yosefa Raz, and Marcela Sulak.[14] Again, I do not put these poets forward to suggest any kind of poetic grouping, with the poets having such different backgrounds, affiliations, poetic sensibilities, and personal and political responses to this region. As the poet and scholar Alkalay-Gut has written, "The imperative of community, the communal experience, simultaneously includes and excludes the Anglo-Saxon writer. We are witnesses to the present, but we do not entirely share all the experiences" ("Poem"). I will add that I consider myself as among these poets, having been raised in New York (Westchester) but living, working, and writing in Tel Aviv for the last two decades. And Whitman happens to be an important intellectual and creative precursor for me. With this tapestry of writers engaged in questions of transnational and hybrid identity, within the multicultural, multilingual milieu of English-language writing, in a region where Hebrew, Arabic, and Russian are the predominant spoken languages, it would be fruitful to examine writing for and against Whitman.

Even this rather lengthy list of poets from early in the twentieth century to the present day does not reflect all the Jewish American poets who have turned to Whitman. Furthermore, one must not discount that there are certainly Jewish American poets whose work does not appear especially informed by or attuned to Whitman. I would argue that all these poetic variations are relevant in their own way when it comes to an intertextual study. Before I turn to the poets explored here, I will point to one other field that this book does not extensively cover: appropriations of Whitman by Yiddish-language poets. Scholars whose work on Yiddish-language poets and Whitman is invaluable include Matt Miller, Julian Levinson, Benjamin Harshav and Barbara Harshav, and Rachel Rubenstein. For the sake of context, later in this introduction, I provide background on some of the major Yiddish poets, translators, and critics, as well as briefly considering how Whitman is represented in H. Leyvik's poem "To America." However, my project focuses on tracing poetic appropriations of Whitman within English-language poetry, as well as dialogues between these English-language poets. These other poets and spheres of influence I leave to readers and scholars to come, in the spirit of Whitman's essay "A Backward Glance O'er Travel'd Roads," which appears at the end of the deathbed edition of *Leaves of Grass*: "the strongest and sweetest songs yet remain to be sung" (438). In other words, there are an infinite number of discoveries still to be made ("the sweetest songs" that "remain to be sung") about Whitman in Yiddish- and English-language poetry. The ever-changing nature of this field of study is what makes it exceptionally dynamic, with new Whitman-related poetry, prose, and criticism being discovered and generated all the time, in no way limited to Jewish writing, of course. That is the appeal hopefully made by this book, not to close a whole arena of investigation but to open one, through an examination and, in some cases, a re-examination, of the work of poets who both align with and resist Whitman.

Moving now to the poets who are the focus of this study: Charles Reznikoff and the Jewish Objectivist poets (chapter 1), Karl Shapiro and Kenneth Koch (chapter 2), Muriel Rukeyser, Allen Ginsberg, and Gerald Stern (chapter 3), and Jewish American women poets Adrienne Rich, Alicia Ostriker, and Marge Piercy (chapter 4). This book traces interpretations of Whitman in Jewish American poetry and presents this network of Jewish American poets who have turned to the paradigmatic poet of America. One finds that Whitman is often represented as a figure whose presence makes these Jewish American poets distinctly Jewish and distinctly American, depending on the poet's aesthetic predilections, literary associations, and historical moment.[15]

In the rest of this introduction, I offer areas of context necessary for a more comprehensive understanding of the main focus of this book, this genealogy across the twentieth and twenty-first century: a critical framework for analyzing

8   INTRODUCTION

Whitman's role among Jewish American poets; perceptions of Whitman by minority, non-Jewish poets in America, like June Jordan and Sherman Alexie; Whitman's role for the nineteenth-century Jewish American poets Emma Lazarus and Adah Isaacs Menken; Whitman's reception among Yiddish-language Jewish poets in America, such as Morris Rosenfeld, I. Leyeles, and H. Leyvik; and Whitman's reception for other Jewish American authors, among them Michael Gold, and by the preeminent twentieth-century Jewish intellectuals Harold Bloom, Leslie Fiedler, Lionel Trilling, and Phillip Rahv. Perceptions of Whitman, as expressed in the writings of these poets, novelists, and critics, intersect in nuanced ways with Whitman's reception within twentieth- and twenty-first-century Jewish American poetry. In the final section of the introduction, I turn to these Jewish American poets—Reznikoff, Shapiro, Koch, Rukeyser, Ginsberg, Stern, Rich, Ostriker, and Piercy—and demonstrate that, collectively speaking, Whitman appears in a multitude of guises: a poetic father, counter-model to conservative and even antisemitic sentiments within High Modernist literary culture, mystic, poet of the Bible, champion of the unjust, political poet, promoter of democracy, glorifier of war, feminist ally, poet of the body, gay ally, radical, and poet of Jewish liturgy—all in relation to the experience of being Jewish in America.

WHITMAN IN JEWISH AMERICAN POETRY: A CRITICAL FRAMEWORK

As a systematic interpretation of Whitman's presence in Jewish American poetry, which explores the breadth of this phenomenon, as well as various poetic, cultural, and political issues at stake, this study is intended to enrich the conversation around Whitman's reception within Jewish American poetry and literature. One challenge of this project is that not only are the poets who adopt Whitman often not seen as connected, but critical discussions can be limited to Whitman's role within the work of individual Jewish American poets. This study seeks to draw together these commentaries, by critics such as Julian Levinson, Ranen Omer-Sherman, Norman Finklestein, Matt Miller, Alicia Ostriker, and Maeera Y. Shreiber, with each one shedding light on elements of Whitman, Jewish poetry, and identity for a plethora of eras and poetic movements in America.

The study *Exiles on Main Street: Jewish American Writers and American Literary Culture* by Levinson—which presents a mapping of the engagement

INTRODUCTION 9

of numerous Jewish American poets and writers (including Emma Lazarus, Mary Antin, Waldo Frank, and Anzia Yezierska) and Yiddish-language poets with Whitman and Transcendentalist thinkers—has provided an especially significant foundation for my own interpretation of this tradition of Jewish American poets. My project is especially indebted to Levinson's findings as to the fruitful dynamics between Transcendentalism and Jewish American literature and how these exchanges grant "Jews with new ways of understanding themselves *as Jews*" (*Exiles* 3).[16] Where I somewhat depart from Levinson is that my examination is focused more on Whitman as a singular, prototypical figure who is appropriated by Jewish American poets in ways that are adjacent to, but also separate from, the Transcendentalist ideals and philosophies more broadly.[17] Whitman was bound up with Transcendentalist figures and doctrines and of course with Emerson's call for a poet of America; as Emerson writes in his essay "The Poet," "the breadth of the problem is great, for the poet is representative. He stands among partial men for the complete man, and apprises us not of his wealth, but of the commonwealth." Whitman famously (or infamously) sent Emerson the first edition of *Leaves of Grass* and inscribed Emerson's letter on the second edition of *Leaves*.[18] Thus aspects of the Transcendentalist movement, such as the divinity of nature and of the individual, informed Whitman's project,[19] but my interest is in Whitman as a distinctive paradigm within American poetry.

Other insightful reflections on Whitman and Jewish American poetry appear in Stephen Paul Miller's hybrid poetic/critical work, titled "Relentlessly Going On and On: How Jews Remade Modern Poetry Without Even Trying," where the speaker asks, "What is Jewish poetry, or, / at least one kind of Jewish poetry?" The poem then offers a response to this very question, in an associative (and self-referentially Whitmanesque) manner, enumerating facets within Jewish American poetry, including Yiddish and Hebrew, Ezra Pound and T. S. Eliot (whose roles will be explored and expanded upon in this book), Objectivism, Theodor Herzl, and Kabbalah. In the first of two references, Miller almost equates Whitman with Jewish American poetry itself:

Whitman
remakes poetry
in a Jewish tradition
that's
unavoidable thereafter. (348–349)

10 INTRODUCTION

Miller seems, first, to be pointing to Whitman's significance within Jewish American poetry and indicating that Whitman's psalmic style appealed to Jewish American poets. Later in the poem is a more overt reference to correlations between Whitman's poetic style and that of the Bible, which is known to resonate for poets: "when the edge of epic / becomes poetry, Whitman / and Biblical poetry cannot be ignored / get more of their due" (349). Miller thus points to another notion within discourse around Whitman's role in Jewish American poetry—how poets are informed by a repetitious poetic style in Whitman that echoes the Bible or Psalms. This idea has been noted by other critics, like Aaron Kramer, who has stated about Eastern European immigrant poets, "[that] as soon as they mastered a new tongue—[they] would recognize Whitman as their poet, both for the Biblical cadences of his lines and the affirmation of individual dignity they had come so far to desperately enjoy" (18).[20] Jewish American poets throughout the twentieth century (including Reznikoff, Rukeyser, Stern, Rich, and Piercy) have certainly declared their appreciation of Whitman's poetic style in connection to the Bible. Yet the modes by which these and other poets incorporate Whitman and biblical form go beyond "cadences," or psalmic-style verse forms that appealed to Jewish American poets familiar with the Hebrew Bible. When the Whitman-biblical correlation is found, these stylistic appropriations frequently overlap with Whitman's role for these poets in assorted realms of identity, culture, and politics.

Miller's poem in "Relentlessly Going On and On" also raises the idea of poets after Whitman encountering his poetry, and therefore Jewish tradition itself. In context with Miller, I would add that Whitman's influence is pervasive but not necessarily "unavoidable"; in other words, entrenched in this project is the idea that the ways Jewish American poets come to adopt Whitman cannot be received without question, especially in relation to Pound and Eliot, also mentioned by Miller. The complex modes in which any poet relates to Whitman are themselves a choice, often with underlying cultural and political agendas. While there are poetic qualities in Whitman's poetry that are significant for many Jewish American poets, I am analyzing these poets' distinct perceptions of Whitman, rather than absolute features of the Whitmanian text. A core tenet of this investigation is that more than Whitman "remaking" poetry in the Jewish tradition (*à la* Miller), it is Jewish American poets who "make" and "remake" Whitman, thereby contributing to Whitman's critical reception into the twenty-first century and likely for generations to come.

As a study of critical reception, this book hopes furthermore to expand the body of research on dynamics of intertextuality.[21] By examining interconnections between poetic intertextuality and cultural phenomena, this book is located within the theoretical sphere of "cultural poetics" or "social formalism," set forth by scholars such as Rachel Blau DuPlessis, Charles Bernstein, and Stephen Greenblatt. These critics have addressed such complications of bridging poetry and culture; as DuPlessis claims, poetry can be (mis)construed as "opposite to society and its discourses" (7). She also argues that research on links between poetry and culture must "struggle deeply and continuously" (8) against the dichotomization of these realms.[22] The Jewish American response to Whitman is a unique case study of analyzing poetic texts as cultural material, which can be applicable to other research into Whitman's reception and other studies of literary reception.

Among individual studies of intertextuality that are outside the area of Jewish American literature and poetry, but are nonetheless formative for this research, is "'Inundated by This Mississippi of Poetry': Walt Whitman and German Expressionism" by Walter Grünzweig, in which allusions to Whitman in German literature are interpreted to be a marker of intertextual exchange in a transnational context:

> Obviously, the mere discovery of Whitman's influence on a given German text may be of little significance, but an evaluation of deficits of understanding and actual misunderstandings of Whitman by a variety of German authors might reveal important insights into the nature of German-American intercultural phenomena. (255)

Grünzweig does not aim for the "mere discovery" of Whitman influence on German-language texts but rather applies these findings to identify "German-American intercultural phenomena." Similarly, Betsy Erkkila's invaluable study, *Walt Whitman Among the French*, investigates the poetic and social significance of Whitman's influence in relation to French authors, including Hugo, Rimbaud, and Apollinaire, arguing, "The relationship between Whitman and the French is also significant both in the history of Franco-American literary relations and in the history of American cultural influence in general" (3). In these analyses of Whitman in German and French literatures, as well as my own analysis in a Jewish framework, interpretations of Whitman are explored with the goal of uncovering cultural and political implications of literary allusions and intertexts.

WHITMAN'S RECEPTION BEYOND
JEWISH AMERICAN WRITING

According to political agendas, historical circumstances, artistic visions, and literary movements, Whitman has been adapted into the work of authors from Iceland, India, South America, Asia, and Israel.[23] As Ed Folsom and Gay Wilson Allen have claimed, "From nation to nation, Whitman's poetry and prose have generated a wide variety of aesthetic, political, and religious responses. . . . [V]arious national cultures have reconstructed Whitman in order to make him fit their native patterns" (2).[24] In the United States, writers of innumerable backgrounds and cultural heritages have been in conversation with Whitman, such as June Jordan, Langston Hughes, Tomás Rivera, Juan Felipe Herrera, Maxine Hong Kingston, Joseph Bruchac, and Sherman Alexie.[25] It is possible to understand the Jewish American poetic engagement with Whitman in terms of these diverse writers, with Whitman assigned contradictory roles of outsider and insider, reflecting tensions related to cultural and national identity, depending on the poet's ideologies and poetic project.

Jordan, a Black woman poet and essayist, for example, identifies Whitman as an influence in her essay "For the Sake of People's Poetry: Walt Whitman and the Rest of Us": "It so happens that Walt Whitman is the one white father who shares the systematic disadvantages of his heterogeneous offspring trapped inside a closet. . . . What Whitman envisioned, we, the people and the poets of the New World, embody. He has been punished for the moral questions that our very lives arouse." Surprisingly, given that Whitman is white and male, Jordan expresses an affiliation with Whitman that she articulates is linked to Whitman's marginalization in America during the High Modernist period of the early twentieth century.[26]

Rather differently, in "Defending Walt Whitman" by the Native American poet, novelist, and essayist Sherman Alexie, Whitman is portrayed as a symbol of ethnocentrism, marginalization, and prejudice within America.[27] The figure of Whitman represents an America at once exploitative and ignorant, as he plays basketball with "Indian boys" on a reservation:

> Walt Whitman cannot tell the difference between
> offense and defense. He does not care if he touches the ball.
> Half of the Indian boys wear t-shirts damp with sweat
> and the other half are bareback, skin slick and shiny.

There is no place like this. Walt Whitman smiles.
Walt Whitman shakes. This game belongs to him. (31)

The idea that Whitman controls the "game," both basketball and America itself, signals Whitman's vision of America as flawed at best and, at worst, deeply discriminatory. Yet, by Whitman's employment thematically and stylistically, there is a resulting reinforcement of Whitman's centrality in American poetry. The themes explored by Jewish American poets, though, are distinct: Jewish immigration, Hebrew, Yiddish, World War II and the Holocaust, the Bible, secularism, Jewish liturgy, and antisemitism. And yet, similar dynamics of simultaneously rejecting and embracing Whitman appear in literature by non-Jewish authors, whereby Whitman might be portrayed as a poet of the minority *and* a poet of the majority, as exemplified by an essay like Jordan's or a poem like Alexie's.

WHITMAN'S NINETEENTH-CENTURY RECEPTION BY JEWISH AMERICAN POETS: ADAH ISAACS MENKEN AND EMMA LAZARUS

Appropriations of Whitman by Jewish American poets did not begin in the twentieth century but long before, around the time Whitman wrote and first published *Leaves of Grass* in the mid-nineteenth century. Two earlier nineteenth-century Jewish American poets are Adah Isaacs Menken and Emma Lazarus. Perceptions of Whitman by Menken and Lazarus are revealed to be quite different, yet for both, Whitman can be said to serve as a mediating figure regarding Jewish American poetry and identity.

Menken—artist, performer, and poet—championed Whitman most publicly. Menken and Whitman were familiar with each other personally from the artist scene of New York City.[28] The collection of poems *Infelicia*, published after Menken's death in 1868, is laden with allusions to Jewish texts and themes and to Whitman. Menken was not born into a Jewish family but came to identify as Jewish later in life. As scholars point out, Menken was married to a Jewish man (Alexander Isaac Menken) and studied Jewish texts but likely did not formally undergo a rabbinic conversion (Levinson, "Seventh Angel" 148).[29] One can therefore observe how Menken (a self-identifying Jewish poet) appropriates Whitman (a non-Jewish poet) to write poetry that is Jewish and American in nature, to put forward her own notions of Jewishness itself. Throughout her

14   INTRODUCTION

poetry, Menken displays a Whitmanesque free verse, filled with repetition and long lines.[30] None exemplifies Whitman more aptly than "Myself" (1868), where Menken puts the experience of the self, the "I," at the center of the poem: "When these mortal mists shall unclothe the world, then shall I be known as I am! / When I dare be dead and buried behind a wall of wings, then shall he know me!" (90–91). Menken's title and language call to mind "Song of Myself": "And such as it is to be of these more or less I am / and of these one and all I weave the song of myself" (41–42). Menken draws on Whitman's "I" as a mode of self-determination that is at once personal ("I [shall] be known as I am") and spiritual or religious ("he"—God—"shall . . . know me").

The connection between Whitman and Jewishness is more explicit in Menken's 1860 essay "Swimming Against the Current" in the *Sunday Mercury*. Menken praised Whitman, despite the editors calling Whitman a "coarse and uncouth creature" (perhaps a semi-veiled reference to Whitman's sexuality). Menken writes, "Look at Walter Whitman, the American philosopher who is centuries ahead of his contemporaries, who, in smiling carelessness, analyzes the elements of which society is composed. . . . He hears the Divine voice calling him to caution mankind against this or that evil, and wields his pen, exerts his energies, for the cause of liberty and humanity!" (1). By equating Whitman's "courage" to "swim against the tide" of society with the "triumph" of Israel, Menken proclaims an optimistic belief that Whitman's "divine" ideas will be one day embraced by society, "rescued from the aqueous grave." So, too, Menken describes Whitman's eventual return as akin to the rise of the Jewish people out of "darkness": "So Judea will triumph, after darkness and ignorance will be utterly dispelled by the radiant sun of divine truth! Israel has swam against the current for thirty centuries and more! Thus it has struggled and combated against the corruptions of all ages in history; Thus is Israel the savior, the Messiah of the nations!" (1). Therefore, Whitman and "Judea" symbolize for Menken open, progressive forces, as opposed to a society that is closed, morally stifled, and "corrupt." As such, Menken envisions a type of Judaism mediated by Whitman that might be open to accepting her.

For Lazarus, born to Sephardic and Ashkenazi parents in New York and renowned for the 1883 poem "The New Colossus," inscribed on the Statue of Liberty, evidence of her connection to Whitman is subtler than for Menken. Nowhere in Lazarus's oeuvre does one find essays lauding Whitman's democratic vision, nor linking her own conceptualization of Jewish American identity to Whitman's poetics. One reason for Lazarus's interest in Whitman being somewhat less palpable[31] is perhaps a well-documented allegiance to Ralph Waldo Emerson, who was a more direct mentor. In 1868, Lazarus wrote to Emerson and described reading a couple of poems by Whitman, still appearing to be somewhat more taken by Thoreau: "I have only been reading Thoreau's Concord River & Letters, & a poem or two of Walt Whitman. . . . But these writers are so in harmony with Nature that they do not take me away from the scene. I no longer wonder at your admiration of Thoreau . . . for he is now more alive to me than many who are living near me" (Levinson, *Exiles* 20–21).

In terms of Whitman's familiarity with Lazarus, in Horace Traubel's commentary from October 9, 1888 (less than a year after her death in October 1887), there is evidence of Whitman expressing curiosity about Lazarus as a prominent woman poet at the time. In volume two of *Walt Whitman in Camden*, Traubel reports that he and Whitman gazed together at a "frontispiece" of Lazarus in the newspaper and that Whitman "had not met Emma Lazarus." Whitman responded, "'I know little about her or her work: but her face is an argument. I must ask Alma Johnston about her: she knows most every woman in New York who does public things'" (456).[32] In commentary from the following day, October 10, Traubel further states that Whitman believed Lazarus to be distancing herself from him, though he was without proof of her doing so:

> W. had been reading some about Emma Lazarus today. "She must have had a great, sweet, unusual nature. I have meant to look more into her work: all I know of her has been casual—the things that come to you here and there in the magazines and newspapers. I never met her—several times came near doing so. It may be gratuitous to say so—no doubt is—but I have randomly, wholly at random, believed she did not wish to meet me—rather avoided me. It may be gratuitous to say this, but I have had reasons for feeling its truth—good reasons, though reasons rather emotional than concrete."[33]

Whitman's claim about Lazarus not wanting to meet him, that he believed, or "felt," that Lazarus avoided him, or was encouraged to do so, is a curiosity. One must ask whether it was Whitman's reputation as a radical gay poet that kept Lazarus at a certain distance. Together with the recent publication of fifteen poems by Lazarus, understood to be same-sex love poems,[34] it is possible to conjecture that she was more soundly in dialogue with Whitman than she would have declared at the time.

16 INTRODUCTION

Despite Lazarus's less explicit embrace of Whitman, and Whitman's account about Lazarus avoiding him, elements of Whitman's free verse style and humanistic philosophy can be observed especially in her later poems. In keeping with Menken, Lazarus can be considered a forbearer in ways of employing Whitman as a mode of defining her Jewish American poetics. I would argue that Lazarus's engagement with Whitman in her poetics does surpass what appears in her letters and that Whitman's voice is a presence positioning her poetry as Jewish and American. Admittedly, some of her most anthologized poems, including "In the Jewish Synagogue at Newport" and "The New Colossus," are not markedly Whitmanian in style,[35] containing fixed meter and regular end rhymes. But the last poem published in her lifetime, titled "By the Waters of Babylon," does display a more Whitmanian style of free verse, which might be taken as a sign of Whitman's significance for Lazarus, as well as a suggestion to rethink other, more formalistic poems by Lazarus through Whitman in retrospect.[36]

In "By the Waters of Babylon" (1887), with the subtitle "Little Poems in Prose," Lazarus narrativizes the Jews being expelled from Spain and symbolically traces them as they are dispersed throughout the world, forever in exile. The structure of the poem, a series of numbered lists, departs from fixed verse forms that Lazarus often employs in earlier poetry. "By the Waters" is divided into five parts, the first of which is "The Exodus," and begins with a Whitmanesque enumeration of figures expelled from Spain, for instance, in sections one and two: "1. The Spanish noon is a blaze of azure fire, and the dusty pilgrims crawl like an endless serpent along treeless plains and bleached high-roads. . . . 2. The hoary patriarch, wrinkled as an almond shell, bows painfully upon his staff" (91). This type of long list cannot but evoke Whitman. Moreover, when the speaker draws the reader's gaze to these figures, there is a compassion expressed for these impoverished outcasts that resonates with the compassion toward those who suffer in Whitman's poem "The Sleepers": "the wretched features of ennuyés, the white features of corpses, the livid faces of drunkards" (325). In the case of Lazarus, however, we cast our eyes on the particularities of the Jewish experience of suffering in exile but, one can argue, with at least a hint of Whitman's expansive, encompassing poetic style.

As the poem continues, Whitman's forms and themes are evident in Lazarus's portrayal of Jewish people being cast out from Spain. In part V, Lazarus writes, "1. Vast oceanic movements, the flux and reflux of immeasurable tides, oversweep our continent" (95), lines that resonate with the language and rhythms of "Mannahatta," Whitman's ode to Manhattan and the immigrants coming to its shores: "Tides swift and ample, well-loved by me, toward sundown . . . Immigrants arriving, fifteen or twenty thousand in a week . . ." (361). With these correlating themes of humanism, as well as formalistic correlations of repetition and anaphora, the entwinement of Lazarus and Whitman is noteworthy.[37] Through this prism, one recalls the inclusive mission in lines from Lazarus's most famous poem on the Statue of Liberty, "The New Colossus": "Your tired, your poor, / your huddled masses" (58). This America is of course Whitman's ideal vision of America, one promoted not just in "The Sleepers" but throughout his poetic project *Leaves of Grass*. I argue that Whitman is an important source in Lazarus's work, especially her later poetry, to promote equality and inclusion in a Jewish context. Although Menken related to Whitman much more directly and Lazarus more indirectly or discreetly, in nuanced manifestations, these Jewish minority women poets write about navigating the experience of being Jewish American, while envisioning through Whitman an America of greater openness and acceptance. Together, the legacies of Menken and Lazarus are really precursors for the many Jewish American poets who would come to adopt Whitman in the subsequent centuries. An analogous egalitarian vision of Jewishness and Americanness will be promoted by poets like Reznikoff and the Jewish Objectivist poets, Karl Shapiro, and Ginsberg, often (though not always) in alignment with Whitman. More specifically, Menken and Lazarus can be understood as having laid the necessary groundwork for the tradition of Jewish American women poets. For example, there is an allusion to Lazarus's "The New Colossus" in a Whitman-themed poem titled "Manahatta" by Ostriker, discussed in chapter 4. With Whitman depicted by Menken and Lazarus as a poet of outsider identity, the body, and politics, with a mission to advance democratic ideals, one finds overlap in many poets of this book, including Rukeyser, Rich, Ostriker, and Piercy.

WHITMAN'S RECEPTION IN YIDDISH-LANGUAGE JEWISH POETRY IN AMERICA

Still another cohort of Jewish poets in America whose writing demonstrates a deep awareness of and commitment to Whitman is Yiddish-language poets, mainly immigrants to New York from Russia and Poland, who wrote in the nineteenth and twentieth centuries. While this book illuminates Whitman's

18 INTRODUCTION

role in English-language Jewish American poetry, references to Whitman in Yiddish-language poetry, translations, and criticism are no less plentiful and no less imperative for understanding Whitman's absorption into the landscape of Jewish American poetry and literature more generally. The Yiddish-language poet Louis Miller (1866–1927) was an important early translator of Whitman's poems.[38] In 1940, another poet by the name of Louis Miller (1889–1967) (who also wrote under the pseudonyms Eliezer Meler, Louis Miler, and L. Miler) translated the first book-length collection of poems from *Leaves of Grass* into Yiddish, titled *Lider fun bukh: "Bletlekh groz"* (*Poems from the book: "Leaves of Grass"*),[39] published by the Yiddish Cooperative Book League.[40] Among poems by Yiddish-language poets that allude to Whitman are Morris Rosenfeld's "Walt Whitman (America's Great Poet)," I. Leyeles's "A Dream Under Skyscrapers," Reuben Ludwig's "Symposium," H. Leyvik's "To America" (which I discuss), and I. J. Schwartz's "Kentucky."[41] One finds many significant parallels between the turn to Whitman by Yiddish-language Jewish American poets and that of English-language ones; for instance, poetic texts in both groups mirror Whitman's long lines, parallelisms, repetitions, and lengthy catalogues. Also, for these groups, Whitman is picked up around issues of outsider identity, with the poet envisioned as a symbol of a more inclusive, democratic America. Yet the Yiddish poets faced the marked distinction of writing in a non-majority language when they did write to, for, about, or against Whitman.

Akin to a central claim in this project about English-language Jewish American poets adopting Whitman, scholarship about representations of Whitman in Yiddish writing has noted that Whitman is conceived as a mediating figure for poets who were navigating experiences of being Jewish immigrants to America, who wrote mainly in Yiddish, and who possessed profound leftist and socialist political affiliations. Rachel Rubenstein, in research about the movement of Yiddish poets in America known as Di Yunge (the Young Ones), writes about dual portrayals of Whitman and Native American figures in the literary journal *Shriftn*; she states, for Di Yunge, Whitman and these Native American figures symbolized an ideal (or perhaps idealized) "authentic" America: "Yiddish interest in the Indian and in Whitman . . . would become acts of interpretation and transformation designed to assert the simultaneous modernism and Americanness of the Yiddish immigrant poet" (438). Furthermore, Levinson has argued about Yiddish poets in America, "[A]s they renewed Whitman's dream, they also imagined . . . that they were staking a claim for a politically progressive Yiddish literary culture in the American of the future"

(*Exiles* 141). Whitman has thus been identified as important within Yiddish poets' navigating of the cultural, political, and linguistic climate of America. Lines from Rosenfeld's ode to Whitman embody this notion of Whitman as a type of American poetic hero for these poets, "immortal bard, I honor thee: I kneel / upon the dust, before thy dust, and sing" (137).[42]

Yet, within the critical conversation around Whitman and Yiddish poets in America and within the framework of reading Whitman in the work of English-language poets, the presence of Whitman could not mark the Yiddish poets in the same way as American (in other words, as insider) to the same degree, even for poets who wrote in the same period as the High Modernist and Jewish Objectivist poets. Since much of their writing was produced in a non-majority language, the outsider position of the Yiddish poets was more pronounced vis-à-vis American culture and the English-language literary world. Poets writing in Yiddish (not just about Whitman) did so from this insulated position; as Benjamin Harshav and Barbara Harshav write, Yiddish poets in America were "quarantined within their alien language" (31), and these struggles with immigration and assimilation are reflected in their poetry:

> Yiddish writing reflected all the modern tensions of a self-ironic society in the process of losing a traditional value system; the throes of urban alienation gripping the scattered descendants of a close-knit feudal community; the tensions of the demands of art on the one hand and the repeated search for new forms of mimesis and expression on the other; and the critical problem of language renewal in a text-burdened culture. All this was magnified by the traumas of Jewish history, from which the poets tried to escape through the forms and myth of modern poetry, and into which they were pulled back by the intimate ropes of their Jewish language. (22–23)

In the background of these "tensions," one unique, distinguishing feature about the Yiddish poetic response to Whitman in America is this sense of heightened outsiderness, being culturally and linguistically more outsider than other English-language immigrant Jewish American poets who also write about experiencing exclusion, as many did. In other words, with this historical, geographical, and linguistic turmoil, Whitman is a poet that in some ways represents not a failed attempt but a limited or complicated attempt to demonstrate the Yiddish poets' insiderness, whereby by claiming Whitman, they would claim or construct their own identity as poets of America.

20 INTRODUCTION

As such, I would point out as part of this discourse that Whitman serves not only as a democratic American hero for Yiddish poets (as is the case for many poets) but also as a symbol of marginalization and exclusion, linked to complexities of having immigrated as Jewish poets to America. In H. Leyvik's poem "To America" (1954), rather than a celebration or affirmation of Whitman, the speaker articulates longing for acceptance by a nation (America) after "forty-one years" of living there but having become disenchanted with America.[43] The speaker writes of this vexed wish to belong with "the hymns of Whitman" at the fore:

> For forty-one years I have lived in your borders, America,
> Carrying within me the bounty of your freedom—that freedom,
> Sanctified and blessed by the blood of Lincoln's sacrifice
> And in the hymns of Walt Whitman. See, how strange it is: to this day
> I seek an answer to the contradictions, to the unrest of my life,
> I wonder, why haven't I sung you, to this day,
> With joy, with praise, with pure admiration— (Harshav and Harshav
> 763)

The poem first expresses an early belief in the "borders" of America—its "freedom" and supposedly democratic ideals. Whitman's poetry is America, "sings" America, representing these values of America. Yet the speaker conveys an equal sense of "unrest" and of alienation from America, alluding to Whitman's "contradictions" in "Song of Myself." Leyvik writes of trying to determine why America has not become a place of inclusion for him, wishing to find "joy" in America, the streets of Manhattan or Brooklyn, "or in his own small world—in Brownsville, or on Clinton Street—." After so many decades of him residing there, Yiddish language is a marker of estrangement: "I tried,—and it is clear: the fault is mine, not yours / that thirty years ago I mourned under your skies / Deep inside me, lamented that I carry my Yiddish song / In fear, through your streets and through your squares" (767).

Even with Whitman—the prototypical American poet—as "captain" (a take on Lincoln as the fallen captain of Whitman's "O Captain! My Captain!"), the speaker describes having difficulty assimilating: "The brave captain shall not betray / His song-of-destiny today. — — — / You see—I am cruel to myself when I say: / It is *certainly* my fault" (767). Moreover, the speaker expresses self-blame for this continual estrangement in an America that he cannot claim and that does not, in his perception, claim him in return. A poem such as

Leyvik's thus highlights how the Whitman of Yiddish poetry is not limited to an embrace of or affinity to Whitman. The dialogue with Whitman within Yiddish-speaking Jewish immigrant poetry is also informed by the realities of this "alien language" of Yiddish, as per Harshav and Harshav. Therefore, there are definite parallels between Whitman's presence in Yiddish- and English-language Jewish American poetry, with these poets often drawing on Whitman as a poet of America to create stronger ties to America itself, as well as distinctions from the English-language tradition, with the Yiddish poets being in certain ways more separate from the majority culture. That said, within High Modernism, Imagism, and Beat poetry, the insider/outsider dynamics, and the dynamics of being for and against Whitman, absolutely reverberate.

WHITMAN'S RECEPTION IN JEWISH AMERICAN PROSE AND CRITICISM

While English- and Yiddish-language Jewish American poets form one context for understanding Whitman's function in Jewish American poetry, responses to Whitman by nineteenth- and twentieth-century Jewish American prose writers and critics, such as Horace Traubel, Anzia Yezierska, Michael Gold, Harold Bloom, and Leslie Fiedler, form another. Whitman is known to have been a favorable figure for many Jewish American writers, who viewed Whitman's rhetoric through an American, democratic, and socialist lens.[44] For one, Wendy Katz has claimed that Whitman was crucial "in [Yezierska's] process of literary 'Americanization'" (155) and that Yezierska identified with his politics, "religious liberalism," and even "proto-feminism" (157). Kenneth M. Price has also examined Whitman's import for the Jewish literary figure Traubel, Whitman's main biographer and author of the biographical volumes *Walt Whitman in Camden*, as well as the political writer Emma Goldman. Traubel and Goldman both, according to Price, "constructed [Whitman] as a semi-miraculous father figure" (71).

In broad terms, Whitman was no less significant for Gold—editor of the journal *New Masses*—than for Traubel or Yezierska; as Richard Tuerk observes, "Gold typically saw Whitman as a major—perhaps the major—part of an American political and literary tradition beginning with the Revolution and leading to a second American Revolution that Gold felt was inevitably to be led by the Communist Party in America, to which he belonged for most

22 INTRODUCTION

of his life" (16). Apt as this notion might be in describing Gold's perception of Whitman, in certain Whitman-informed texts by Gold, Whitman is not portrayed simply as the representative of an ideal, progressive America, or as a "semi-miraculous father figure" (71), as Price has noted about Traubel and Goldman. For instance, Gold's poem "Ode to Walt Whitman" is not a straightforward tribute to Whitman (a contrasting poem would be the ode to Whitman by the Yiddish-language poet Morris Rosenfeld, "Walt Whitman (America's Great Poet)," which more wholly embraces Whitman's legacy). In Gold's poem, the speaker identifies himself as one of Whitman's sons, and a son of Manhattan, but a Manhattan in which the city is foul and gritty: "And me a son of Walt Whitman / A son of Manhattan the bitch / Born on Rat and Louse Street / Near Tuberculosis avenue—" ("Ode" 168–171). Similar resonances of Whitman are found in Gold's novel *Jews Without Money*, which depicts scenes of impoverishment on the Lower East Side of Manhattan: "A parrot cursed. Ragged kids played under truck-horses. Fat housewives fought from stoop to stoop" (357). In the enumeration of symbols of poverty, for instance, Whitman's listing is echoed, and therefore, the passages in Gold's poem and his novel can be read considering the complexities of Whitman's reception for Jewish American writers, whereby Whitman represents a certain ideal version of America and yet likewise, at times, represents the realities of an America that was far from equal for all.

Alongside these Jewish American prose writers, opinions of Whitman can be found in various essays by Leslie Fiedler, Lionel Trilling, Harold Bloom, and Phillip Rahv, among the major twentieth-century Jewish American literary and cultural critics. In some of these works about Whitman's poetry and legacy, the opinions expressed are less than complimentary, with Whitman accused of being phony, uncouth, and overblown, as illustrated by Fiedler's assertion that "Whitman is the slyest of artificers" (172). In "Paleface and Redskin," where Rahv conceptualizes Henry James and Whitman as "two polar types" (1), both authors are deemed deficient, with one side of the spectrum (James) being too elitist and exclusionary and the other side (Whitman) being too crass and, worse, lowbrow. In Trilling, furthermore, one encounters a dislike for the linguistic liberties that Whitman was known to have taken in his poetry and a subtle derision of some of Whitman's language and vocabulary: "[W]e hear of 'the ostent,' of 'orbic barbs' of 'literatuses'" (207).

Despite such perceived flaws in Whitman, Trilling signals an approval of what he believes to be Whitman's attempt to impact society through literature itself: "He [Whitman] is in the great romantic tradition, and he shares as fully as possible the large romantic belief in the political mission of the 'literatus'" (208). Such notions of Whitman's significance for society at large are in line, moreover, with notions put forward by Bloom, who, among these Jewish American critics, conveys the most vigorous support for Whitman and his potential function within American literature and culture; as Bloom states, "Whitman centers the American canon because he changes the American self and the American religion by changing the representation of our unofficial selves and our persuasive if concealed post-Christian religion" ("Walt" 283). For Bloom, part of Whitman's significance stems from this possibility of a shifting "self," whereby neither individual nor national identities are fixed but are fluid and, by extension, can be adapted for the betterment of society and used to challenge exclusionary and (to Bloom) dogmatic religious forces, specifically Christian ones, which would exclude Bloom himself. This idea of Whitman as an agent of possibility and transformation aligns with comments by Fiedler, who, in the same essay where he criticizes Whitman, also takes note of how Whitman is being wielded as a symbol or "weapon" against various elitist factions within High Modernism: "And Whitman has become a weapon in the hands of those who (Van Wyck Brooks is an example) condemn Eliot or Pound on the grounds that he has rejected all that Whitman affirms. . . . We shall not return to the same Whitman from which we started; twenty-five years of dissent cannot be undone" (170–171). As such, Bloom's and Fiedler's commentary on Whitman is in keeping with Jewish American poets like Reznikoff, Shapiro, Koch, and Rukeyser, who have employed Whitman as a mode to challenge conservatism in society, in the context of High Modernism, precisely as a "weapon" against the High Modernist forces of which Fiedler speaks.

REDRAWING THE MAP: TWENTIETH- AND TWENTY-FIRST-CENTURY JEWISH AMERICAN POETS RESPOND TO WALT WHITMAN

With these intricate appropriations of Whitman by American non-Jewish minority poets, nineteenth-century Jewish American poets, nineteenth- and twentieth-century Yiddish-language poets, and prominent Jewish American authors and intellectuals in mind, I turn to the poets at the heart of this study. While Jewish American poetry has tended to receive less scholarly consideration than Jewish American prose, this study joins a rich critical conversation on Jewish American poetics, undertaken by Jonathan N. Barron, Eric Murphy Selinger, Charles Bernstein, John Hollander, Norman Finkelstein, Stephen Fredman, and Maeera Y. Shreiber, who have sought to illuminate the formalistic, thematic, and cultural attributes that constitute Jewish American poetry as an entity onto itself, exploring its "various identity positions, aesthetic dilemmas, and formal innovations" (Shreiber, "Jewish American Poetry" 150). Such a turn relies upon the notion of Jewish American poetry having been conceptualized by scholars as a distinct category, albeit with loosely defined boundaries, often containing themes of Jewish identity and culture, religiosity and secularism, Jewish liturgy, the Holocaust, Yiddish and Hebrew, immigration, assimilation, antisemitism, and engagement with a majority, non-Jewish culture of America.[45] I contend that this book, which explicates recurring responses to a singular non-Jewish figure by Jewish American poets across more than a century—with Whitman being formative in the poetic oeuvres of so many individual poets and with the nature of these responses being so often intertwined—bolsters the borders of the tradition as such (as shifting and evolving as they continue to be).

Using a model that is mostly (though not solely) generational, with a delineation according to thematic and formalistic modes in which Whitman's vision is manifest, reveals how Whitman has been perceived over time by poets who write of straddling Jewish and American culture(s), negotiating notions of and conflicts around Jewish identity, in keeping with political, historical, and social shifts in America. The following chapters provide an infrastructure for interpreting Whitman—one that is applicable to Jewish American poets not featured centrally in this study and even for poetry yet to be written. A central goal of this study is to establish that from the 1855 publication of *Leaves of Grass* onward, any response by a Jewish American poet to Whitman can be read in relation to this network of poets, which stretches as much backward into the past as it does forward into the future. My objective is not to determine the extent to which Whitman might be received favorably or unfavorably by a given poet but to probe how these interpretations reflect the poets' experiences of Jewish culture and identity in America. For some of the poets discussed here, the connection to Whitman is more recognized by readers and scholars (like Allen Ginsberg, Gerald Stern, and Alicia Ostriker), and for some, the connection is lesser known (like Charles Reznikoff, Muriel Rukeyser, and Marge Piercy), but all these poets can and should be seen as part of this larger genealogy of Jewish American poets turning to Whitman.

Chapter 1, "Charles Reznikoff, the Jewish Objectivist Poets, and Walt Whitman," situates Whitman among the Jewish Objectivist poets, with an emphasis on Charles Reznikoff (1894–1976). Reznikoff was born in Brooklyn, New York, to Jewish parents fleeing pogroms in Russia. His first collections of poetry were titled *Rhythms* (1918) and *Rhythms II* (1919), and among his well-known later volumes of verse are *Testimony: The United States, 1885–1890: Recitative* (1965) and *Testimony: The United States, 1891–1900: Recitative* (1968). Reznikoff also wrote longer works of prose (some with notably Whitmanesque titles), such as *By the Waters of Manhattan: An Annual* (1929). In this chapter, Reznikoff's work is presented as emblematic of how the early twentieth-century Jewish Objectivist poets—Reznikoff, Louis Zukofsky, Carl Rakosi, and George Oppen —embraced Whitman, despite being closely entwined with Ezra Pound and other High Modernist poets, who often held complicated attitudes toward Whitman (except for William Carlos Williams, who more patently embraced Whitman). Still more vexing for these Jewish Objectivist poets were the conservative and anti-Jewish sentiments expressed within the milieu of High Modernism, with Pound himself openly expressing such views.

Reznikoff's poetic style, in keeping with the Modernist and Imagist aesthetics promoted at the time, often with pared-down language and short lines, does not appear to reflect Whitman's longer, anaphoric, repetitive poetic forms. Additionally, in various sources, Reznikoff and other Objectivist poets claim not to be engaged in the Whitman tradition, identifying themselves as more strongly aligned with Pound. Yet, taken together, the allusions to Whitman throughout Reznikoff's oeuvre, both explicit and implicit, reveal a profound allegiance to the paradigmatic American poet, as exemplified by poems such as "A Compassionate People" (1944) and the autobiographical poem "Early History of a Writer" (1969). I highlight two poetic arenas in which Reznikoff appears to draw on Whitmanian themes and forms: first, the trope of the poet walking through Manhattan (as Reznikoff and Whitman both do), where the speaker draws the reader's gaze upon figures oppressed by society, with the goal of making them visible; and second, Reznikoff's adoption of Whitman as juxtaposed with the seventeenth-century Jewish philosopher Baruch Spinoza. I claim thus that any allusion to Whitman in Reznikoff can be read as a strategy of navigating the position of writing as a Jewish poet within the High Modernist period in America.

Chapter 2, "Whitman versus High Modernists: On Karl Shapiro and Ken-

26 INTRODUCTION

neth Koch," examines two Jewish American poets who championed Whitman throughout the mid- to late twentieth century: Karl Jay Shapiro (1913–2000) and Kenneth Koch (1925–2002). Far from the subtler incorporations of Whitman by Charles Reznikoff are the parallel enlistments of Shapiro and Koch, who boldly criticize and attack poets perceived as elitist within High Modernist culture, above all Pound, Eliot, and Yeats. Both Shapiro and Koch wrote numerous essays and poems criticizing these Modernist poets, while promoting the more democratic, inclusive model they thought Whitman offered. Shapiro was born in Baltimore, Maryland, and raised, he says, "Jewish, Depression, intellectual, poetic. . . . I was a Baltimorean, a 'Southerner'" (Slavitt 554). Among Shapiro's works is the seminal, Jewish-themed collection *Poems of a Jew* (1958). In these poems, as well as essays like "The First White Aboriginal," Shapiro articulates a sense of being marginalized as a Jew in America and, likewise, depicts Whitman as a figure who was egregiously sidelined within American culture. Shapiro's depictions of Jewish people in the introduction to *Poems of a Jew* echo his descriptions of Whitman, with both Whitman and Jewish people envisioned by Shapiro as eternally in exile and "beyond" time and place. Therefore, in both his poetry and prose, there is a conceptualizing of Whitman that parallels Shapiro's conceptualizations of Jewish figures.

In the work of Kenneth Koch, born in Cincinnati, Ohio, and recognized as a leading figure of the New York School of poets, Whitman is frequently identified as a celebrated influence; for example, Koch declares in a 1996 interview, "After I read Whitman, I felt I could write about anything" ("Interview" 188–189). I interpret Koch's embrace of Whitman and resistance to High Modernist figures, such as appears in the poem "Fresh Air," through two lenses. The first is Koch's position among the New York School of poets, a group that generally favored Whitman, especially Frank O'Hara. The second is Koch's Jewish American identity, which, I argue, is significant in terms of understanding Koch's oeuvre in general, as well as his perceptions of Whitman. While, unlike in Shapiro's case, Jewish themes are almost absent from Koch's *Collected Poems* (2005), in his penultimate collection of poems, titled *New Addresses* (2000), two poems are laden with an intersection of Jewish themes and Whitmanian themes and forms: "To Jewishness" and "To Jewishness, Paris, Ambition, Trees, My Heart, and Destiny." Thus, very much akin to Shapiro, Whitman is evoked by Koch "against" the literary environment of Modernism in the context of writing about being Jewish in America.

Chapter 3, "Whitman's Poetics of Witness: Muriel Rukeyser, Allen Gins-

INTRODUCTION 27

berg, and Gerald Stern," presents three Jewish American poets from across the twentieth century, with unique thematic concerns and aesthetic orientations, to reveal how a thread of Whitmanian poetics of "witness"—or the speaker's humanistic gaze—is evident within each poet's poetic project. In complex ways, this poetry of witness is a mode of countering High Modernist politics that was similarly undertaken by Charles Reznikoff, as well as by Karl Shapiro and Kenneth Koch. In Muriel Rukeyser (1913–1980), one finds a Jewish American woman poet and leftist political activist who was deeply immersed in Whitman's poetics and comes to serve as a crucial foremother for later Jewish American women poets discussed in chapter 4: Adrienne Rich, Alicia Ostriker, and Marge Piercy. The scope of Rukeyser's poetic project has invited comparisons to Whitman (including by Rich, in the essay "Beginners"), with her mission to write prophetic poetry that seeks to correct social injustices in various sites. Rukeyser was raised in an upper-middle-class, German Jewish community of Reform Judaism, and Whitman's democratic ideologies can be detected as part of Rukeyser's resistance to the social ignorance that—in the essay "Under Forty"—she writes of having experienced. Moreover, writing amid High Modernism of the 1930s, 1940s, and 1950s, Rukeyser's engagement with Whitman is partly a response to the Modernist aesthetics that she considered to be "static" and non-egalitarian. Poems such as "The Road" and "The Book of the Dead" from *The Book of the Dead* (1938) and the "Akiba" poems from *The Speed of Darkness* (1968) exemplify how a Whitmanian poetics witnessing is adopted into Rukeyser's mission, which is to create a democratic poetics that is both Jewish and American and that would shape society itself.

By reexamining Whitman's reception by the Beat poet Allen Ginsberg (1926–1977) within the genealogy presented here, I set out to establish that Ginsberg's affiliation to Whitman was not isolated but inseparable from his Jewish American identity (as articulated in poetry and other textual sources), as well as informed by a dialogue with Reznikoff and High Modernist poets like Pound and Williams. Ginsberg was born in Newark, New Jersey, to parents Louis and Naomi Ginsberg, of Russian Jewish descent (like Reznikoff). Ginsberg, father of the Beat generation who wrote poetic anthems like "Howl" and "Kaddish," is by far the most famous poet to have centered Whitman as a poetic father and comrade, celebrating the body and homoerotic intimacy and emulating Whitman's long poems and anaphoric rhythms, as evident in Ginsberg's "A Supermarket in California": "What thoughts I have of you tonight, Walt Whitman" (*Collected Poems* 136).[46] I explore Ginsberg's appropriation of

Whitman within the mapping of Jewish American poets turning to Whitman, focusing on the poetics of witnessing that I argue are in line with Rukeyser's and Stern's. This turn to Whitman is also connected to nuanced dynamics in relation to Reznikoff, Williams, and Pound. These are not the exact dynamics of Shapiro and Koch; in Ginsberg, one does not find sustained attacks against Pound or High Modernism. Instead we find Ginsberg responding to Whitman through an appreciation of the Objectivist poetics of Reznikoff, and Reznikoff's own modes of witnessing and clear representation, and what Ginsberg describes as his "photographic accuracy and precision of detail" ("Reznikoff's Poetics" 142). The Ginsberg-Whitman-Reznikoff line is, moreover, informed by the poetic "empathy" that Ginsberg attributes to both Whitman and Williams (Pacernick 155). Four poems by Ginsberg are presented as case studies of his notions of Whitman and the interplay of a Whitmanian/Reznikoff/Modernist poetics of witnessing: "Improvisation in Beijing," "Yiddishe Kopf," "After Whitman & Reznikoff," and "Waking in New York."

The final poet in chapter 3 is Gerald Stern (1925–2022), born in Pittsburgh, Pennsylvania. Stern is the author of numerous volumes of poetry, among them *Lucky Life* (1977) and *This Time: New and Selected Poems* (1992), as well as essay collections, such as *What I Can't Bear Losing: Notes from a Life* (2009). In Stern's poetry and essays, Whitman emerges as an instrumental predecessor—acknowledged by Stern in essays from *What I Can't Bear Losing* —to be a figure that he both "loves" ("What I Have to Defend" 319) and "resists" ("Ginsberg and I" 266). I suggest that, as with every poet in this book, Stern's affiliation with Whitman is inseparable from his position of being at once Jewish and American. Though Stern's first collection of poems (*Lucky Life*) appears after the height of Anglo-Modernism, the Jewish Whitman that Stern receives has roots in Ginsberg and in the Objectivist-Modernist legacy of Reznikoff, Pound, and Williams. I trace a strand of the poetics of witness in Stern's long poem titled "Hot Dog," in the collection *Odd Mercy* (1997), focused on a young, impoverished girl compelled to be homeless. The poem contains themes of New York City, Jewish identity, America, the Holocaust, poverty, and questions of mortality. Strikingly, the poem also features Whitman as a main character, whom the speaker "follows through half of Camden" (87). As such, it serves as a site where the aspects of the Stern-Whitman-Jewish-Modernist line is evident.

Chapter 4, "Jewish American Women Poets Respond to Whitman: Adrienne Rich, Alicia Ostriker, and Marge Piercy," explores Whitman's critical reception by three Jewish American women poets, with Muriel Rukeyser as a guiding foremother. The chapter considers notions of Whitman in the poetry, scholarship, and interviews of Adrienne Rich (1929–2012), Alicia Ostriker (b. 1937), and Marge Piercy (b. 1936). It is no surprise that in their work, collectively speaking, Whitman is imagined in radically complex and often contradictory ways: as a figure of poetic and personal liberation, as a feminist ally, and no less as a symbol of an ailing, failing (or already failed) America. Rich is the author of seminal collections of poetry, like *Diving into the Wreck: Poems 1971–1972* and *An Atlas of a Difficult World* (1991), and essays on Jewishness, identity, and sexuality like "Compulsory Heterosexuality and Lesbian Existence" (1980) and "Split at the Root: An Essay on Jewish Identity" (1982). Rich was born in Baltimore, Maryland, to parents of divergent cultural backgrounds: her mother was non-Jewish and southern and her father of Jewish descent. Conflicts around a multiplicity of identities are at the core of Rich's response to Whitman. In the 1987 essay "The Genesis of 'Yom Kippur 1984,'" Rich writes of a "considerable dialogue" with Whitman (255). Critics from varying orientations have offered valuable interpretations of this engagement with Whitman's poetics.[47] Largely, though, Rich's imagining of Whitman has yet to be contextualized within the wider Jewish American poetic tradition. I extend this conversation on Rich and Whitman by examining Rich's essay "The Genesis of 'Yom Kippur 1984,'" as well as the poems "Yom Kippur 1984" and "Tattered Kaddish," arguing that in the framework of Rich's "split" identities, Whitman (though very far from being an ideal democratic figure) informs Rich's mission to shape a more democratic poetics and a more open, tolerant society.

For Alicia Ostriker, a Jewish American poet and scholar born in Brooklyn, New York, her work at its essence is political; as she has claimed, "All art is political. Either it is political or it is wallpaper" (Pacernick 229). The political is evinced in her many collections of poetry, among them *The Book of Seventy* (2009) and *Waiting for the Light* (2017), and her scholarly volumes, such as *Stealing the Language: The Emergence of Women's Poetry in America* (1987), *The Nakedness of the Fathers: Biblical Visions and Revisions* (1997), and *Dancing at the Devil's Party: Essays on Poetry, Politics, and the Erotic* (2000). Ostriker has clearly articulated an allegiance to Whitman, having been "powerfully influenced by the Whitman, Williams, and Ginsberg line" (Pacernick 224–225). Ostriker also talks about first encountering with Whitman as a girl of thirteen ("To read Whitman was to experience self-recognition") and a child of Jewish Russian immigrants in the essay "Loving Walt Whitman" (25–26). However,

30 INTRODUCTION

views of Whitman in Ostriker's essays can be read as layered (as in Rich), whereby Ostriker takes issue with Whitman, especially what she perceives as nationalistic proclivities and a glorification of war in Whitman's *Drum-Taps*. I explore this complex interplay of Jewish American identity and Whitman evident in Ostriker's poems "Manahatta" and "Dry Hours: A Golden Shovel Exercise," from *Waiting for the Light* (a collection replete with Whitmanian themes and allusions), as well as "Elegy Before the War," from the earlier collection *No Heaven* (2005).

Finally, for Marge Piercy, political themes likewise pervade her more than twenty volumes of poetry, novels, and works of science fiction, among these *Breaking Camp* (1968), *Stone, Paper, Knife* (1983), *Woman on the Edge of Time* (1985), *What Are Big Girls Made Of* (1997), and *The Art of Blessing the Day: Poems with a Jewish Theme* (2000). Piercy—born and raised in Detroit, Michigan—like the other poets in this chapter, has been engaged in a lifetime of activism, with much of her work informed by the tenet of "being of use" (from the oft-cited poem "To Be of Use," in the 1973 collection by the same title). In keeping with Rich and Ostriker, in overlapping arenas of poetry, politics, and identity, Whitman's intertext appears, for example, in "How I Came to Walt Whitman and Found Myself" (1992), an essay where Piercy writes of having discovered in Whitman "permission to be where I was and who I was" (99). This idea of self-determination extends to her Jewish self, noting "a confirmation of earlier rhythms from Jewish liturgy and the Torah and the psalms" (99). Such discoveries by Piercy in Whitman—the personal, the poetic, the Jewish, and the liturgical—together constitute what I would argue is Whitman's unique role in Piercy's poetry, whereby Whitman's poetics are reflected in liturgical texts composed for the purpose of Jewish services and rituals, connected to the Reconstructionist movement of Judaism (the progressive Jewish movement in America with which Piercy identifies), as well as containing a general, universal appeal beyond a Jewish readership.[48] I explore Whitman being adopted into Piercy's prayer-poems in two texts from *The Art of Blessing the Day*, "The Art of Blessing the Day" and "Nishmat" (1993). The last poem I discuss in Piercy's work is "Praise in Spite of It All," from *On the Way Out, Turn Off the Light* (2020); "Praise" likewise evokes a prayer-like, liturgical style, which I suggest has aspects of being Jewish and Whitmanian, as reflected in the last line of the poem: "I have loved many / and some have even loved me. Amein."

In the conclusion, I revisit a few of the contemporary responses to Whitman by Jewish American poets mentioned the introduction, which are outside the scope of this book, like Jerome Rothenberg, Charles Bernstein, and C. K. Williams. These poets, and others enumerated earlier in the introduction, write for, about, and against Whitman and thus represent an extension of the intricate network of Jewish American poets who look to Whitman. Together, they reflect what Whitman might have conceived of in the poem "To Foreign Lands," where he writes, "I heard that you ask'd for something to prove this puzzle the new world / And to define America, her athletic Democracy, / Therefore I send you my poems that you behold in them what you wanted" (11). Many Jewish American poets continue to "behold" Whitman, in modes that reflect what each poet "wants." This investigation, in its totality, illuminates a realm of exchange whereby Whitman as an American poet shapes Jewish poetry and Jewish poets in America, in turn, shape Walt Whitman.

CHAPTER ONE

Charles Reznikoff, the Jewish Objectivist Poets, and Walt Whitman

> I had been bothered by a secret weariness
> with meter and regular stanzas
> grown a little stale. The smooth lines and rhythms
> seemed to me affected, a false sense on words and syllables—
> fake flowers
> in the street in which I walked.
>
> —CHARLES REZNIKOFF, "Early History of a Writer"

In 1973, Charles Reznikoff (1894–1976), when asked whether he had read Walt Whitman and been influenced by him, replies, "I had read Whitman, but I don't particularly care for him." Reznikoff elaborates, stating that Ezra Pound, too, was thought to have been influenced by Whitman, when in fact Pound had been more impacted by free-verse French poets, the "Anglo-Saxons," and the Bible (Sternburg and Ziegler 116). With such a remark, Reznikoff appears, first, to distance himself from the tradition of the nineteenth-century American poet; and second, to align himself more directly with Pound, a poet known for his own complicated views of Whitman. If Reznikoff's statement were to be taken as the final word on the matter of Whitman, the nuances of the Reznikoff-Whitman (and Poundian) relationship might be readily overlooked. An investigation of appropriations of Whitman by Reznikoff reveals a more dynamic narrative—one in which Reznikoff subtly yet pervasively aligns with Whitman, which I argue is related to Reznikoff's position as a Jewish poet in America amid High Modernism. Moreover, these dynamics can be extended to the other members of the Jewish Objectivist group, of which Reznikoff was a member: Louis Zukofsky, Carl Rakosi, and George Oppen.

Ostensibly quite distinct from Whitman's characteristically long and repetitious poems, Reznikoff's poetics—reflecting Modernist and Objectivist verse forms—tend to be concise and precise; as Reznikoff claims about his own writing, "I'm a great believer in clarity and I try to practice it" (Dembo and Reznikoff 198). Yet Reznikoff did draw upon Whitman, often modestly but pervasively and, I would argue, as a mode of navigating the position of being a Jewish American poet within a Poundian, High Modernist milieu.[1] In the following sections, I explore Reznikoff and the other Jewish Objectivist poets in the context of Pound and of William Carlos Williams. I then examine some explicit allusions to Whitman, as well as more implicit manifestations of this connection, in relation to Reznikoff's Jewish-themed poems, such as "A Compassionate People" (1944); poems containing motifs of Jewish outsider identity, immigration, and assimilation, as in the biographical "Early History of a Writer" (1969); poems informed dually by Whitman and philosophies of the seventeenth-century Jewish philosopher Baruch Spinoza, such as "Poland: Anno 1700" (1934); and finally, in poems by Reznikoff whereby the speaker serves to witness and document the subjects that he sees and, in doing so, casts a Whitmanesque, humanistic, compassionate gaze upon them, as in "Walking in New York" (from *Last Poems*)[2] and "Sunday Walks in the Suburbs" (1921).[3]

WHITMAN, HIGH MODERNISM, AND JEWISH OBJECTIVIST POETICS

Investigating Whitman in the context of High Modernism and the Jewish Objectivist poets is laden with complexity, starting with Ezra Pound, who, in a contradictory manner, championed Jewish American poets of the pre–World War II period yet was known for his elitism, right-wing politics, and antisemitic sentiments.[4] Furthermore, Pound disapproved of Whitman to a large extent,[5] as articulated in the 1909 essay, "What I Feel About Walt Whitman"; as Pound writes, "He *is* America. His crudity is an exceeding great stench, but it *is* America." Pound's sentiments toward Whitman were also infamously articulated in the poem "A Pact":

34 CHAPTER ONE

I make a pact with you, Walt Whitman—
I have detested you long enough.
I come to you as a grown child
Who has had a pig-headed father;

Such unflattering descriptions of Whitman in prose (the "stench") and a poetic "pact" that is all but unresolved signify an attitude with High Modernism and among Imagist poets, expressed by poets like Amy Lowell, who claimed their poetic sensibilities to be far more refined than Whitman's.[6]

It was William Carlos Williams who regarded Whitman more favorably than Pound or Lowell, writing about how *Leaves of Grass* inspired him as a young poet: "But modern poetry, what there was of it, and especially the free verse of Walt Whitman, opened my eyes" (Preface). James Breslin notes that Williams had early notebooks containing thoughts on Whitman, which Pound—unsurprisingly perhaps—"denounced" (615). Williams maintains a more approving stance toward Whitman in terms of Whitman's aesthetics, as well as his role in the tradition of American poetry at large. As Stephen Tapscott has shown in his work on Williams's poetic adoptions of Whitman in the context of Modernism, Williams conceives of a "protomodernist Whitman . . . the Whitman he thinks he and his contemporaries need" (7).[7] Indeed, one finds this notion of the "protomodernist Whitman" in "An Essay on *Leaves of Grass*," where Williams observes, "Whitman's so-called 'free-verse' was an assault on the very citadel of the poem itself. . . . It is a challenge that still holds good after a century of vigorous life during which it has been practically continuously under fire but never defeated" (22). Williams, therefore, was an exception among the Modernist poets in his more total embrace of Whitman.

Within this literary and cultural moment, whereby Whitman's legacy was in flux, the Jewish Objectivist poets emerged, spearheaded by Zukofsky, alongside Pound, Williams, and the Imagist poets. The Jewish Objectivists were deeply informed by a dialogue with Pound and Modernism, as reflected in the pared-down style of Objectivism, with sharp language used to depict objects, subjects, and feelings; as Stephen Fredman writes, Objectivists favored an "elevation of the image" (*Menorah* 5).[8] In 1970, Reznikoff himself gave a definition of "Objectivist" in a London anthology: "Images clear but the meaning not stated but suggested by the objective details and the music of the verse; words pithy and plain; with the artifice of regular meters; themes, chiefly Jewish, American, urban" (qtd. in Ray 914).[9] Fredman notes that Pound was a chief mentor to

REZNIKOFF, THE JEWISH OBJECTIVIST POETS, AND WHITMAN   35

Zukofsky and could not be ignored as a literary guide,[10] since Pound facilitated the publishing of Zukofsky's major work, "Poem Beginning 'The,'" as well as paved the way for Zukofsky to edit the 1931 issue of *Poetry Magazine* titled "Program: Objectivists, 1931," in which Zukofsky highlighted Objectivist-style poets (*Menorah* 3).[11] Pound, Williams, and Marianne Moore were included in the issue.[12] While Reznikoff, Oppen, and Rakosi were never as close to Pound as Zukofsky, both directly and through Zukofsky, Pound played a significant role in the poetic and professional trajectories of each poet.[13]

It is salient to read the near-dismissals and ambiguous responses to Whitman that one finds expressed not just by Reznikoff but also by Oppen and Rakosi within this context. For example, Matt Miller examines Oppen's relationship to Whitman, quoting a letter in which Oppen rather plainly disavows Whitman: "Tho Whitman has been no use to me" ("Getting" 153). Yet, as Miller identifies, Whitman appears as a rather clear influence in Oppen's poem "Of Being Numerous" (153–154). Carl Rakosi, too, when asked about his influences in an interview, names all the Jewish Objectivist poets, as well as Pound, Williams, Shakespeare, Chaucer, Blake, and others, but never states Whitman by name (Pacernick 30). However, in Rakosi's poem titled "Manhattan, 1975," which speaks of a love for New York City, the body, nature, Jewishness, and sensuality, one finds a line in parentheses gesturing to Whitman: "(impossible to keep Whitman out of this)" (*Collected Poems* 282). These semi-renunciations of Whitman by Oppen and Rakosi resonate precisely with Reznikoff's seeming denial of Whitman, whereby the poets do not categorically reject Whitman, despite their claims to having done so.

WHITMAN IN REZNIKOFF'S JEWISH AMERICAN POETRY

Given these layered poetic and political forces, the extent to which Whitman is found in Reznikoff might be thought unlikely; yet there are numerous thematic and formalistic references to Whitman that reveal Reznikoff as having been quite steeped in Whitman's poetics. Before turning to some of these references that are woven more implicitly into Reznikoff's verse, I will touch on some of the more explicit allusions to Whitman. First, what might be considered the most extended incorporation of Whitman into a Jewish-themed poem by Reznikoff is "A Compassionate People" (1944) (vol. 2, 61),[14] which celebrates the survival and "compassion" of the Jewish people after terrible oppression

36   CHAPTER ONE

throughout history and is directly in dialogue with Whitman's poem "Out of the Cradle Endlessly Rocking."[15] In "A Compassionate People," Reznikoff writes of the Holocaust as but one of the many persecutions against Jewish people, out of which they rise to become "a people of love."[16]

In the last section of the poem (number 6), one is met with the unmistakable language and syntax of the opening of Whitman's "Out of the Cradle" ("Out of the cradle endlessly rocking"):

Out of the strong, sweetness;
and out of the dead body of the lion of Judah,
the prophecies and the psalms;
out of the slaves of Egypt,
out of the wandering tribesman of the deserts
and the peasants of Palestine,
out of the slaves of Babylon and Rome,
out of the ghettos of Spain and Portugal, Germany and Poland,
the Torah and the prophecies,
the Talmud and the sacred studies, the hymns and songs of the
Jews;
and out of the Jewish dead
of Belgium and Holland, of Rumania, Hungary, and Bulgaria,

[. . .]

a generous people;
out of the wounded a people of physicians;
and out of those who met only with hate,
a people of love, a compassionate people.

In a poem that seeks to find redemptive "compassion" born of the Jewish people themselves having experienced persecution across history, Whitman is clearly evoked. In terms of form, Reznikoff's twenty-three-line stanza with no full stops corresponds to the structure of the first section of Whitman's "Cradle," a twenty-two-line poem with no full stops. The phrasing "out of" is drawn from Whitman's "Out of the cradle endlessly rocking, / Out of the mocking-bird's throat, the musical shuttle, / Out of the ninth month midnight" (196). Reznikoff's poem also echoes "Cradle" in the way it links a series of incomplete clauses with anaphora and semicolons.[17] Reznikoff's listing of places ("of Belgium and Holland, of Rumania, Hungary, and Bulgaria") likewise emulates Whitman's use of repetition and anaphora with the phrase "out of," as well as being the places where Jewish massacres took place.

Moreover, there is a thematic similarity between Reznikoff's and Whitman's poems, which is the possibility of salvation that emerges from death. Whitman, in the penultimate stanza of "Cradle," writes of the sea whispering the word "death": "the low and delicious word death, / And again death, death, death, death." Yet, out of "death," Whitman writes, the "word of the sweetest song" comes forth, which are his "songs" or poems: "My own songs awaked from that hour . . . / The word of the sweetest song and all songs, / That strong and delicious word which, creeping to my feet, / . . . The sea whisper'd me" (201). Reznikoff's echoing Whitman's language ("sweetness") in the first line of the passage ("out of the strong, sweetness") can represent that Reznikoff, too, derives poems and songs from death. Whitman's notion of death is "melodious," "strong," and "delicious"—a kind of glorifying of death, while Reznikoff's death of the Jewish people is not beautiful or longed for—the result of historical violence against the Jewish people, to which the speaker alludes. Still, the poem's main thrust is a hope that light can come from darkness, people "met only with hate" become "a compassionate people." With the insistence that Jews have always persevered (and will always do so) after the tragedies that befall them, Reznikoff thus writes Whitman into an account of Jewish history.

A poem in which Whitman is not only integrated but identified by name and acknowledged as an influence is "Early History of a Writer" (1969), a long poem in which Reznikoff's speaker narrates his coming of age in New York as a Jewish American immigrant poet. In section seventeen, the speaker writes of having lost interest in fixed verse forms and coming to embrace Whitman's "irregular rhythms":

I had been bothered by a secret weariness
with meter and regular stanzas
grown a little stale. The smooth lines and rhythms
seemed to me affected, a false sense on words and syllables—
fake flowers
in the street in which I walked.

[. . .]

The brand-new verse some Americans were beginning to write—
after the French "free verse," perhaps,

38   CHAPTER ONE

or the irregular rhythms of Walt Whitman,
the English translations of the Hebrew Bible
and, earlier yet, the rough verse of the Anglo-Saxons—
seemed to me, when I first read it,
right:
not cut into patterns, however cleverly,
nor poured into ready molds,
but words and phrases flowing as the thought;
to be read just as common speech
but for stopping at the turn of each line—
and thus like a rest in music or a turn in the dance. (vol. 2, 171)

Even as Reznikoff adopts a concise, Objectivist, non-Whitmanesque style, there is a nod to the inspiration of poets writing in non-fixed verse forms, or "brand-new verse." Though Reznikoff does not specify other poets, it is Whitman who corresponds to "French free verse" and "English translations of the Hebrew Bible," with a distinction made between the Whitmanesque "rhythms"—a "burst of song and sudden dancing" that seemed to him "right"—and the "stale" metered stanzas carried over by British Romanticism. This mention of Whitman is notable because "Early History" was published in 1969, a few decades after Pound and High Modernism ceased to be the most dominant literary forces. Reznikoff is not found to allude to Whitman in such an overt fashion earlier in his work, when acknowledging Whitman's "words and phrases flowing as the thought" might transgress against certain Modernist viewpoints. By extension, when Reznikoff valorizes Whitman's biblical style, he also openly marks his own tradition as a Jewish American poet.

A second, similar engagement in Whitman's poetics, specifically *Leaves of Grass*, is evident in a later passage of the poem:

I also knew a Chinese proverb
that one who can work ten years without recognition
will be known everywhere
and in the tradition in English verse of private publication
as the "Rubaiyat" was published and "Leaves of Grass." (vol. 2, 176)

These lines contain the single explicit mention of Whitman's *Leaves of Grass* in Reznikoff's poetry. The reference is doubly meaningful because it relates to Whitman's self-publishing of his writing, which Reznikoff did also, and points to Whitman's legacy in the "tradition of English verse." I suggest it is no mere coincidence that only in Reznikoff's final book, signifying his maturation as a poet, is Whitman identified as an influence on his poetic vision.

WHITMAN IN REZNIKOFF'S JEWISH-OUTSIDER POEMS

Tracing Whitman further into Reznikoff's poetry, we find Whitman acting in Reznikoff's portrayals of immigrant identity, as appears in Reznikoff's biographical poems about being Jewish in America in general and in New York in particular.[18] Whitman is employed frequently in Reznikoff's poetry of New York City—its streets, environment, and citizens. Biographically speaking, to escape the pogroms, Reznikoff's Yiddish-speaking parents, Sarah Yetta (Wolwovsky) Reznikoff and Nathan Reznikoff, immigrated to America in the 1880s and settled in Brooklyn, where Reznikoff was born, working in the garment industry (Poetry Foundation, "Charles"). Reznikoff's first two books of poetry, *Rhythms* (1918) and *Rhythms II* (1919), are not overtly concerned with Jewish (or Whitmanian) themes; however, Reznikoff's third volume, *Uriel Accosta: A Play and a Fourth Group of Verse* (1921), contains biographically informed work about an immigrant Jewish boy and his family living in Brownsville, Brooklyn. In the books of poetry that follow, Reznikoff seems to become more progressively engaged in Jewish texts, languages, and history, as demonstrated by his fourth book, *Five Groups of Verse* (1927), which includes the oft-quoted section containing the lament of "exile" from Israel and the Hebrew language: "How difficult for me is Hebrew: / even the Hebrew for *mother*, for *bread*, for *sun* / is foreign. How far have I been exiled, Zion" (vol. 1, 72).

In the poem "Autobiography: New York" from *Going To and Fro and Walking Up and Down* (1941), Whitman is quite evident in the recurring motif of Reznikoff being caught between Jewish and American identities;[19] for example, Reznikoff's speaker assumes a Whitmanesque persona of the urban outsider, who is at once a part of and separate from the crowds on the streets of New York City:

III

Walking along the highway,
I smell the yellow flowers of a shrub,
watch the starlings on a lawn, perhaps—

40   CHAPTER ONE

but why are all these
speeding away in automobiles,
where are they off to
in such a hurry?
They must be going to hear wise men
and to look at beautiful women,
and I am just a fool
to be loitering here.

IV

I like the sounds of the street—
but I, apart and alone,
beside an open window
and behind a closed door. (vol. 2, 26)

Reznikoff, solidly in the tradition of Whitman, often took walks through New York; as Milton Hindus writes, he was "a true 'walker in the city,' and the city to him was Whitman's Mannahatta in which he walked for many miles each day, even after he had fallen victim [to a crime]" (*Man* 31). In section three of "Autobiography: New York," the position of being both an insider and outsider is reflected in the way the speaker describes being *in* the city, ("walking along the highway"), while at the same time distracted by nature—"the yellow flowers of a shrub" and "the starlings on a lawn." The speaker calls himself "a fool" for this distraction. These natural elements are in contrast with the city environment, and this engagement with nature sets him apart from "these / speeding away in automobiles." The passage recalls a Whitmanian manner of describing nature in the industrialized city of "Mannahatta": "Numberless crowded streets, high growths of iron, slender, strong, light, splendidly uprising toward clear skies, / Tides swift and ample, well-loved by me, toward sundown" (361).

In the following section of "Autobiography," Reznikoff's speaker is part of the cityscape, listening to "the sounds of the street," which call up the sounds of Whitman's "Mannahatta": "vehicles, Broadway, the women, the shops and shows, / A million people—manners free and superb—open voices." Reznikoff, too, hears these sounds but remains "apart and alone." While the standard syntax of line two might be thus—"But I [*am*] apart and alone"—instead a tone of tension around the speaker's sense of place and displacement is generated. By omitting an expected verb ("am"), Reznikoff thrusts upon the reader something of the distress experienced by the speaker. Whitman is, therefore, woven into the poem as a mediating presence in the speaker's problematical position of what I read as referencing being an outsider in New York.

In another poem, "Autobiography: Hollywood" (based on the period in which Reznikoff lived in Hollywood working as a writer), the speaker again introduces descriptions of nature in an urban setting as a symbol of outsiderness. In this case, nature is a symbol of double outsiderness; that is, being a Jewish person in America as well as a New Yorker in Los Angeles. This time, the longing is for the Whitmanian streets of Manhattan, which, in comparison, he describes as being more connected to, in terms of familial, cultural, and linguistic identity:

> I
>
> A street of strange trees
> thick with small leaves; a grove of dark pines
> with heavy branches thick with needles;
> a sparrow that flutters to the sunny ground
> unlike the brisk birds that I know.
>
> I like the streets of New York City, where I was born,
> better than these streets of palms.
> No doubt, my father liked his village in Ukrainia
> better than the streets of New York City;
> and my grandfather the city and its synagogue,
> where he once read aloud the holy books,
> better than the village
> in which he dickered in the market-place.
>
> I do not know this fog,
> this sun, this soil,
> this desert;
> but the starling that at home
> skips about the lawns
> how jauntily it rides a palm leaf here! (vol. 2, 38)

The first stanza has a reflection upon the "strange trees" and the "sparrow" in Los Angeles being markedly different than the "starlings" in New York. Residing in Los Angeles brings about a nostalgia for New York, conceptualizing New York

42   CHAPTER ONE

as "home," where the speaker was "born." The poem moves chronologically backward, as the speaker writes that his father must have liked the "village in Ukrainia" better than "the streets of New York City" and that his grandfather must have liked "the city and its synagogue / . . . / better than the village / in which he dickered in the market-place." In the last stanza, Reznikoff employs the enumerative listing of Whitman to reinforce his own alienation from Los Angeles: "I do not know this fog / this sun, this soil, / this desert." Reznikoff observes a starling in Los Angeles moving awkwardly, "jauntily," while a New York starling "skips about the lawns." Besides the formalistic nods to Whitman, Reznikoff's juxtaposition of themes of rootlessness—the loss of, and longing for, an imagined home—and the setting of New York echoes Whitman's engagement with New York and the natural world within it.

Finally, to return to Reznikoff's autobiographical poem "Early History of a Writer" (1969), Whitman's poetics are palpable in Reznikoff's depiction of growing up as a Jewish child in America and becoming a poet. In a notable instance from section 1, Reznikoff describes a trip to the park with his mother but is chastised by a policeman for walking on the grass. It is the iconic symbol of "grass" associated with Whitman that appears in Reznikoff's lines:

1

My mother and I were going to the park
and as soon as I smelled the earth I could no longer walk sedately
but ran away—as fast as I could—
upon the forbidden grass;
up, up
a steep slope
until I had to stop for breath.
I turned to look proudly down at my mother
far below.
The tall policeman, who stood in the middle of the drive
among the horses and carriages
and who, it seemed to me, had never as much as glanced at us,
was walking slowly towards my mother
scolding her.
She called me back sharply
and I came down from the heights
to walk meekly beside her

along the asphalt path;
guilty and ashamed,
unworthy to be trusted among the splendors of the park. (vol. 2, 137)

Reznikoff depicts New York—and America, by extension—as alluring and seductive, with two grass-related images, "splendors of the park" and "the earth." The word "splendor" is one that Whitman often uses, such as in "Crossing Brooklyn Ferry": "Gorgeous clouds of the sunset! Drench with your splendor me."[20] The poem "Early History" contains themes other than Jewishness, such as domestication, the world of prohibition, and childhood (perhaps no child, whether Jewish or not, would be welcome on the grass). Yet to apply this universal reading is to minimize Reznikoff's subjective position, as well as the centrality he attributes to being Jewish in many contexts of his work. From the perspective of Reznikoff as a Jewish American child, grass is not Whitman's "hopeful green stuff woven" but an emblem of what he is thwarted from occupying fully. Whitman's grass itself is "forbidden" to the speaker in his memory.[21] When the authority figure of the "policeman" reprimands Reznikoff's mother, deeming Reznikoff "unworthy" to be in the park, and he is forced "meekly" back to the "asphalt path," the grass can be further recognized as a sign of being marginalized within America. Whitman's grass, and Whitman more broadly, symbolizes the America in which Reznikoff lives and writes but, as a Jewish immigrant, he is not fully included.

REZNIKOFF'S WHITMAN AND REZNIKOFF'S SPINOZA

A strand of secular, spiritual Jewishness that informs Reznikoff's poetic vision is still another arena where Whitman can be found to operate. Moreover, it appears that Reznikoff may have found synchronicity between Whitman's ideas of God and humanity and analogous notions in the philosophies of the radical seventeenth-century rabbi Baruch Spinoza, who was excommunicated for promoting ideas of God that were transgressive to the Orthodox Jewish community (Nadler). Here the term "secular" is not used to signify a lack of engagement with Jewish tradition or God by Reznikoff; rather, it refers to a resistance to institutionalized religion, or a dogmatic God of the Hebrew Bible, more in keeping with Whitman's God in "Song of Myself" ("I hear and behold God in every object"). The affinity between Whitman and Spinoza did not escape nineteenth-century reviewers of Leaves of Grass, with one going

44   CHAPTER ONE

so far as to call him "a genuine disciple of Spinoza."[22] Critics, from time to time, observe this duality of Whitman and Spinoza in Reznikoff's poetry, such as Hindus, who writes that God in Reznikoff's poetry is less Jewish than Spinozistic and Whitmanian:

> Reznikoff's religious sentiments, which are unmistakably present in many of his poems . . . are difficult to define precisely. His God, except in direct translations from the Bible, is perhaps nearer to the God of Spinoza and of Whitman than He is to the God of the Jewish tradition. (*Critical Essay* 20)

Along Hindus's lines, Whitman and Spinoza are representative for Reznikoff's presenting Jewishness as a realm malleable and open to individual interpretation and self-definition. I claim that for Reznikoff, the non-Jewish Whitman together with the Jewish Spinoza serve as dual figures through which a more open, self-defining mode of Jewishness in America is advanced in Reznikoff's poetry.[23]

This section briefly explores the Whitmanian and Spinozistic philosophies that reverberate in Reznikoff's poems, often with God as found not in a synagogue or in the Bible but in nature. For example, a section of the poem "Jerusalem the Golden" titled "Spinoza" speaks to the idea of God being found everywhere and in nature, which can be read as very Whitmanian:

> *Spinoza*
> He is the stars,
> multitudinous as the drops of rain,
> and the worm at our feet,
> leaving only a blot on the stone;
> except God there is nothing. (vol. 1, 113–115)

The poem attests to a more universal God, the God in all things, in the "stars," "drops of rain," "a blot on the stone," and all living beings. By employing the word "multitudinous," one cannot miss a reference to Whitman's quintessential line "I contain multitudes" in "Song of Myself" (78) in the notion that godliness resides in the natural world, not in a strictly religious setting with the accompanying dogmatic rituals and practices.

The "Spinoza" section in "Jerusalem the Golden" can inform a reading of section six of "Poland: Anno 1700" from the collection *In Memoriam: 1933* (1934). This collection gives voice to figures from Jewish history, starting with a "sentry" in "Samaria Fallen: 722 B.C.E." (vol. 1, 133). "Poland" is another example of the phenomenon in which Whitman and Spinoza can be read as merged in Reznikoff's Jewish verse; for instance, in a passage with dialogue about God that takes place between an "old Jew" and a "young Jew":

> *A Young Jew.* You look at the world through printed pages—
> dirty panes of glass;
> and even if the pages are the Talmud
> and those who have written wrote with diamonds,
> the more they are scratched, less clearly we can see. (vol. 1, 159)

The young Jew is skeptical of religion and chastises the old Jew for "looking at the world through printed pages." The pages of the Talmud ("dirty panes of glass") prevent the old Jew from "seeing clearly." The young Jew then articulates his own reimagined notion of God (perhaps closer to Reznikoff's own ideologies):

> I see neither rag nor bark,
> flesh nor leaf,
>
> [...]
>
> I see God only and my spirit brightens
> like a mirror;
> I touch Him touching all I touch;
> on earth I am as close to Him as those in Heaven.
> Could I teach myself to want nothing,
> nothing could be taken from me;
>
> [...]
>
> Cold and hunger, pain and grief
> do not last,
> are mortal like myself;
> only the joy in God has no end—
> that it is in the wind
> that showers the petals upon the grass,
> whirls up the glistening snow,
> or sweeps the dust along the streets before the storm;
>
> [...]

46 CHAPTER ONE

tasting God in the salt water
and the sweet rain,
I sink and my feet have nothing to rest on,
I rise and my hands find nothing to hold,
and am carried slowly,
now swiftly,
towards night and towards noon. (vol. 1, 159–160)

In contrast to the old Jew, the young Jew thus claims that God exists everywhere: "I touch Him touching all I touch" and "tasting God in the salt water / and the sweet rain." The young Jew's experience of God is reminiscent of the themes in the earlier poem "Spinoza," where God resides in nature, in the "stars" and "the worm at our feet." The experience of God for the young Jew comes likewise from nature, the "wind," "petals," and "salt water." Furthermore, there is an interplay between the young Jew and Whitman: "I see neither rag nor bark / flesh nor leaf," and "I see God only and my spirit brightens / like a mirror." These lines by Reznikoff can readily evoke the passage of "Song of Myself" aforementioned, where Whitman puts forth his notion of a universal God: "I hear and behold God in every object, yet I understand God not in the least, / Nor do I understand who there can be more wonderful than myself . . . I see something of God each hour of the twenty-four, and each moment then, / In the faces of men and women I see God, and in my own face in the glass" (76). Reznikoff's Spinoza, Reznikoff's Whitman, and Reznikoff's young Jew, therefore, experience God as a permeating presence, whose sources are nature and the individual self rather than a text that suggests an antiquated and oppressive religious authority, the old Jew's "Talmud."

In "Spinoza" and "Poland," the speakers thus surrender to a divine sense of nature as a godly realm. The idea of nature as God is not a Jewish idea but a pantheistic one that Reznikoff seems to import from Whitman and Spinoza to augment or broaden his vision of Jewishness. The "Poland" poem ends with the young Jew being transported into a transcendent realm through a relationship and merging with nature, in a way that Whitman's speaker does in the last section of "Song of Myself." There, Whitman assumes a godlike form of nature: "The last scud of day holds back for me, / It flings my likeness after the rest and true as any on the shadowed wilds, / It coaxes me to the vapor and the dusk. / I depart as air" (78). The God of Reznikoff, Spinoza, and Whitman is similarly found everywhere and not dictated, defined, or determined by a religious authority—neither rabbi nor priest.

WHITMAN IN REZNIKOFF'S POETICS OF WITNESS

The final realm examined in relation to Whitman is Reznikoff's poetics of witnessing, or casting a poetic gaze upon vulnerable figures in society and, in turn, making these figures seen and visible to the reader.[24] This mode of representing those who are outsider and marginalized is quite foundational to Reznikoff's conception of Jewishness, which is democratic in nature.[25] As Ranen Omer-Sherman crucially writes, Reznikoff's experience of being marginalized in American society, as well as his Jewish experience of exile or "homelessness," can be read as being adapted into a poetic interest in, and concern for, various Others:

> [T]he Jewish experience with homelessness provides him with an imperative to address the needs of others. Reznikoff became the rare kind of modernist poet who, by virtue of his outsider status, somehow knew he was emblematic of America, that America was full of aliens like himself, and that through "the sheer plurality of perspectives" these represented, they undermined univocal notions of the nation. (*Diaspora* 160)

This conviction that Omer-Sherman identifies, and with which I agree, is expressed in a number of Reznikoff's poems in which the speaker serves as a witness, or what Whitman calls a poetic "seer" in the preface to *Leaves of Grass* (*Whitman: Poetry and Prose* 9–10).[26] Reznikoff's mode of identifying with the Other is rarely, if ever, in the spirit of Whitman, manifest in the speaker transforming himself *into* the Other, as in Whitman's classic poem of witness "The Sleepers": "I am ... the emigrant and the exile, the criminal that stood in the box" (326). Reznikoff, in a Modernist-Objectivist fashion, strives for imagistic accuracy and emotional distance between the speaker and the subject(s) of the poem.[27] Taken together, though, Whitman's and Reznikoff's perceptions of the role as poet-witnesses similarly contain a moral dimension, thus employing the act of witnessing as an act of inclusion of, and articulating empathy for, the stranger, the outsider, and the Other.[28]

Section 1 of "Walking in New York" from *Last Poems* exemplifies just how Reznikoff employs Whitman, and the symbol of the photograph, as a strategy for representing marginalized figures in society, highlighting social injustices, and promoting humanistic values. Reznikoff's speaker—with Whitman as an implicit compatriot—observes and documents an old woman on Fifth Avenue in Manhattan, who is mostly being ignored by everyone but the poet himself:

48   CHAPTER ONE

Fifth Avenue has many visitors
and many of these have cameras:
they take pictures of themselves, of course,
or of buildings,
and even of trees in Central Park.

But I have yet to see anyone
taking a photograph of the old woman
who stands on the sidewalk
wearing the blanket in which she has slept on a bench:
her stockings fallen
and showing her naked legs
streaked with black dirt;
her grey hair disheveled
and her face also streaked with smudges. (vol. 2, 208)

In the first stanza, Reznikoff offers an image of the "visitors" on Fifth Avenue, who take photographs of themselves, of "buildings" and "trees." The phrase "of course" in line three ("they take pictures of themselves, of course") hints at the visitors' disregard of the surrounding poverty and marks the poem's social criticism. In the second stanza, this criticism is more overt, as the gaze of the speaker and reader are drawn to a destitute woman on the street. Reznikoff writes that he has never seen "anyone" taking that woman's picture, or recording "her naked legs / streaked with black dirt."[29] As is characteristic of Reznikoff, the speaker does not interject with overtly subjective statements (or feelings) about what he sees; yet the poem, through Whitman, does the work of making the invisible visible through a clear depiction of the scene.

With Reznikoff's poem itself serving to capture the scene, the same way the "camera" is used by the visitors, this poem underscores an intersection for Whitman and Reznikoff of poetry and photography. Whitman was himself photographed many times, with portraits often featured in the different editions of *Leaves of Grass*. As Ed Folsom states, Whitman was curious about the photograph because "he liked the idea that technology had arrived at a point where it seemed almost to have gained a soul, a sensibility" (*Native Representations* 101). Moreover, Whitman maintained that the photograph was a more accurate, and equalizing, representation of "reality" than other art forms; he sought to translate the egalitarian quality of the photograph in his poetry, stating that the "work" of the poet was akin to that of the photographer: "The great poet is he who performs the office of the camera to the world, merely reflecting what he sees—art is mere reproduction" (qtd. in Folsom, *Native Representations* 103). Whitman's photographic eye (or "I") thus provides not only an aesthetic but also a moral grounding for his poetics. In the context of "Walking in New York," Reznikoff, too, seems to subscribe to Whitman's notion of photography, whereby the photograph provides a moral grounding, and democratic social agenda, entwined with his very ideas of Jewishness.

Section seven from the collection *Rhythms* (1918) provides another textual example of a poem of witness; in this case from much earlier in Reznikoff's work, it is similarly laden with Whitmanian references. In this poem, the speaker "crosses" between Manhattan and Brooklyn (with a clear reference to Whitman's famous poem "Crossing Brooklyn Ferry"), and the speaker is the solitary witness to a man's death on the Brooklyn Bridge:

> On Brooklyn Bridge I saw a man drop dead.
> It meant no more than if he were a sparrow.
>
> Above us rose Manhattan;
> below, the river spread to meet sea and sky. (vol. 1, 14)

Like the earlier case of "Walking in New York," it is the speaker alone (possibly in a crowd) who is witness to the moment of the man's death on the bridge: "I saw a man drop dead." The "sparrow" can be read as Reznikoff's compensation for society's refusal to acknowledge this death, and that death is insignificant in the scheme of humankind, the grandeur of nature, and the passing of time.[30] Whitman, too, amid the masses in "Crossing Brooklyn Ferry," is alone: "Flood-tide below me! I see you face to face! / . . . / Crowds of men and women attired in the usual costumes, how curious you are to me!" (129). When Reznikoff writes, "Above us rose Manhattan; / below, the river spread to meet sea and sky," Whitman's own glorifying of these grand elements resonates: "Flow on, river! flow with the flood-tide, and ebb with the ebb-tide!" (133). The ebb-tide symbolizes the rush of humanity, the beauty of nature, and the progression of time. Reznikoff and Whitman, from a distance, gaze upon these "flood-tides," finding beauty and meaning in them. Whitman, in "Crossing," claims to be like the men and women he observes: "Just as you feel when you look on the river and sky, so I felt" (130). However, Whitman observes the life teeming around him from a certain distance. Reznikoff's speaker is situated at a similar distance, between New York and Brooklyn, acting as a singular witness to the man who dies, and whose significance is barely registered, except within the poem.

50   CHAPTER ONE

A final case of Whitman's poetics of witness being incorporated into Reznikoff's poetics of witness appears in "Sunday Walks in the Suburbs," a poem from *Uriel Accosta: A Play and a Fourth Group of Verse* (1921). These passages are focused on the impoverished, decaying neighborhoods, which Reznikoff likely observed on his walks through New York:

1

On stones mossed with hot dust, no shade but the thin, useless
     shadows of roadside grasses;
into the wood's gloom, staring back at the blue flowers on
     stalks thin as threads.

The green slime—a thicket of young trees standing in brown
     water;
with knobs like muscles, a naked tree stretches up,
dead; and a dead duck, head sunk in the water as if diving.

The tide is out. Only a pool is left on the creek's stinking mud.
Someone has thrown a washboiler away.
On the bank a heap of cans;
rats, covered with rust, creep in and out.
The white edges of the clouds like veining in a stone.

2

Scared dogs looking backwards with patient eyes;
at windows stooping old women, wrapped in shawls;
old men, wrinkled as knuckles, on the stoops.

A bitch, backbone and ribs showing under the sinuous back,
sniffed for food, her swollen udder nearly rubbing along the
     pavement.

Once a toothless woman opened her door,
chewing a slice of bacon that hung from her mouth like a
     tongue.

This is where I walked night after night;
this is where I walked away many years. (vol. 1, 41–44)

Several Whitmanesque features stand out in the poem; notably in the first line, where Reznikoff subverts Whitman's trademark "grasses" into the "roadside grasses" that signify the decrepitude and poverty of these places. The poem features lines that are uncharacteristically long (for Reznikoff) to convey endless suburban poverty, thereby emulating, while also subverting, the long lines Whitman often uses to convey the very beauty and grandiosity of America. The act of witness is introduced in the couplet at the end of section 2, where Reznikoff employs the refrain "this is where I walked." For Whitman, "walking" is never a mere physical act but a moral, divine endeavor, as in "Song of Myself": "Pleasantly and well-suited I walk, / Wither I walk I cannot define, but I know it is good, / The whole universe indicates that it is good" (337).

In Whitman's stead, Reznikoff's walking "night after night" is symbolically his way of doing "good," another part of his moral imperative as a Jewish poet. The more realistic the representation, the more "good" Reznikoff's poems seek to do. Reznikoff does not shy away from decrepit images of nature ("green slime," "naked trees," and "stinking mud"), animals (rats, "scared dogs," and the "bitch"), and people (the "old men" and the "toothless woman . . . chewing a slice of bacon that hung from her mouth like a tongue").[31] The poem realizes Whitman's drive for inclusiveness but fails to find beauty in the subjects Reznikoff witnesses. Reznikoff's gaze on the particular does not lead to the kind of romanticized beauty that Whitman oftentimes portrays. However, the essential foundation for Reznikoff's "horrible picture" is the drive to elicit the "truth" of humanity as accurately as possible, which he does in this case through a dialogue with Pound's Modernist tradition, together with Whitman's "walking" and "seeing," on the streets in which Reznikoff, in a poetic, philosophical, and one might say spiritual way, "walked at night for many years."

Hopefully, the analysis aforementioned reflects the depth and breadth of Charles Reznikoff's turn to Whitman and adds nuance to Reznikoff's seemingly adverse comment not to "care" for the American poet. Across Reznikoff's oeuvre, in Jewish-themed poems, outsider poems, poems influenced by Baruch Spinoza, and poems of witness that signify a Jewish responsibility to the Other, Whitman resides. The extent to which Whitman is intrinsic to Reznikoff's work is more meaningful within the literary, historical, and political background of Ezra Pound's often anti-Whitman and exclusionary High Modernist setting. Such allusions to Whitman are markers of identity as Jewish American poets writing amid High Modernism, not only for Reznikoff but for the other Jewish Objectivist poets: Louis Zukofsky, George Oppen, and Carl Rakosi.

In the later part of the twentieth century and into the twenty-first century, responses to Whitman in the context of Pound and High Modernism are evident for poets as varied as Karl Shapiro, Kenneth Koch, Muriel Rukeyser, Gerald Stern, and Allen Ginsberg. In fact, Reznikoff's poetics will come to serve as an imperative foundation for Ginsberg's famous appropriation of Whitman. As discussed in chapter 3, Ginsberg's alignment with Whitman can be far better understood in the framework of his engagement with and appreciation of Reznikoff's Jewish Objectivist poetics. As I will establish, for all these poets, with respect to how Whitman is imagined in varying and unique ways, there is a shared strategy of appropriating the poetics of Whitman to negotiate the position of writing as Jewish poets, who write toward a more egalitarian America.

CHAPTER TWO

Whitman versus High Modernists:
On Karl Shapiro and Kenneth Koch

Walt Whitman has had more influence on my poetic
thinking than anybody.

—KARL SHAPIRO, from *The Madness of Art*

After I read Whitman I felt like I could write about
anything—I love Whitman's tone.

—KENNETH KOCH, "Interview with Jordan Davis"

KARL SHAPIRO, KENNETH KOCH, AND WALT WHITMAN

Throughout the mid- to late twentieth century, Walt Whitman was championed by two Jewish American poets: Karl Jay Shapiro (1913–2000) and Kenneth Koch (1925–2002). Shapiro is well-known as the author of the seminal, Jewish-themed collection *Poems of a Jew* (1958), and Koch as a founding member of the New York School of poets, with his first collection, *Poems*, appearing in 1953. Evidence of Shapiro's and Koch's embrace of Whitman appears in essays, interviews, and poetry, as signified by the epigraphs noted, where Shapiro claims Whitman to be his most valuable predecessor, and Koch to have been poetically liberated by Whitman. That poets Shapiro and Koch, with Jewish America backgrounds, wrote in the same period, but operating in somewhat

54 CHAPTER TWO

different literary spheres, makes their shared appreciation for Whitman especially noteworthy.

More remarkable still is the poets' parallel enlistments of Whitman to boldly attack elements within High Modernist groups they perceived as elitist, especially Ezra Pound, T. S. Eliot, and William Butler Yeats, among the leading literary figures of the time. Shapiro and Koch wrote poetry and prose essays portraying these and other poets as conservative and exclusionary, while promoting Whitman's poetics as a more democratic model. This embrace of Whitman on the one hand and rejection of aspects of High Modernist culture on the other has roots in the alignment with Whitman by Jewish American poets of an earlier generation discussed in chapter 1, such as Charles Reznikoff and the other Jewish Objectivist poets Louis Zukofsky, George Oppen, and Carl Rakosi. However, as previously explored, Reznikoff's alignment with Whitman, although quite pervasive in his poetry, was far subtler, having been more connected to Pound and the High Modernist milieu, within which views of Whitman were frequently ambivalent.

Though also of an overlapping generation, Shapiro and Koch neither appear to turn to Whitman in the mode of Allen Ginsberg (1926–1997). Ginsberg is recognized for turning to Whitman as a model of counterculture, sexual politics, and homoerotic kinship, most famously in poems such as "Howl" and "Kaddish." Shapiro, in fact, professed a dislike of aspects of Ginsberg, and Ginsberg's employment of Whitman, stating, "I am not crazy about the Whitman element in Ginsberg; it seems to me Ginsberg knew what Whitman was doing, but Ginsberg is a programmer and a propagandist and a politician. His poetry has suffered very badly. There's some great stuff—poetry of lamentation and so on—but so much of it is theatrical and phony" (Phillips 56). Regarding Koch, and salient for this context, in an interview between Ginsberg and Koch in the *New York Times* in 1978, Ginsberg himself inquires as to an affinity between his own poem "Howl" and Koch's poem "Fresh Air," comparing the two poems to Whitman: "I thought we hit on the same explosion of fearless humor, poetic energy, expansive and unchecked, as the Good Grey Poet might say." In response, Koch states, "I don't know. I supposed I trust my associations the way I imagine a composer of music would trust his" ("Writing" 185). Shapiro's and Koch's adoptions of Whitman thus do not mirror Ginsberg's. And yet, in Shapiro's and Koch's confrontations with High Modernist poets, Whitman is designated as a poet far more open and democratic; in significant respects, Shapiro and Koch will be demonstrated as far more in line with Ginsberg's adoption of Whitman than might be apparent at first.

With respect to the uniqueness of each poet's aesthetics, relationships to Jewish American identity, and views of Whitman, this chapter examines how Shapiro and Koch similarly imagine Whitman against elitism in the literary world (and beyond). Shapiro, expressing a sense of being marginalized as a Jew, also imagines Whitman as marginalized in American society. Shapiro's portrayals of Jews and Jewishness parallel his portrayals of Whitman, thus coming to imagine Whitman *as* a Jew. In the case of Koch, the embrace of Whitman and resistance to High Modernism is read through binary lenses. The first lens is his position among the New York School of poets, with a focus on Frank O'Hara, who collectively embraced Whitman and resisted High Modernist elitist figures. The second is Koch's Jewish American identity, which I would argue is more influential in reading Koch's work and his alignment with Whitman than is often recognized. By juxtaposing Shapiro and Koch, I hope to illuminate a genealogical branch of Whitman's absorption into the Jewish American poetic tradition in which Whitman himself is transformed, politicized, and "ethnicized."

KARL SHAPIRO—JEWISH AMERICAN POET IN EXILE

With scholars noting his idiomatic language and depictions of middle-class American life, Karl Shapiro was considered by certain critics to be a proto-typical American poet.[1] Hayden Carruth states, "Shapiro was derivative but never imitative. He was an American" (4).[2] *V-Letter and Other Poems* (1945), the Pulitzer Prize–winning collection Shapiro wrote during his military service in World War II, further solidified his reputation as a distinctly American poet; according to Hilene Flanzbaum, the various personas assumed by Shapiro in his war poetry made him appealing: "Shapiro has written poems about being Jewish and Christian, Native-American and Black, wounded and healthy, and it is indeed part of his point that as the composite American—and most important, as the ideal American soldier—he can be any of these things" (263). Thus, Shapiro was perceived as an American poet, not necessarily a Jewish one.

Shapiro cultivated the role of the American poet to some degree. In the essay "Notes on Raising a Poet," for instance, his description of an ideal American poetry seems to reflect not only his own poetic style but a collective to which he belonged: "What would American poetry be like, to deserve a name? Answer: It would be nonsensical, hilarious and obscene like us. Absurd like us.

56   CHAPTER TWO

. . . It would be mystical, savage and drab" (130).[3] However, Shapiro at times minimized, or outright denied, the designation of the American poet:

> Words like "spokesman" and "touchstone" took me completely by surprise.
> . . . Not only had I been out of the country when my first two books were published, but I have always been "out of the country" in the sense that I never had what ordinarily is thought of as a literary life, or been part of a literary group. . . . I never had any of that and still don't. (Phillips 50)

This resistance to serving as a "spokesman" for, or representative of, America bespeaks an outsider position, being American and yet "out of the country" in a literal and symbolic way. Shapiro referred to this outsiderness in regard to institutional affiliations, holding positions that placed him ostensibly in the echelons of American poetry—a professor at several major universities, the editor of *Poetry Magazine*,[4] and poetry consultant at the Library of Congress in 1946: "I have a sort of special status around English departments. I'm not really a professor, but sort of a mad guest" (Phillips 62).

A major reason for Shapiro's sense of outsiderness was having been Jewish—an outsiderness compounded by his own complex and troubled attitude toward Jewishness itself. Born in 1913, Shapiro writes that he was raised "Jewish, Depression, intellectual, poetic. . . . I was a Baltimorean, a 'Southerner'" (Slavitt 554). Shapiro was not religiously observant, unlike others in his family. When Robert Phillips asks Shapiro, "What has being Jewish done to your work?" Shapiro describes resisting Judaism, to the point of considering conversion to Christianity:

> Just everything. I went through a period, like many middle-class Jews, in which I consciously drew away from religion and everything Jewish in my life. And I think for a long time, say in the 1930s, I felt completely cured of the religious virus. (Phillips 60–61)

Shapiro's cynicism as to the "virus" of religion typifies an attitude held by many secular, left-wing Jewish American intellectuals, authors, and artists of the period.[5] As such, Jewishness was a crucial element of Shapiro's self-identification, one that pervaded his writing, but it was a cultural identity rather than a traditional, religious one.

The outsider condition of being Jewish for Shapiro was mirrored, moreover, in the outsider condition of being a poet, with both as sources of tension: "I have always had this feeling—I've heard other Jews say—that when you can't find any other explanation for Jews, you say, 'Well, they are poets.' There are a great many similarities. This is a theme running through all my stuff from the very beginning. The poet is in exile whether he is or he is not" (Phillips 60). With this notion of exile, Shapiro is likely alluding to Marina Tsvetayeva's oft-quoted statement "All poets are Jews." Shapiro's expression of "exile" also evokes John Hollander's well-known concepts of exile in the essay "The Question of American Jewish Poetry"; first, Shapiro claims that Jews are "outsiders, by nature itinerant no matter how locally rooted," and second that Jews exist in "a kind of linguistic *galut*" (40, 43). This theme of *galut* (the Hebrew term for exile or Diaspora) appears throughout Shapiro's work. In "Poet," he writes that the Jew and the poet "shall be always strange" (42). In another poem, "Travelogue for Exiles," the theme of outsiderness is evident in the title ("exile"), as well as in the repeated line "this is not your home" (*Poems of a Jew* 18). Such a line can be read as a reflection on the human condition of outsiderness; however, in context with the Jewish themes of Shapiro's work, it must also be understood to reference a particularly Jewish sense of exile.[6]

Returning to Whitman, the following sections demonstrate how Shapiro perceives Whitman to be positioned in a liminal place in America. Somewhat in parallel to Shapiro, Whitman sought to situate himself as America's poetic spokesperson, "commensurate with a people," as written in the preface to *Leaves of Grass* (*Whitman: Poetry and Prose* 6–7). As we will see, Whitman was pushed to the margins, or as per Shapiro, somewhat in exile, by several leading High Modernist figures, the very figures who contributed to Shapiro's own sense of exile as a Jewish poet. As intimated earlier, Shapiro's perception of Whitman as a force against certain High Modernists is even more significant when juxtaposed with the Jewish American poet Kenneth Koch. Koch describes his experience with Jewishness in America as complex and in a few texts praises and celebrates Whitman, while simultaneously criticizing High Modernist poets such as Pound, Yeats, and Eliot.

Shapiro's Attack on High Modernist Poets

In "The First White Aboriginal," Shapiro asks, "What has happened to Whitman in the century since *Leaves of Grass* was published?" (160). This query, ostensibly straightforward, signifies layers of Shapiro's critique of Whitman's diminished reputation in that period of High Modernist dominance, as well as the glorification of Whitman that one encounters throughout Shapiro's essays. Later in "The First White Aboriginal," Shapiro writes, "The power of

58   CHAPTER TWO

Walt Whitman in the world is incalculable" (173). In "Is Poetry an American Art?," an essay published several years later, Shapiro declares, "We [America] have given birth to only one poet before the present century—Walt Whitman. There are a few false starts, such as Poe and Emily Dickinson. The rest is padding" (399). Indeed, among the "padding"—in other words, the many writers that Shapiro held in high esteem, such as William Carlos Williams, Emily Dickinson, W. H. Auden, D. H. Lawrence, Henry Miller, Randall Jarrell, and Hart Crane—it is Whitman that Shapiro singularly places on a pedestal.[7]

As highly as Whitman is extolled by Shapiro, Shapiro's aversion to the aesthetics and politics of the right-wing High Modernist milieu is made clear: "Once upon a time there was a thing called poetry; and . . . it was very beautiful and . . . people tried to bring it to our shores in boats, but it died" ("Is Poetry" 405).[8] Shapiro often employs a humorous tone when conveying his otherwise serious grievances against Pound, Eliot, and Yeats above all. In *The Poetry Wreck*, Shapiro condemns "the political simple-mindedness and viciousness of the great trio of Pound, Eliot and Yeats," voicing acute disapproval of their ideologies (xv):

> Never mind their fascism, with or without the large F. . . . The real triumph of these famous old poets was of course never in the world of politics but in the Academy. They defined an attitude toward literature and gave it an intellectual sanction. (xvi)

Shapiro deliberately describes each member of the "trio"; regarding Pound, he maintains, "Any way you look at it, writing about Ezra Pound and his poetry is unpleasant business. . . . Pound is not the kind of writer who once did something wrong and can now be forgiven in the mellowness of time. . . . He is righteous about his wrongness; he forces his worst upon us whenever we meet him, and there is no escaping it" (29). In "The Death of Literary Judgment," Shapiro also denounces Eliot: "[Eliot] resembles one of those mighty castles in Bavaria which are remarkably visible, famed for their unsightliness, and too expensive to tear down" (35). William Carlos Williams was an exception among the prominent High Modernist figures; about him Shapiro wrote far more favorably, stating that Williams had protested the "sell-out poetry" of High Modernism ("Hockey" 285). Shapiro's admiration of Williams is in keeping with other Jewish American poets, like Reznikoff, Ginsberg, and Koch, who viewed Williams favorably compared to Pound. Williams was far more embracing of Whitman than Pound and other High Modernists, as discussed in chapter 1.

In 1948–1949, the rift between Shapiro and these poets deepened when Williams's *Paterson* and Pound's *Pisan Cantos* were both nominated for the 1948 Bollingen Prize. The prize committee, composed of major literary figures including Shapiro, Eliot, Auden, and Lowell, voted to give the award to Pound. The next day Shapiro changed his vote, stating he could not "endorse an anti-Semite" for the prize (Rubin, "Karl Shapiro" 111). Shapiro reports that the circumstances around the Bollingen Prize were a "turning point" in his life, as well as "a great blow to me, the publicity and the scandal. I was suddenly forced into a conscious decision to stand up and be counted as a Jew" (Phillips 61). Shapiro states that if not for "the anti-Semitic and anti-American propaganda" in *Pisan Cantos*, he would have voted for Pound, despite supporting Williams (Phillips 61).

Shapiro's denunciation of Pound and Eliot was thus born from his belief that they propagated an exclusionary culture, one that not only kept him, a Jew, as an outsider but also imprisoned poetry in the academy, withdrawing it from the popular realm. As Flanzbaum notes, by resisting the New Critical hold on the academy, Shapiro resisted the "inaccessibility" of poetry: "For Shapiro, poetry heals and unites, it has a social function, it makes community, and is central to the well-being of America" (264). Shapiro argued that Eliot, for example, led American poetry away from the people, at a time when poetry "had got into the street, into the open air. People, even newspapers understood that America was beginning to write its own poetry" ("Hockey" 285). Shapiro went so far as to equate "Newcrit" with Orwell's "Newspeak" ("Hockey" 285). Shapiro also wrote disparagingly of the New Critical movement as being intolerant to writers of color and other marginalized groups: "The highbrow magazines, always on the side of power-culture, refuse to recognize the existence of a revolt. . . . The Academy observes a kind of token assimilation of the Beat, just as the big Southern universities admit three Negroes a year. A few professors like myself are permitted to hang on, but nobody knows when the knock is coming at the door" ("Hockey" 285).

And it was not only Shapiro for whom the "knock" at the door was coming, but Whitman too. According to Shapiro, Whitman was "sent packing" as soon as Eliot began to "manipulate" poetry ("Hockey" 285). Shapiro believed the High Modernist poets' dismissing of Whitman to be radically hypocritical, because these same poets minimized the significance of Whitman's influence on their poetry: "And what are we to make of the paradox, for example, of Pound's dependence on Whitman's prosody while rejecting the *sense* of Whitman's poetry. And Hart Crane's identification with the sense of Whitman, while

60 CHAPTER TWO

rejecting the revolutionary forms?" ("Is Poetry" 397). In "Notes on Raising a Poet," Shapiro underscores this hypocrisy: "[A]ll other American poetry tries, though most would deny it, to measure up to *Leaves of Grass*. It can be argued that *The Waste Land* and even the *Cantos* are redactions of *Leaves of Grass*" (130). Elsewhere, he makes clear the reason for this hypocrisy, that Whitman's pluralistic vision threatens the poets' elitist culture:

> Whitman had the greatest insight after all. This might account for his unpopularity in America. For Whitman is unpopular not only with Americans at large—nonexistent would be a better word—he is also unpopular with poets. Whitman is dangerous to American poets, like a pesticide. ("Is Poetry" 397)

Given Shapiro's antipathy to the elements of New Criticism that he perceived as problematic, it is unsurprising that Shapiro's spokesman of America—Whitman, the "pesticide"—would become a contrasting symbol of equality and egalitarianism.

In "The First White Aboriginal," Shapiro seeks to reconsider so-called misunderstandings about Whitman—and to revitalize his reputation, in other words—which had been wounded by the High Modernist milieu. Shapiro compliments Lawrence for valuing Whitman and "acknowledging him with love" (157). He also states that Lawrence was "inferior" to Whitman (159) and that Whitman was the true democratic poet of America: "At a single stroke, apparently without preparation, Whitman became the one poet of America and Democracy" (157). Therefore, it is Whitman's liberal ethos that Shapiro puts forth as a corrective to the elitism he associates with Pound, Eliot, and Yeats.

Shapiro lauds Whitman not only as a poet of democracy but as the inventor of an American prosody as well; for example, in a passage from *Essay on Rime*, he writes,

> Whitman's metric is maladroit, at times
> As flaccid as the gentle curve of Longfellow's
> *Evangeline*, but at its best the strongest
> Link in American prosody. In fact,
> If any one poet fathered a new form
> And freed us from the traditional. . . . (16)

In terms like "flaccid" and "gentle," hints of discomfort with Whitman's sexuality may be detected, and though Whitman's sense of meter is criticized, Shapiro nevertheless names Whitman as the "father," the "strongest link," the hero whose free-verse poetry liberated America from "traditional" verse forms.

While Shapiro considered Whitman quintessentially rooted in America, he believed Whitman to be a mystic with a vision transcending nation, culture, and religion. Shapiro refers frequently to Whitman's mystical nature. In response to Phillips's query, "In the middle or late fifties, Whitman became very important to you—almost in religious terms. Can you comment on that? And what about Poe?" Shapiro states,

> Poe was the father of symbolism, so Poe never appealed to me. . . . On the other hand, there was Whitman. Whitman to me is the most fascinating of American poets. Whitman started to write the great poetry from scratch after he had written all that junk for newspapers, the sentimental lyrical poetry. All of a sudden, he wrote *Leaves of Grass*. . . . I was completely bowled over by this, not having been able to explain how Whitman came to write "Song of Myself," which is unlike anything not only in American literature, but unique in all the world. The parallels to it are mystical literature. (Phillips 55–56)

In "Cosmic Consciousness," Shapiro alludes again to the idea of Whitman as mystic, describing *Leaves of Grass* as a "mystical document," which "plunges into the central mystical experience of Whitman's poetry" (30–31). Earlier in the same essay, Whitman is said to possess "cosmic consciousness."[9] Shapiro writes that Whitman's cosmic consciousness marked him as "a member of a new species of the [human] race. He is characterized by a state of moral exaltation, enhanced intellectual power, a feeling of elevation" (31). Elsewhere, the mystic turns prophet: "[Whitman] sprouted . . . vegetated . . . loafed out of nowhere into the role of prophet and seer. . . . [H]e is the one mystical writer of any consequence America has produced" ("First White Aboriginal" 157). Shapiro therefore comes to think of Whitman as all-American *and* a prophet, roles with a strong exilic dimension. Whitman is American, yet not perceived by the majority as the father of American poetry. Whitman is also a prophet, but one whose orientation is more dissident than participant.

Ascribing Jewish connotations of prophecy to Whitman is noteworthy, especially when coming from Shapiro. By understanding Whitman as a prophetic poet, presumably like any of the Jewish prophets of the Bible with extraordinary knowledge and insight, Shapiro positions Whitman in a Jewish context. These dual attributes, being an American and a prophet, are Shapiro's

62   CHAPTER TWO

explanations for the Modernists' rejection of Whitman, a rejection that Shapiro himself wrote of facing as a Jew. Shapiro therefore perceives Whitman to be a poet in exile, a role Shapiro designated for himself and which was imposed upon him. As the next section will address, there is great gain for Shapiro in turning Whitman into a prophetic poet and thus a quasi-Jew.

Shapiro's Whitman, Shapiro's "Jew"

With Shapiro locating Whitman as an American poet in exile, is it surprising that his vision of Whitman evokes his vision of the "Jew" and Jewishness itself? This Whitman-Jewish correlation is evident in Shapiro's introduction to *Poems of a Jew*, a collection where each poem explores some aspect of Jewishness—language, culture, the Holocaust, and Israel. Ironically, Shapiro claimed there not to be "concerned" with "The Jewish Question," "Judaism," "Jewry," or "Israel" (ix), a contradiction reflective of a certain inconsistency, whereby Shapiro particularizes Jewishness on the one hand yet generalizes it on the other. Shapiro infers that the "undercurrent" of the poems in the collection is the Jew and that the Jew is at the "center" of the collection. At the same time, he insists that the poems are intended to be "universal":

> [These poems] are not for poets. They are for people who derive some strength of meaning from the writings of poets and who seek in the poet's mind some clue to their own thoughts. . . . These poems are documents of an obsession. This obsession, I believe, is universal and timeless; the Jew is at its center, but everyone else partakes in it. (ix)

Shapiro describes the uniquely Jewish nature of the collection but equates the Jew with "universality" and "timelessness." Richard Slotkin comments on the association between Jewishness and human suffering, that for Shapiro, the Jew is "a modern man . . . a humanist intimate with God through his intimacy with the pain, suffering, humiliations and joys of the world" (220). Admittedly, Shapiro's statement has an implicit ethnocentricity, whereby the Jew is at the center of his "obsession" for others to "partake in," revealing some lack of self-reflection regarding his conception of Jewishness. This aside, Shapiro attempts to bring Jews from the margin to the center by theorizing the Jewish condition as that of human suffering, of "everyman."

In a later passage Shapiro writes that being Jewish is to possess an "inescapable state of consciousness," contradicting the earlier notion that the Jewish experience represents a broader, human one:

No one has been able to define *Jew*, and in essence this defiance of definition is the central meaning of Jewish consciousness. For to be a Jew is to be in a certain state of consciousness which is inescapable. As everyone knows, a Jew who becomes an atheist remains a Jew. A Jew who becomes a Catholic remains a Jew. Being a Jew is the consciousness of being a Jew, and the Jewish identity, with or without religion, with or without history, is the significant fact. (*Poems of a Jew* x)

By claiming that the Jew is permanently "inescapable" from himself as a Jewish person (here treading on the problematic territory of *essentialism*), Shapiro infers that Jewishness is a unique state of being. Subsequently, Shapiro reverts to his previous position, of Jews being a "divine" or transcendent people:

The Jew is absolutely committed to the world. This people beyond philosophy, beyond art, virtually beyond religion, a stranger even to mysticism, finds itself at the very center of the divine manifestation—man. The Jew represents the primitive ego of the human race. . . . [T]he Jew cannot be erased from human consciousness, even by force. (x)

Shapiro vacillates between emphasizing what he sees as the uniqueness of the Jew and at the same time conceptualizing the Jew as representative of the "human race."[10] He goes so far, in *Poems of a Jew*, as to suggest that Jews who suffered in the Holocaust represent the suffering of all mankind:[11]

The hideous blood purge of the Jews by Germany in the twentieth century revived throughout the world the spiritual image of the Jew not as someone noble and good, or despicable and evil . . . but as man essentially himself, beyond nationality, defenseless against the crushing impersonality of history. (x)

Shapiro intimates that the victimization of Jews in the Holocaust is at the core of the universalizing potential that Jews possess, whereby the "evil" faced by Jews is the same evil faced by humanity at large.[12]

Shapiro's rhetoric about the Jew being at once a particular and a universal figure shares various parallels with rhetoric about Whitman. As discussed earlier, Shapiro thought of Whitman as transcending any nation, culture, or aesthetic. Whitman, Shapiro declares, "looked beyond literature and beyond the greatness of art. His true personality went out beyond America, beyond religions and even beyond mankind. . . . Whitman accepted death. . . . [H]e triumphed over it. He saw beyond history and beyond America" ("First White Aboriginal" 171–172). Later, Shapiro again employs the term "beyond": "Because Whitman is beyond the law of literature he is condemned to extinction from generation to generation . . . Whitman is beyond the reach of Criticism, beyond Congress and the Church, and yet there, right under your nose" ("First White Aboriginal" 174). In *Poems of a Jew*, Shapiro bestows the same term upon Jews: "beyond philosophy," "beyond art," "virtually beyond religion." Therefore, the trait of being "beyond" marks the Jew and Whitman as outsiders yet insiders, members of the very context that they supposedly also transcend. For Shapiro, Whitman is inherently American (and implicitly Jewish), while Jews are inherently Jewish (and implicitly American).

In addition to his essays, Shapiro's conflating of Whitman and the figure of the Jew is reflected in poetry. Shapiro does not identify Whitman as a stylistic influence, often employing un-Whitmanian devices, such as structured stanzas, short lines, and spare language. However, in a number of collections, among them *Person, Place and Thing* (1942), *V-Letter and Other Poems* (1945), *Trial of a Poet* (1947), *Poems of a Jew*, and *The Bourgeois Poet* (1964), one detects the thematic and formalistic imprint of Whitman. "I Am an Atheist Who Says His Prayers," from *The Bourgeois Poet*, can be taken to exemplify the poetic conjoining of Shapiro's Whitman and Shapiro's Jew (*Collected Poems* 180–181). The speaker of the poem, overtly Jewish and American, assumes a variety of identities, refusing to abide by religious, cultural, and social categories. In the opening lines, the speaker celebrates these contradictions, as Whitman does famously in "Song of Myself." With a Whitmanian "I" and catalogue, and Shapiro's trademark sense of (Jewish?) humor, the speaker enumerates these identities:

I am an atheist who says his prayers.

I am an anarchist, and a full professor at that. I take the loyalty oath.

[. . .]

A physical coward, I take on all intellectuals, established poets, popes, rabbis, chiefs of staff.

I am a mystic. I will take an oath that I have seen the Virgin. Under the dry pandanus, to the scratching of kangaroo rats, I achieve psychic onanism. My tree of nerves electrocutes itself.

[. . .]

How beautifully I fake! I convince myself with men's room jokes and epi-
grams. I paint myself into a corner and escape on pulleys of the un-
known. Whatever I think at the moment is true. Turn me around
in my tracks; I will take your side. (180–181)

Throughout the poem, Shapiro assumes a myriad of selves, like Whitman,
"beyond" privileging any one singular self. The first line, "I am an atheist
who says his prayers," bespeaks the paradox of a secular Jewish poet resisting
religious tradition yet partaking in religious ritual. In line 2, Shapiro presents
another paradoxical identity, being as an "anarchist" against institutions, yet
part of one as a "professor" (which biographically Shapiro was). By line 3, the
speaker expresses, even embraces, his nonconformity, adding, "I am a deviate."
This plurality of selves is carried throughout the poem with the Whitmanian
anaphora of "I": "A physical coward, I take on all intellectuals, established
poets, popes, rabbis, / chiefs of staff." Moreover, with this Whitmanian "I,"
the speaker claims to be a "mystic," and a Jewish/Christian one at that: "I am
a mystic. I will take an oath that I have seen the Virgin." As discussed earlier,
Shapiro believes Whitman to be a mystic, able to reach a higher psychical
plane, as a Jew, an American, and an everyman.

Jewishness is explicitly referenced only once in the poem, when Shapiro
writes in a later stanza, "O Israel," a recognizable Jewish credo. It is the rec-
itation of the speaker's changing self that marks him as a Jew, as long as we
understand the Jew, as Shapiro does, to represent everyman in a symbolic
sense. The shifting "I" and Shapiro's cataloguing of identities clearly call to mind
the Whitmanian persona in "Song of Myself": "I am of old and young, of the
foolish as much as the wise, / Regardless of others, ever regardful of others, /
Maternal as well as paternal, a child as well as a man . . . / . . . I resist anything
better than my own diversity" (42). With this plethora of selves possessed
by the speaker, he possesses many but perhaps none wholly or permanently.
The speaker regards the transience of this condition with humor, though the
humorous tone can be read as a veil partly masking an underlying distress
about his complicated status, for examples, in lines such as "How beautifully
I fake! . . . / Whatever I think at the moment is true. Turn me around / in my
tracks; I will take your side." The idea of immutability in "I Am an Atheist" is
crucial to Shapiro's notions of Whitman and Jewishness, whereby the speaker
is an American insider and a Jewish outsider, "beyond" categorization, and
his own Jewish Whitman "I."

"A RESCUER OF ME FROM THE FLATNESS OF MY LIFE": KENNETH KOCH, JEWISH AMERICAN POET IN THE NEW YORK SCHOOL

An abiding appreciation for Whitman pervades the work of Kenneth Koch. As seen in the chapter epigraph, in a 1996 interview with Jordan Davis, Koch declares, "After I read Whitman, I felt I could write about anything." About lines from "Song of Myself," he states, "[Whitman's] lines seem to rise from the pages of a book like trumpet sounds from microscopic chips embedded there" (188–189). In "Whitman's Words," an essay exploring the pedagogical possibilities in the themes, imagery, and language of "Song of Myself," Koch describes Whitman as "interesting," "suggestive," and "exciting" (36–37). In poems, too, Koch identifies Whitman as an influence, such as "Fresh Air," the poem widely recognized for Koch's criticism of the dominance of certain High Modernist figures, such as Ezra Pound, and of aesthetics. There Whitman appears, along with Mallarmé, Shelley, and Byron, as a progenitor of "the new poem of the twentieth century" (123) and thus representing a counter to High Modernist conservatism.[13] Broadly speaking, Koch's forms and themes are frequently Whitmanesque in nature—long, associative poems that depict New York City and rejoice in the beauty of nature.[14] These explicit references and allusions to Whitman in Koch's writing represent a high regard for Whitman—held likewise by Karl Shapiro—and expressed in a manner that is as equally uncompromising and blunt.

The embrace of Whitman by Koch can be understood in terms of two separate but related contexts: First, Koch was among the founding members of the first generation of the New York School of poets, often considered to be Koch, John Ashbery, Frank O'Hara, James Schuyler, and Barbara Guest, who were active in New York City beginning in the 1950s and 1960s.[15] It is fairly well documented that the poets of the New York School promoted and emulated Whitman, presenting him as a counter-figure to the High Modernist, New Critical establishment. Second, Koch was Jewish, and in fact the sole poet with a Jewish background from the first-generation New York School poets. As I argue, Koch's Jewish American identity informs a reading of his responses to Whitman within the context of Shapiro's and the wide network of Jewish American poets from the mid-nineteenth century to the contemporary period. Furthermore, Koch's praising of Whitman and employing Whitman to attack High Modernist figures and poetry—both actions in keeping with Shapiro's mode of doing the same—solidifies Koch's position within the Jewish American tradition, in which Whitman is enlisted in a poetic struggle for national, cultural, and literary inclusion.

Arguably, the poets most recognized today from the New York School are Ashbery and O'Hara. A certain level of critical neglect of Koch has been attributed to his open attacks on major literary figures and the use of humorous elements in his poetry.[16] Yet Koch played a central role among the group of poets who shared a poetic, artistic, and ideological sensibility, writing nonformalistic, experimental poetry with humoristic elements, seeking to depict life in New York City. The poets famously collaborated with musicians, artists, and abstract painters, like Jackson Pollock and Willem de Kooning (Poetry Foundation, "Introduction"). In addition to Whitman, major poetic influences include Shelley and Yeats, Pound, Eliot (despite his expression of a complicated attitude toward these poets), French surrealists, and Italian poets. The delineation of the New York School remains in flux; as Josh Schneiderman writes, "The New York School of Poets has always been a contested label" (346).[17] But the poets' impact on one another, personally, creatively, and professionally, was tremendous—as Koch himself stated about Ashbery and O'Hara, "We inspired each other, we envied each other, we emulated each other, we were very critical of each other, we admired each other, we were almost entirely dependent on each other for support" ("Interview" 213).

Collectively, the poets' engagement with the establishment of High Modernism and New Criticism could be openly antagonistic, challenging poets they associated with the intellectual elite. Schneiderman has noted that, "far from being indifferent to it, the New York School was founded on both an attack on and a direct engagement with the establishment" (350). As for Shapiro, these High Modernist figures are namely (though not limited to) Pound, Eliot, and Yeats. The type of poetics the New York School poets worked to promote is epitomized by a defense of Koch's poetry by O'Hara that appeared in *Poetry Magazine* in March 1955. In July 1954, Harry Roskolenko, a poet and critic known for conveying conservative viewpoints, had written negatively in *Poetry Magazine* about Koch's first collection, *Poems*, claiming that Koch's "word combinations" were unserious and immature, and did not reflect the elevated material of poetry itself" (O'Hara 349).[18]

In response to Roskolenko, O'Hara starts by defending not just Koch but other poets of the New York School group, claiming, "It is amusing to think of the number of gifted (even great!) poets my epigraph [from Roskolenko's

68   CHAPTER TWO

review of Koch] applies to" (349). Regarding the qualities that O'Hara views as favorable in Koch's poetry, O'Hara asserts:

> Mr. Koch's poems have a natural voice, they are quick, alert, instinctive. . . . His technique is opposed to that Academic and often turgid development by which many young poets gain praise for the "achievement," an achievement limited usually to the mastery of one phase of Yeats (and usually the last). (349)

O'Hara further endorses Koch by labeling him a poet of the tradition of Whitman:

> Poetry in our time may be distinguished without being frozen. I find Koch close to the light sensuality of the Cavalier poets; there is a debt, too, to those catalogues of Whitman in which the poet warmly embraces the vulgar and inanimate objects of everyday life and to the syntactical abbreviations of early Auden. (350)

As opposed to the old-fashioned, close-minded, and static poets described by O'Hara, Koch's poetry is fluid, organic, humorous, and informed by poetic tradition, such as Auden's, but without being confined by their legacy. O'Hara's letter reveals much about his position toward these poets, as well as about Whitman's position in America at the time. As David Eberly states, "Confronting a poetry scene as stultifying as Whitman did his own, O'Hara sought to sabotage the rigid concept of the poem then enforced by the New Critics, who he believed had 'ruined' American poetry to a great degree" (72–73).[19] O'Hara, through supporting Koch by identifying him as Whitmanian, symbolically pulls Koch and Whitman from the margins; thus, Whitman comes to elevate the New York School of poets as part of a defense of their own inclusion.[20]

Again, when I interpret Koch's views of Whitman, it is within these dynamics of the New York School at large. As a member of the New York School especially, Koch's poetry and legacy have received a fair amount of critical attention.[21] The arena given somewhat less critical attention is the expression of Jewishness in Koch's writing. This relative neglect is perhaps attributable to Jewishness not appearing as a dominant motif in his poetry or other writings (unlike the case of Karl Shapiro).[22] Regarding Koch, who was born and raised in Cincinnati, Ohio, one does not find Jewish themes or motifs foregrounded in *The Collected Poems* (2005). However, in *New Addresses* (2000), the penultimate collection within *The Collected Poems*, two relatively long poems are replete with Jewish themes: growing up Jewish in America, the Bible, Hebrew, and antisemitism. These poems are titled "To Jewishness" (611) and "To Jewishness, Paris, Ambition, Trees, My Heart, and Destiny" (617).[23] Both poems, in which Koch's speaker describes the richness and complications of Jewish American hybrid identity and the experience of being excluded at times from non-Jewish society, reveal various layers of engagement with Whitman's poetry, as I discuss later.

To look for a moment at the former poem (putting Whitman briefly aside), Jewish themes and outsider identity are on display in ways that evoke Shapiro's poems about outside identity, with a range of sentiments toward Jewishness, from the joyful to the conflicted to the painful.[24] Passages that represent a more affirming attitude toward Jewishness include a comical anecdote in the opening lines about Jewishness being "contained" in a kiss from "Louise Schlossman." The speaker later describes Jewishness as bestowing him with enthusiasm and strength in lines such as "At which I felt / Chagrined but was energized by you." Finally, at the end of the poem, within an extended dialogue that takes place between the speaker himself and Jewishness, Jewishness asks the speaker, "But / why not admit that I / gave you the life of the mind as a thing / to aspire to?" The speaker, responding reflexively to himself, declares, "I do know your good qualities / [. . .] I / Was excited by you, a rescuer / Of me from the flatness of my life." Koch's speaker therefore depicts Jewishness as an element that protects and "rescues" him from a potentially lackluster, unintellectual, uninspiring life.

The speaker also describes a sense of exclusion from American society, ranging from incidents with subtle discrimination to more overt antisemitic encounters. For instance, after the speaker recounts the kiss, the poem takes a more solemn, serious turn; Koch writes, "Ah, you! / Dark, complicated you!" Jewishness results in his family being treated as Other: "Kept my parents and me / Out of the hotels near Crystal Lake / In Michigan and you resulted, for me, in insults." The speaker relays yet another antisemitic exchange that occurred during his army service: "One night in a foxhole / On Leyte a fellow soldier / Said Where are the fuckin Jews? / Back in the PX." In that exchange, Koch writes of having had to pass or "conceal" his Jewishness.[25] The complicated hybridity of Jewishness conveyed in "To Jewishness" can inspire one to revisit Koch's Jewish and American writing, as well as Koch's views of Whitman, with these issues being intertwined, in line with Shapiro and other poets within this Whitman/Jewish mapping.

Koch (and Whitman) versus "The Strangler"

Deviating somewhat from the deep dislike that Karl Shapiro expresses about Pound and Eliot, Koch occasionally credits these Modernist poets as having been impactful on his writing; for example, Koch writes that Pound made him aware of poets from other cultures outside of the US: "Without Pound I don't know if I would have ever read Provencal poetry or ever have read Chinese poetry and Japanese Noh plays so seriously. As it was he made them part of the great secret literary fiesta of my time" (187–188). However, Koch's nod to Pound as a poetic influence also contains some minor sarcasm: "Pound's writing had a way of moving right into my head and bossing me around" (188). With a similarly sardonic quality, Koch also compliments Eliot, with reservations: "I remember being spellbound when I first read the *The Wasteland*. . . . In an Eliot-dominated poetic ambiance, even the slightest sensations of happiness or pleasure seemed rare and revolutionary poetic occasions" ("Interview" 188).

Mainly, however, very much in keeping with Shapiro, one finds Whitman's model of poetry presented as a challenge to poets who represent (to Shapiro and Koch) the intellectual establishment. Speaking out against many of the leading poets of the day, in the long poem "Fresh Air," Koch refers to these figures as "assembled mediocrities," "the professors," and "the dumb, the deaf, and the creepy" (122).[26] In the same poem, Koch also laments the outsize influence of High Modernist poets and New Criticism. In a passage that echoes Shapiro's declaration as to the "viciousness of the great trio of Pound, Eliot, and Yeats," Koch points out Yeats, Auden, and Eliot as grave threats to the value of poetry itself:

> Who are the great poets of our time, and what are their names?
> Yeats of the baleful influence, Auden of the baleful influence, Eliot of the
>   baleful influence
> (Is Eliot a great poet? no one knows), Hardy, Stevens, Williams (is Hardy
>   of our time?) (123)

In response to these poets, Koch envisions a figure he calls "the Strangler," who will (with a note of irony) "strangle several bad poets": "Here on the railroad train, one more time, is the Strangler. / He is going to get that one there, who is on his way to a poetry reading" (124). In section 4 of the poem, Koch also mocks "the deans of Columbia College," "T. S. Eliot," and "Ezra Pound," to whom one cannot "complain" (125).

The concepts Koch presents to offset the problematic, "baleful" poets and what Koch perceived as the elitist literary culture of the time (in other words, the "fresh air" of openness, fluidity, inclusion, and equality) can be traced to Whitman, in terms of an expansive free-verse form and themes of nature. In its entirety, this poem by Koch emulates Whitman's manner of repetition and cataloguing (also identified by O'Hara as a Whitmanian characteristic in Koch's poetry), as such offering a sort of poetic alternative to the more fixed, closed verse forms that Koch laments.[27] Thematically, Whitman resonates in the symbols of nature—nature that provides the literal "fresh air," which the speaker suggests (with some dark humor) as a way to cure these "ill-contented souls," for example, in section 5, with "sun" and "air":

> Sun out! perhaps there is a reason for the lack of poetry
> In these ill-contented souls, perhaps they need air!
>
> Blue air, fresh air, come in, I welcome you, you are an art student,
> Take off your cap and gown and sit in the chair. (125)

It hardly bears mentioning that Whitman is not the only poet to write of nature, but it is impossible to miss an allusion in Koch's language ("Sun out!") to lines where Whitman greets the sun, from "Song of Myself": "The feeling of health, the full-noon trill, the song of me rising from bed and meeting the sun" (30). The elated, exclamatory tone of Koch's lines ("perhaps they need air!") echoes Whitman, as does the "welcoming" of the air itself: "Blue air, fresh air, come in, I welcome you." The Whitmanian fresh air continues throughout the poem as a model through which to soothe the harm caused by the "baleful influence," as Koch phrases it. In the last several lines, which likewise intimate that a Whitmanian celebration of nature can cause these constrictive influences to loosen, the speaker (again, with some irony) indicates that not just the sun represents beauty and joy but also the "sea," in which these other poets will figuratively "drown":

> Hello, sea! good morning, sea! hello, clarity and excitement, you great expanse of green—
>
> O green, beneath which all of them shall drown! (128)

Here, one finds a joyful greeting similar to that of the sun by the speaker ("Hello, sea!"), which can represent poetry and art rooted in "clarity and excitement."

72 CHAPTER TWO

If this is embraced, the other poets will "drown," disappear, or perhaps one day fall out of relevance. Thus, in "Fresh Air," Whitman's poetics are put forth as a possible antidote to the literary and cultural forces criticized by Koch in "Fresh Air" and elsewhere, a similar way of drawing upon Whitman as in the poetry and essays of Karl Shapiro.

Whitman in Koch's Jewish American Poems

In the two main poems by Koch in which Jewish American identity is foregrounded, "To Jewishness" and "To Jewishness, Paris, Ambition, Trees, My Heart, and Destiny," while there are no explicit references to Whitman in these poems, I would argue that there is a definite interweaving of Jewish themes, symbols, and images together with Whitmanian poetic forms and motifs. Firstly, "To Jewishness" employs an extended anaphora throughout, evident in the speaker's enumeration of sensory images related to growing up Jewish in America; for instance, the repetition of "Oh" and "Of," "Oh the soft smell / Of the pine / Trees of Michigan / And the gentle roar / Of the Lake!" With this listing of olfactory, visual, and aural images, when the speaker goes on to define his sense of Judaism, there is a contradiction displayed that I suggest resonates with Whitman's prototypical idea of contradiction, in "Song of Myself" famously: "Do I contradict myself / Very well then I contradict myself" (78). In Koch's poem, Jewishness is depicted as an entity at once inextricable from the speaker's selfhood ("the one who goes with you") and yet elsewhere, Other, detached from the speaker ("Oddly separated / From you"):

> But Judaism, the one who goes with you
> And is your guide, supposedly,
> Oddly separated
> From you, though there
> In the same building, you
> In us children, and it
> On the blackboards
> And in the books—Bibles
> And books simplified
> From the Bible. How
> Like a Bible with shoulders
> Rabbi Seligmann is! (612–613)

The contradiction around Jewishness in this case is not quite the open embrace of contradiction in "Song of Myself." Jewishness in Koch's poem is conveyed as a more elusive facet of the speaker's identity, as a "guide" that permeates the speaker's formative memories and experiences ("children," "books," "blackboards," and "Bibles") and yet carries an aura of estrangement. As Koch's poem engages with questions around Jewish identity, with the American Whitman at hand, Whitman resonates in writing about the Jewish American experience and, I would argue, in more and less overt ways.

The motif of contradiction with associations to Jewishness and Whitman continues to develop in the poem, as Koch's speaker presents an imagined dialogue between himself, with a humorous third-person reference to himself ("Kenneth"), and Jewishness itself (with Jewishness serving as the speaker—"I"). In this passage, Jewishness declares to Kenneth:

> I'll be
> Here if you need me and here
> After you don't
> Need anything else. HERE is a quality
> I have, and have had
> For you, and for a lot of others,
> Just by being it, since you were born. (615)

It is Jewishness that gets the last word of this dialogue (which is, in fact, a monologue, with the speaker speaking/writing to himself in the voice of Jewishness). The idea of Jewishness being available to the speaker when he needs it ("I'll be / Here if you need me and here / After you don't") reflects the contradictory quality of Jewishness mentioned earlier, with Jewishness being infinitely present and infinitely absent. Again, lines from Whitman that hint at this very duality come to mind, specifically from the last stanza of "Song of Myself": "Failing to fetch me at first keep encouraged, / Missing me one place search another, / I stop somewhere waiting for you" (79). If Jewishness, the "guide," is permeating, elusive, tangible, and intangible, the same can be said of how Whitman appears in Koch's Jewish-themed poems.

The second poem by Koch with Jewish themes, "To Jewishness, Paris, Ambition, Trees, My Heart, and Destiny," is an exploration of these attributes (with Jewishness first in the list) and, additionally, an implied tribute to Whitmanesque themes and forms. Here Jewishness itself is depicted in a more affirming light than in the previous poem, while the poet still expresses

74 CHAPTER TWO

a certain ambivalence toward Jewishness. "To Jewishness, Paris" opens with the speaker addressing the six elements in the title (Jewishness, Paris, and so forth), declaring, "It's almost too exciting to have all of you here—" (617). As Koch's speaker muses about life, the body, spirituality, the self, the origins of Jewishness (as to whether it was "destiny" that brought Jewishness to the speaker), and eventually "Hebrew melodies," Whitman's poetic intertext is infused into the lines, for example, in this section:

> Now that you all have gathered here to talk with me,
> Let's bring everything out into the open.
> It's almost too exciting to have all of you here—
> One of you physically and another spiritually inside me,
> Another worn into me by my upbringing, another a quality
> I picked up someplace west of here, and two of you at least fixed things
>   outside me,
> Paris and trees. Who would like to ask the first question?
> Silence. Noble, eternal-seeming silence. Well, destiny, what do you think?
> Did you bring Jewishness here or did it bring you, or what? (617)

With the ideas of the "physical" (referring to the heart) and the "spiritual" (Jewishness), the poem gestures to the well-known Whitmanesque binary of the body and soul, which leads directly into the idea of that specific element—presumably Jewishness—"worn into me by my upbringing." The phrasing "worn into" suggests some of the ambivalent tone toward Jewishness in the previous poem. Indeed, after a "silence," the speaker moves to the very beginnings of Jewishness; Koch's speaker states, "Did you [destiny] bring Jewishness here ... or what?" Though I would not claim that Koch is referencing Whitman directly here, I do find a curious correlation to the question posed by Whitman's speaker in "Song of Myself": "A child said, *What is the grass?*" Whitman provides possible answers to this question ("it must be the flag of my disposition" or "the handkerchief of the lord"), but a definitive answer is never provided; Whitman writes, "How could I answer the child? / I do not know what it is any more than he" (33). Likewise, though Koch questions "destiny" (somewhat facetiously) as the reason that Jewishness is part of him, a definitive answer is not offered. In the context of the previous poem, "To Jewishness," Jewish identity is bestowed upon Koch and his upbringing and remains with him, almost beyond his own choice or agency. The question about Jewishness in "To Jewishness, Paris" turns out to be rhetorical, so ultimately, the questions in Koch's poem, as well as in Whitman's, are unanswerable.

In a subsequent passage, Koch's speaker continues to muse with the six elements at the core of the speaker's self. The poem moves from the amusing idea of them going out to lunch together (in a personified way), to a Whitmanian type of celebratory song or poem, then back to the idea of Jewishness, and into a Hebrew song or "melody." In these lines, the "song" can be read as a Whitmanesque celebration of these elements (with the obvious reference to Whitman, "I celebrate myself, and sing myself"):

> Should we go to lunch? Just sit here? Or, perhaps, sing
> A song about all of you. "Including you?" one of you speaks for the first
> time (617)

With an undercurrent of "Song of Myself," in the context of Koch's Jewish American writing, the speaker reiterating and listing the elements of the heart, Paris, and trees, Jewishness comes back onto the scene. The "song" transforms into a Hebrew one, in which the speaker conveys not ambivalence but joy and pleasure:

> And it is you, my heart, a great chatterbox all the same! And now you,
> Jewishness, chime in
> With a Hebrew melody you'd like us to enjoy and you Paris and trees step
> out
> Of the shadows of each other and say "Look
> At these beautiful purple and white blossoms!" Destiny you wink at me
> and shrug (617)

Jewishness returns with a Hebrew melody, with Paris and with trees and lots of nature, "purple and white blossoms," ambition and destiny, thus symbolically coming "out of the shadows" and embraced by the speaker. As the poem progresses, the speaker seems to move away from hesitancy and ambivalence toward a clearer celebration of the self. At the very end of the poem, the speaker rejoices much more openly and readily the idea of Jewishness, destiny, the "trees" (and implicitly the model of Whitman):

> "To be with Jewishness and trees and destiny at the same time makes me
> leap up!" (617)

After much musing and deliberating in this poem (and in fact both of these Jewish-Whitman poems), there is a final exclamatory ("leap up!"), a singing of himself and of destiny, precisely as a Jewish poet, now in a more exuberant mode, I suggest via Whitman. In an environment of the "baleful," "ill-contented" poets—to return to Koch's words in "The Strangler"—and the literary and political forces in America that he wrote of being exclusionary, with Koch writing directly about Whitman in his criticism and with indirect but often unmistakable characteristics of Whitman evident in Koch's Jewish writing, Whitman is a poet not just to examine the Jewish experience but, for Karl Shapiro and Kenneth Koch and so many other poets in this book, through which to construct a more liberated idea of Jewishness.

Reading Karl Shapiro's and Kenneth Koch's dual engagements with and imaginings of Whitman reveals an individual and collective mission of challenging perceived exclusion by the High Modernist milieu and America at large. For Shapiro, Whitman effectively becomes a Jewish poet, or is assigned a position as a Jewish poet that is akin to Shapiro's own experience of being a Jewish outsider in America. Koch puts forth Whitman against the same culture, as part of the New York School of poets, who endorse Whitman, seeking inclusion as poets and intellectuals. Koch writes of discrimination and antisemitism, with Whitman's poetic model permeating his poetry in general and his Jewish-themed poetry in particular. Together, Shapiro and Koch bring Whitman to the fore as part of their own ideas of a more liberal American society, one that includes them as well. Shapiro's and Koch's ways of turning to Whitman differ, as well as they differ from Ginsberg's, as will be discussed in chapter 3. Yet, declarations by Shapiro aside, Shapiro, Koch, and Ginsberg adopt Whitman to similar ends, which is to confront literary, political, and cultural exclusion. In the story of the Jewish American appropriation of Whitman, these efforts are part of a poetic navigation of hyphenated identity. Thus, in context with the Jewish American poets of earlier and later generations, Shapiro, Koch, and even Ginsberg partake in the shaping of Whitman's reputation in America, in conjunction with an ever-shifting Jewish American identity. The Jewish appropriation of Whitman underscores a deeply American notion (and ideal) —the possibility of transformation.

CHAPTER THREE

Whitman's Poetics of Witness: Muriel Rukeyser, Allen Ginsberg, and Gerald Stern

> I have no mockings or argument, I witness and wait.
>
> —WALT WHITMAN, "Song of Myself"

Walt Whitman wrote often of "seeing" or "witnessing" his subjects, as in poems such as "The Sleepers" ("I wander all night in my vision" 325) and "Song of Myself," which contains the line "I witness and wait" (32). This chapter traverses the twentieth century to study Whitman's function in the oeuvres of three Jewish American poets, each with different thematic concerns and poetic styles, as well as manners of imagining Whitman: Muriel Rukeyser (1913–1980), Allen Ginsberg (1926–1977), and Gerald Stern (1925–2022). I seek to shed light on the multifaceted ways in which all three poets (not only Ginsberg, as frequently assumed) adore, integrate, and "resist" Whitman (as per Stern's essay "Ginsberg and I"). This chapter also highlights a Whitmanian poetic strategy of witnessing—casting a humanist gaze on his most vulnerable subjects—which can be detected in the work of the poets individually and collectively. The poets' varying strategies of turning to Whitman, including the poetics of witness, are markers of their being situated in the genealogy of Jewish American poets in this project, in particular Charles Reznikoff, who subtly incorporates Whitman's poetics of witness, as surveyed in chapter 1. In fact, among the poets discussed in this chapter, one finds they frequently

78 CHAPTER THREE

turn to each other when it comes to Whitman (Ginsberg to Reznikoff, Stern to Ginsberg, and Adrienne Rich, Alicia Ostriker, and Marge Piercy to Rukeyser). Also, in nuanced ways, the literary and political culture of High Modernism continues to resonate for Rukeyser, Ginsberg, and Stern.

MURIEL RUKEYSER

Whitman is a "bad" influence; that is, he cannot be imitated.
He can, in hilarious or very dull burlesques, be parodied;
but anyone who has come under his rhythms to the extent of
trying to use them knows how great a folly is there.

—MURIEL RUKEYSER, *The Life of Poetry*

Almost two decades before Allen Ginsberg's *Howl and Other Poems* (1956) appears, in her first book, *Theory of Flight* (1935), Muriel Rukeyser could be found challenging or "rebelling" against thematic and formalistic poetic conventions, à la Walt Whitman: "Rebellion pioneered among our lives / viewing from far-off many-branching deltas, / innumerable seas" ("Poem Out of Childhood" 3).[1] Rukeyser's indebtedness to Whitman might be surprising for several reasons. What does Rukeyser, a poet who began writing amid High Modernism in the 1930s, find in the nineteenth-century American Romantic poet? What does the male Whitman offer Rukeyser, who is invested patently in female identity? And what does Rukeyser, a self-consciously Jewish American writer, take from Whitman, a non-Jewish one?[2]

Yet one finds Rukeyser, a German Jewish, radical, political, socialist poet, engaging with Whitman's poetics and ethos across her oeuvre. In Whitman, Rukeyser found a paradigm that traversed boundaries of history, gender, and culture. As such, Rukeyser is a fundamental cornerstone of this investigation, both in her individual adoption of Whitman and in her place within the Jewish American poetic tradition more widely. This chapter explores some of the main arenas in which Rukeyser draws from Whitman in the context of her discontent with Reform Judaism (her personal Jewish background) and Modernist aesthetics and culture (which she viewed as equally problematic).

Observations have been made about Rukeyser's connection to Whitman, with one by a woman poet who will come to engage Whitman as significantly as Rukeyser herself: Adrienne Rich. By situating her in line with Whitman and

Dickinson, Rich underscores Rukeyser's poetic achievements: "Twenty-one years after the death of Whitman, twenty-seven years after the death of Dickinson, another poet is born. Her name is Muriel Rukeyser" ("Beginners" 15). At times, these affinities are expressed as if Rukeyser is Whitman reborn: "a twentieth-century Whitman,"[3] "a woman Whitman,"[4] "an embodiment of Whitman,"[5] an "inheritor" of Whitman.[6] Whitman has even been called Rukeyser's "hero."[7] These types of characterizations, though intended very much as praise of Rukeyser, by extension identify her as secondary to Whitman, whether in terms of gender (a "woman Whitman"), generation (an "inheritor"), or poetic ability (an "embodiment").[8] This study highlights the active nature of Rukeyser's appropriation of Whitman and the positioning thereof in relation to her Jewish American identity.

Rukeyser was among the most prolific American poets of the twentieth century, with Jewish and non-Jewish writers claiming her influence, as exemplified by Anne Sexton's letter to Rukeyser, which states that she is "mother of everyone."[9] Unfortunately, for much of the latter half of the century, Rukeyser's work has suffered some critical neglect.[10] More recently, scholars such as Louise Kertesz, Jan Heller Levi, Janet E. Kaufman, Anne F. Herzog, Kate Daniels, Maeera Y. Shreiber, and Shira Wolosky have made significant strides in combatting this oversight.

Here, in the context of this rich research on Rukeyser and the notion of the poet as a "mother of everyone," I undertake a past-due close investigation of Rukeyser's dialogue with Whitman, who has long been considered the "father" of American poetry. One detects Whitman's influence on Rukeyser in several major areas in her poetic project: the role of poet-as-prophet, the intimacy between speaker and reader, the impact of poetry on society, the coupling of poetry and democracy, the role of the poet-as-witness (a focus of this chapter in line with Allen Ginsberg and Gerald Stern), and a celebration of the body, including the poems "The Road" and "The Book of the Dead" from *The Book of the Dead*, featured in *U.S. 1* (1938), and the "Akiba" series from *The Speed of Darkness* (1968).[11] Beyond poetry, Whitman features in Rukeyser's *The Life of Poetry* (1968) (a series of critical essays about the "responsibility" of the poet in society[12]), as well her biography of the late nineteenth-century scientist Willard Gibbs. Whitman's influence also comes up in interviews. Taken together, these writings and texts reveal that despite being cautious about the "folly" of "imitating" Whitman, as per the epigraph for this section, Rukeyser held a sustained engagement with Whitman—one that pervades her work.[13]

80   CHAPTER THREE

In Rukeyser's poetry and prose, one finds a conflation of the apolitical High Modernist tradition, the political Marxist tradition, the Whitman tradition, and Jewish tradition. Like Charles Reznikoff, Karl Shapiro, and Kenneth Koch, Rukeyser began writing Jewish American poetry amid High Modernist literary culture. Rukeyser conveyed an aversion to strict Modernist forms, writing in *The Life of Poetry* about the "wretched and static condition" of the "New" group (178). Moreover, in the context of what she calls the "static mechanics" of Modernist poetry, she states, "In poetry, the relations are not formed like crystals on a lattice of words, although the old criticism (which at the moment is being called, of course, the New Criticism) would have us believe it so. . . . [O]ne evidence after another shows they are thinking in terms of static mechanics" (177).

As with Reznikoff and Shapiro, Whitman's place in her poetry can be seen as a marker of her delineation from the ("wretched and static") High Modernist tradition. Yet Rukeyser's appropriation of Whitman does diverge from Reznikoff's and Shapiro's in several ways. First, Rukeyser was more concerned with inventive, experimental poetic forms than either of them. Second, Rukeyser's Jewish American identity was forged in the upper-middle-class, German Jewish community of Reform Judaism, while Reznikoff and Shapiro (and Ginsberg and Stern) were born into Yiddish-speaking, Eastern European immigrant families. Though German Enlightenment values of reason were an influence for Rukeyser, she did resist the social and political values she encountered in that community. Rukeyser, at the core, embarked upon a project of humanist poetry that can be compared to Whitman's *Leaves of Grass*, with a mission to counteract elitism and injustice in sites such as the High Modernist milieu, the conservative culture of her parents' Judaism, and American society at large.

Rukeyser's Political Jewish American Identity

In the essay "Under Forty: A Symposium on American Literature and the Younger Generation of American Jews," Rukeyser writes, "My parents did not migrate from Europe, but from America" (5).[14] Although Rukeyser has stated rather famously that being Jewish was one of the four pillars of her identity, along with being a poet, a woman, and an American, she found aspects of this Jewish American milieu to be greatly problematic.[15] Her parents' connection to Jewishness (or lack thereof) was quite typical of that era, whereby, in order to distinguish themselves from the impoverished Eastern European and Russian Jews immigrating to America, German Jews were inclined to assimilate.[16] Rukeyser wrote extensively of perceiving her parents to be disconnected from their Jewish heritage: "The young man my father and the young woman my mother had no cultural resources to strengthen them. There was not a trace of Jewish culture that I could feel—no stories, no songs, no special food—but then there was not any cultural background that could make itself felt" ("Under Forty" 5).

Rukeyser did not merely lament the absence of Jewish tradition in her family; she detected grave spiritual, moral, and intellectual deficiencies in the German Jewish Reform movement.[17] This linkage between Rukeyser's political activism and her sense of Jewish identity is noted by Jo-Ann Mort, who traces Rukeyser's passion for social justice to a "Deuteronomic call 'intrinsic to Judaism': Justice, justice shalt thou follow, that thou mayst live, and inherit the land which the Lord thy God gaveth thee" (20). Shira Wolosky also aptly points out that Rukeyser's "reaction against" her parents' type of Jewishness "resulted" in her political activism (216).[18] Rukeyser's impetus to make poetry a site of political activism is evident in "Under Forty," whereby the community's desire to remain "invisible" was (to Rukeyser) a refusal to engage in the inequities and tragedies occurring throughout the world:

> I think that many people brought up in reformed Judaism must go starving for two phases of religion: poetry and politics. The sermons I heard were pale and mechanically balanced talks. I grew up among a group of Jews who wished, more than anything else, I think, to be invisible. (6)

The qualities that Rukeyser assigns to this "group of Jews"—intellectual stagnation, denying one's Jewish heritage, and remaining blind to social injustice—are precisely the qualities Rukeyser promotes in the inseparable realism of Jewishness, politics, and poetry.[19] As Shreiber claims, Judaism for Rukeyser "[took] the form of an ongoing commitment to the sociopolitical demands of history" ("Jewish American Poetry" 157).[20] Rukeyser's desire to challenge these qualities was therefore not just as a poet but as a self-consciously Jewish one.

One of Rukeyser's responses to those who "refused" their Jewishness was to employ her poetry and other writing to combat prejudice that she encountered in many places, including the milieu of Reform Judaism. For this mission, Rukeyser drew upon an American poetic predecessor from the nineteenth century, Whitman, whom she envisioned to be likewise grappling with conservative, anti-democratic elements in America. At the core of Rukeyser's

82 CHAPTER THREE

and Whitman's seeking for poetry to have authority is their notion of the "prophet" or "seer," the poet who possesses special insight and disseminates this insight to society at large. Shreiber has written that Rukeyser is "taking up a spiritual charge" ("Jewish American Poetry" 156). In the poem "Letter to the Front," Rukeyser identifies poets, poetry, and women to be prophets of "truth." As such, she implicitly labels herself a prophet: "Women and poets see the truth arrive" (239). As evident in *Willard Gibbs*, Rukeyser was familiar with Whitman's idea of the poet as the bearer of wisdom for society: "Whitman was completely conscious of the meaning of his work in relation to the republic. He wrote: I look upon *Leaves of Grass* as my definitive *carte visite* to the coming generations of the New World" (258).

A feature in Rukeyser's work with roots in Whitman is a poetic speaker that transcends place and time and speaks directly to the reader. The nature of this speaker is reflected in Whitman's "prescient poet," described in the preface to *Leaves of Grass*: "The prescient poet projects himself centuries ahead and judges performer or performance after the changes of time" (*Whitman: Poetry and Prose* 24). Whitman also "projects" his presence across time, as in 1860–1861 edition of "Crossing Brooklyn Ferry," where he addresses his future readers: "I am with you, you men and women of a generation, or ever so many generations hence; / I project myself—also I return—I am with you, and know how it is" (380).[21] With this timeless presence, Rukeyser accepted a model offered by Whitman for her poetic "I," who likewise addresses her reader of the present and future. A Whitmanian present-prescient speaker appears, for instance, in Rukeyser's poem "Then." As Herzog states, Rukeyser "constantly practices a poetics of heightened relationship that accentuates the active writer-reader connection within the rhetoric of her text" (38). In "Then," the heightened relationship is that of "love" for her reader during the speaker's life and after death.

> When I am dead, even then,
> I will still love you, I will wait in these poems,
> When I am dead, even then
> I am still listening to you.
> I will still be making poems for you
> out of silence;
> silence will be falling into that silence,
> it is building music. (561)

The speaker's relationship to her reader is conveyed as continuous and infinite, not just in this poem but in "these" poems, alluding to Rukeyser's poetry itself. In what follows, Whitman resides in Rukeyser's poetry of democracy and liberalism and poetry of witness (like Reznikoff and so many others), making the invisible visible. Each allusion to Whitman is an element of Rukeyser's poetics of democracy, which both poets sought to promote within their time and into the future.

Whitman's Camera in Rukeyser's Poetics of Witness

In Rukeyser's poetic series *The Book of the Dead*, the speaker is a poet-photographer-documentarian who sets out to shed light on the 1929 Hawk's Nest Tunnel tragedy in West Virginia, where miners, mostly Black, became ill or died after inhaling silica dust. The collection in its entirety imparts a responsibility to bear witness—part of the moral code that underlies Rukeyser's work.[22] In the poems that bookend this series, "The Road" (73–74) and "The Book of the Dead" (106–110), Whitman's explicit presence is detected. These two poems are journeys deep into West Virginia, as described in the first line of "The Road": "These are roads to take when you think of your country." A version of this line is repeated in stanza 5: "These roads will take you into your own country."[23] This refrain alludes to Whitman's "Song of the Open Road": "Afoot and light-hearted I take to the open road, / Healthy, free, the world before me, / The long brown path before me leading wherever I choose" (120). Rukeyser thus appears to channel Whitman's all-encompassing eye (and I) to convey her critique of America. Tim Dayton has noted the comparison between "The Road" and "Song of the Open Road," stating that Rukeyser is critical of Whitman and that her poem "was both a statement of affiliation with Whitman and his America . . . and a corrective to it, in light of historical experience and new knowledge" (32). While I agree that Rukeyser's response to Whitman is a marker of "affiliation," whether it is also a "corrective" is a bit in question. Whitman's poem does not only portray America in a celebratory light but calls for an active fight against injustice; as Whitman writes, "My call is the call of battle, I nourish active rebellion." I would contend that Rukeyser enlists Whitman to perform this "active rebellion," and as such, Whitman serves as a partner more than a model to subvert.

Moving to how a Whitmanian symbol of the camera functions in Rukeyser's poetic "rebellion," in the first poem of *The Book of the Dead*, "The Road," Rukeyser employs a camera as a symbol of the responsibility to "see" and be

84 CHAPTER THREE

witness: "Now the photographer unpacks camera and case, / surveying the deep country, follows discovery / viewing on groundglass an inverted image" (74).[24] As Ed Folsom claims, for Whitman, the photograph was a more exacting representation of "reality" than other artistic forms; therefore, "photography was the harbinger of a new democratic art, an art that would not exclude on the basis of preconceived notions of what was vital, of what was worth painting" (*Native Representations* 102). Rukeyser, like Whitman (and like Reznikoff), portrays this notion of the photograph as an inherently democratic medium, whereby the photographer (or poet, in the context of poetry) can serve as a witness to all and document everything within the entity of a poem.[25]

With the idea of the poet-photographer who "unpacks camera and case," Rukeyser seems to evoke Whitman's poetic lens to reveal the inequities of class, gender, and race in America, as embodied by the circumstances at Hawk's Nest Tunnel. The speaker in the poem "Gauley Bridge," for example, also from *The Book of the Dead*, gazes with a camera on a scene of poverty and racial inequity: "Camera at the crossing sees the city / a street of wooden walls and empty windows, / the doors shut handless in the empty street, / and the deserted Negro standing on the corner" (77). Returning to the poem "The Book of the Dead," Rukeyser echoes the photographic gaze of Whitman to expose the "lie" of America inherent in such scenes: "seeing America / lie in a photograph of power, widened / before our forehead." The "lie" of America is encapsulated in the poetic photograph. The notion of seeing and "sight" itself becomes Rukeyser's strategy to expose this imbalance of power:

Defense is sight; widen the lens and see
standing over the land myths of identity,
new signals, process:

Carry abroad the urgent need, the scene,
to photograph and to extend the voice,
to speak this meaning. (110)

Here, the ability to "see"—to observe the "land" and its "identity"—is Rukeyser's "defense" against bias and the "evils" inflicted by the Union Carbide company. There is Whitmanesque listening of images to "speak" the voice and "meaning" of the Other throughout the poems "The Road" and "The Book of the Dead." Whitman is therefore profoundly resonant in Rukeyser's employment of the symbol of the camera, and more broadly in the link between poetry and photography.[26]

In a related notion, Rukeyser writes in *The Life of Poetry* of the importance of the "visual" and "seeing" in poetry: "The visual imagination may be spoken of as including the eyes. The imaginative function includes the senses. It includes, easily, a kind of seeing; we are perhaps most used to having sight invoked in the telling of stories and poems" (82). Rukeyser identifies this exact "visual imagination" in Whitman and describes his lists as a series of unfolding images: "These successions are not to be called catalogues. That name has thrown readers off; it is misleading. What we are confronted with here, each time, is not a list, but a sequence with its own direction" (84). Rukeyser offers lines from Whitman's poem "Song of the Open Road" to illustrate this point: "The birth, the hasting after the physician, the beggar's tramp, the drunkard's stagger, the laughing party of mechanics" (84). Rukeyser comments on the "sequences" of Whitman's formal poetics; however, the concept of Whitman as a "film editor" echoes what Rukeyser calls the "ethical communication" in "the cutting of films" (*Life* 150–151). Rukeyser claims, "As far as the making of films goes, when the functions are identified so that there is again . . . a writer-director-editor, some unity of imagination may appear in the finished work" (*Life* 152). Whitman served for Rukeyser as a model of the writer-director-editor, and therefore as a point of departure for Rukeyser's own "directing" of poems of "ethical" witness.

This act of witnessing in poetry is directly related to the High Modernist tradition. Passages in *The Book of the Dead* do reflect a Modernist (and Objectivist) poetic style, like "Mearl Blankenship," which contains sparse, factual language to describe a man afflicted with silicosis: "He stood against the stove / facing the fire— / Little warmth, no words, / loud machines" (82). If Rukeyser is able to make the reader aware of this man's suffering ("he stood" and "little warmth"), it is, to a large extent, a result of the fusing of the Modernist-Objectivist style with a type of poetic gaze that Rukeyser encountered in Whitman.[27] Together, these poems from *The Book of the Dead* illustrate how Rukeyser's engagement with Whitman, and a poetry of witness, sets her apart from the German Jewish Reform community, as well as the High Modernist poetics, both of which to her represented closure and confinement.

Whitman in Rukeyser's "Akiba" Poems

Rukeyser's "Akiba" poems (454–460), from the book *The Speed of Darkness*, reflect the aspects of Whitman's influence that I have discussed in this chapter—the Bible, the prophetic voice, the intimate relationship between poet and reader,

86 CHAPTER THREE

poetry's ethical role in society, the act of bearing witness, the contradiction of good and evil, "courage and possibility," and the body. All of these come together here in an extensive poetic exploration of Jewishness. These themes are evident in every section of "Akiba," but I will look specifically at "The Witness," the poem that concludes the "Akiba" series. In the essay "The Education of a Poet," Rukeyser relates that her mother would tell her a "legend" about their family being descendants of Rabbi Akiba, a legend Rukeyser describes as a "gift":

> Akiba the martyr who resisted the Romans in the first century and who was tortured to death after his great work for the Song of Songs. He was flayed with iron rakes tearing his flesh until at the end he said "I know that I have loved God with all my heart and all my soul, and now I know that I love Him with all my life." Now this is an extraordinary gift to give a child. (226)

The poem was commissioned by the Union of American Hebrew Congregations in 1960, a Reform organization, at a time when "a dramatic shift had occurred in American Jewry, from shame born of the European genocide to pride in identification with the . . . [strong] state of Israel" (Kaufman 53). In the five poems of this series, Rukeyser evokes the figure of Rabbi Akiba, turning his mythical devotion to God into a devotion to resisting social tyranny, while imagining Judaism as a realm of intellectual curiosity, social justice, political activism, and gender and sexual equality.

In the poem entitled "Akiba Martyr," which precedes "The Witness," Akiba passes away, "the old man saying Shema. / The death of Akiba" (459). After Akiba's passing, Rukeyser begins "The Witness" with a question: "Who is the witness? What voice moves across time, / Speaks for the life and death as witness voice? / Moving tonight on this city, this river, my winter street?" (459). This voice of witness is at the heart of Rukeyser's poetic vision. The voice that "speaks for life and death" is a Whitmanesque, prescient poet who transcends space and temporality. The three witnesses in the poem—the speaker ("Myself"), Akiba, and the reader ("You")—are each assigned the role of Whitman's prescient poet. In the second stanza, Rukeyser imagines herself and Akiba in a "meeting," leading to a scene where Akiba transfers his roles as prophet and witness to the speaker:

> He saw it, the one witness. Tonight the life as legend
> Goes building a meeting for me in the veins of the night
> Adding its scenes and its songs. Here is the man transformed,

WHITMAN'S POETICS OF WITNESS   87

The tall shepherd, the law, the false messiah, all;
You who come after me far from tonight finding
These lives that ask you always Who is the witness— (459)

Rukeyser places the responsibility of being witness not only on the Jew but on all of humanity: "You who come after me far from tonight." Rukeyser bestows the responsibility of acting as witness to the poem itself, and she "implicates and invests each reader to his or her responsible witnessing" (Wolosky 213). Rukeyser also acknowledges the contradictory nature of man—the existence of good and evil embodied in "the tall shepherd," "the law," and "the false messiah." In the fourth stanza, Rukeyser commands the reader to "take" from the "acts of encounter" between herself and Akiba, to learn from the lessons they "wake to attempt":

Take from us acts of encounter we at night
Wake to attempt, as signs, seeds of beginning,
Given from darkness and remembering darkness,

Take from our light given to you our meetings.
Time tells us men and women, tells us You
The witness, your moment covered with signs, your self. (459)

Rukeyser then speaks directly to "You / the witness," employing Whitman's "you" that appears from the earliest lines of *Leaves of Grass*, inviting a spiritual and physical connection between speaker and reader: "What I assume you shall assume, / For every atom belonging to me as good belongs to you" (29). Rukeyser creates the poetic encounter as a space of the corporeal, where the reader "takes" from "our light" to become "the witness."[28] The thrust of the poem is to transfer to the reader full agency as witness.

The notion of "signs" that "cover" the reader is Rukeyser's main symbol of transferring this responsibility. The "sign" pervades the "Akiba" poems, beginning in the first text, "The Way Out": "The night is covered with signs. The body and face of man, / with signs, and his journeys" (454). The signs have strong connotations in the Jewish context; Kaufman identifies the passage in Deuteronomy where the Israelites are warned not to follow "the signs and wonders" of false gods (55). Wolosky has elucidated the connection between the "signs" and the Jewish "letteristic culture, constituted of texts and responses to them"; she writes that Rukeyser "embraces linguistic materiality, with its historicity, physicality, immanence" (213, 215). I would add to these observa-

88　CHAPTER THREE

tions that reading the poem through the prism of Whitman and his recurrent use of the term "sign" confers an additional layer of meaning to the term in Rukeyser's poem, which might be separate from specifically Jewish "letteristic" culture. The link to Whitman is evident in Rukeyser's own definition of the sign in "The Way Out": "taking for signs the signs of all things, the world, the body / which is part of the soul, and speaks to the world." The lines allude to Whitman's duality in "Song of Myself": "I am the poet of the Body, / I am the poet of the Soul" (45). With this duality, Whitman contains all and is witness to all. Whitman also gives a "sign": "I speak the password primeval. . . . I give the sign of democracy; / By God! I will accept nothing which all cannot have their counterpart of on the same terms" (48). Whitman's sign is therefore a sign of democracy, the very thing that Rukeyser strives for in her sense of Judaism. At the heart of Rukeyser's signs is "truth," which she believes is embodied in the self of the poem and the self of the reader (You):

> Tell us this moment, saying You are the meeting.
> You are made of signs, your eyes and your song.
> You dance the dance, the walk into the present. (460)

The idea that her readers "dance the dance" conveys a belief that humanity itself is holy; as Rukeyser writes in *Willard Gibbs*, "[Whitman] felt of himself that he was the ritual, and that the dance was holy; that through it the dancer was on the way to holiness" (359). The poem ends on this note of dancing and holiness, a full acceptance of the self and, by extension, the Other:

> All this we are and accept, being made of signs, speaking
> To you, in time not yet born.
> 　　　　　　　　　　The witness is myself.
>
> 　　　　　　　　　　　　　　　　　　And you,
> The signs, the journeys of the night, survive. (460)

The vision of faith and justice—or courage and possibility—that Rukeyser saw represented by Akiba is shifted completely onto herself and the reader, those now and "in time not yet born." Just as Whitman proclaimed, "I witness and I wait," Rukeyser is a continual witness. Signs held up by Whitman, Akiba, and Rukeyser herself lead to no less than human greatness, or at least its possibility. Turning now to Allen Ginsberg, and then to Gerald Stern, I also identify various responses to High Modernism, and a poetry of witness, through Whitman, with Whitman offering a model of poetics that was fluid, open, and democratic.

ALLEN GINSBERG

> I write poetry to talk back to Whitman, young people in ten
> years, talk to old aunts and uncles still living near Newark,
> New Jersey.
>
> —ALLEN GINSBERG, "Improvisation in Beijing"

Interpreting the American Beat poet Allen Ginsberg (1926–1977)—author of *Howl and Other Poems* (1955) and *Kaddish and Other Poems* (1961)—within the map of Jewish American poets who look to Whitman is by no means an attempt to downplay the unique importance of Ginsberg's ties to Whitman. Ginsberg is already extremely famous among readers and scholars for having looked to Whitman (by far the most famous of the poets in this project); he expresses a near-total embrace of the paradigmatic American poet: "the old soldier, old sailor, old writer, old homosexual, old Christ poet journeyman" ("I Love Old Whitman So" 900).[29] In the essay "Allen Ginsberg on Walt Whitman: Composed on the Tongue," Ginsberg articulates a grandiosity that he finds in Whitman's humanistic, democratic poetic vision: "There was a man, Walt Whitman, who lived in the nineteenth century, in America, who began to define his own persona, who began to tell his own secrets, who outlined his own body, and made an outline of his own mind, so other people could see it" (329). Modes by which Ginsberg adopted Whitman are evident in Ginsberg's earliest poems from *Empty Mirror: Gates of Wrath, 1947–1952*, to the last posthumous collection, *Death & Fame: Poems 1993–1997*. Whitman's "outline" is identifiable in themes, forms, and ideologies throughout Ginsberg's oeuvre: Americanness, Jewishness, poetic and personal freedom, anti-capitalism, anti-conservatism, queerness, outsider identity, and the body.

Major influences for Ginsberg, aside from Whitman, include numerous others, among them writers of the Beat movement, like Jack Kerouac, Neal Cassady, William S. Burroughs, and Gregory Corsco; Charles Olson; his parents, Louis and Naomi Ginsberg; Zen Buddhist philosophy; William Blake; Ezra Pound and William Carlos Williams; and the Bible itself. It is Whitman, though, who permeates Ginsberg's writing most pervasively. Critics have written extensively about Ginsberg's stylistic and thematic integrations of Whitman,[30] such as Alicia Ostriker, who has broached the Whitman-Jewish connection in Ginsberg: "From America Allen takes Whitman. The manly love of comrades, the open road, the democratic vistas stretching to eternity, and also the eyes of America

90   CHAPTER THREE

taking a fall, which he plants, later, in his mother's head. America will always be, for him, infinite hope and infinite disappointment. That's very Jewish" ("Poet as Jew" 118). Ostriker's observation is quite apt, since Ginsberg does display a Whitmanian view of America that is at once optimistic and pessimistic—a quality that can be considered Jewish from a cultural standpoint. By reexamining Ginsberg's affiliation to Whitman within the Jewish American poetic tradition at large, this research hopes to deepen the understanding Ginsberg's adoption of Whitman (such as Ostriker's), in relation to Ginsberg's identity as a Jewish American poet, through the lens of Ginsberg's responses to the earlier Jewish American poet Charles Reznikoff explored in the essay "Reznikoff's Poetics."

With recognition of the Whitman-Ginsberg line, I suggest a repositioning of Ginsberg alongside the poets in this chapter—Muriel Rukeyser and Gerald Stern—and a corresponding mode of poetics of witness with roots in Whitman. Moreover, Ginsberg's engagement with Whitman is interwoven with dynamics of High Modernism. Also, as I will illuminate, Ginsberg's integration of Whitman is crucially informed by Reznikoff. There are dynamics in the Ginsberg-Whitman relationship that are akin to Jewish American poets before and during Ginsberg's time, who have employed Whitman as a symbol to negotiate writing as Jewish poets in America. For instance, as in the case of Reznikoff, Rukeyser, Koch, and Shapiro, Ginsberg's response to Whitman is mediated by William Carlos Williams and Ezra Pound and the poetics of High Modernism. These phenomena are an inextricable facet of Ginsberg's turn to Whitman more broadly, as well as to a mode of poetic witnessing (as per Rukeyser and Stern), as evident in essays such as "Reznikoff's Poetics" and "Allen Ginsberg on Walt Whitman: Composed on the Tongue." I present three poems as emblematic of the Whitman/High Modernist/Objectivist style: "Yiddishe Kopf" (1991), "After Whitman & Reznikoff" (1980), and "Waking in New York" (1964). These three are distantly informed by the combined poetic traditions of Whitman (and Reznikoff), marking how Ginsberg, as a self-consciously Jewish American poet, at once receives, responds to, and even challenges aspects of High Modernist literary culture.

Ginsberg's (Russian) Jewish American Whitman

Before investigating these intersections between Ginsberg, Whitman, Reznikoff, and High Modernism, it is salient to touch upon "Yiddishe Kopf" (or "Yiddish Brain"),[31] a poem in which Ginsberg's speaker reflects on his Russian Jewish

American immigrant identity and in which Whitman's repetitious poetic model resonates. Ginsberg was born in Newark, New Jersey, son of Louis and Naomi Ginsberg. Naomi (née Livergant) was raised until she was ten years old in a village in western Russia (Nevel). In 1905, she immigrated with her family to the United States. Louis's parents, Pinkus and Rebecca (née Schulman), met in Newark after Pinkus settled in the US in the 1880s (Schumacher, *Dharma* 4).[32] Although Ginsberg did not speak or write Russian, perhaps being steeped from a young age in Russian language, politics, and culture led him to state in a 1993 interview, "I am basically a Russian poet, put in an American scene" (Lauridsen and Dalgard 28).[33] In the poem "Yiddishe Kopf," the speaker enumerates various elements that comprise his Jewishness, an identity that is in itself fundamental, having been bestowed by so many earlier generations of Russian Jewish ancestry: "I am Jewish because love because my family matzoh ball soup / I'm Jewish because my father mother uncles grandmothers said 'Jewish,' all the way back to Vitebsk & Kaminetz-Podolska via Lvov" (1013).[34] Thus Jewishness—represented by food ("matzoh ball soup")—family, humor, language (Yiddish), pogroms, and immigration to America are the core elements of Jewish American identity in Ginsberg's poem.[35]

The extent to which Ginsberg seems to rely upon the Whitman tradition to convey such elements of Jewish identity is intriguing (and is in keeping with other poets in this book who do so). The first third of Ginsberg's poem is based on repetition of the phrase "I'm Jewish because" and "Jewish because," along with Whitmanian catalogues employed within the lines themselves: "Jewish because reading Dostoyevsky at 13 I write poems at restaurant tables Lower East Side, perfect delicatessen intellectual. . . . Jewish because violent Zionists make my blood boil." Craig Svonkin has also noted that this anaphora evokes Whitman: "Ginsberg's use here of anaphora, or opening repetition, a common Hebrew poetic device borrowed later by Walt Whitman, demonstrates simultaneously his attempt to identify as a Jewish poet and his poetic syncretism, given that this form so clearly identifies with Whitman" (184). Certainly, the anaphora calls up biblical-style rhetoric and Whitmanian forms found in Ginsberg. Ginsberg has declared his engagement with the Bible and emulation of cadences from Ecclesiastes, the Psalms, and the Song of Songs (Pacernick 144). To take this point about the repetition still further, the presence of Whitman's anaphora serves as a marker of mediating these disparate parts of Ginsberg's identity—the Jewish and the American. A poem constructed in the style of Whitman, such as "Yiddishe Kopf," gestures toward the identities that Gins-

92 CHAPTER THREE

berg was compelled to straddle and integrate. While the speaker of "Yiddishe Kopf" describes not being able to choose his Jewishness, as an American, he is able to choose his poetic associations—namely, the poet Walt Whitman.

Ginsberg, Whitman, Reznikoff, and High Modernism

Regarding Ginsberg's alignment with Whitman more broadly, one finds this alignment quite enmeshed with Reznikoff and Objectivist tradition, as well as with the High Modernist milieu of Pound and Williams. This intertextual landscape was equally resonant for poets who came before Ginsberg—like Reznikoff and the other Objectivist poets, Koch, Shapiro, and Rukeyser—whereby Whitman comes to represent an alternative model to what was offered by the milieu of High Modernism, what with Pound's conservatism, antisemitic leanings, and ambivalence toward Whitman. Ginsberg's views of the High Modernist movement, Modernist poetry, and its associated figures are found to be distinct from preceding Jewish poets, like Reznikoff or Koch. First, unlike in the case of Koch, Shapiro, or Rukeyser, Ginsberg's writings do not display avidly anti-Modernist sentiments, and certainly not about Williams, whom Ginsberg describes as the "old soul kind and meek" ("Death News" 305).[36] Williams contributed the introduction for Ginsberg's collection *Empty Mirror*, then later for *Howl*. In these introductions, Williams seems to acknowledge the sources of Ginsberg's poetics as both Jewish and American and does not shy away from Ginsberg's overt themes of sexuality. About *Howl*, Williams states, "This poet sees through and all around the horrors he partakes of in the very intimate details of his poem. He avoids nothing but experiences it to the hilt. . . . Hold back the edges of your gowns, Ladies, we are going through hell" ("Introduction" 820). Ginsberg also claimed Williams as an important predecessor,[37] looking to Williams as a model of "empathy" in poetry—in context, in fact, with Whitman; as Ginsberg would claim in an interview, "I'd like to be remembered as someone who advanced, actually advanced the notion of compassion in open-heart, open-form poetry, continuing the tradition of Whitman and Williams" (Pacernick 155).

Pound appears as a more problematic figure for Ginsberg (again, in line with numerous poets in this research). Viewpoints of Pound are expressed in Ginsberg's poem "War Profit Litany" (494), which contains the epigraph "To Ezra Pound." The poem lists the companies that profited from the Vietnam War: "These are the names of the companies that have made money from this war." Presumably, the poem is a not-so-subtle critique of Pound's dissemination of fascist attitudes.[38] In spite of this awareness of Pound's politics, Ginsberg maintains a congenial—one might say forgiving—attitude toward Pound, identifying in Whitman, Pound, and Williams a poetic "wisdom" and acknowledging all of them as poetic influences: "A wisdom inherited by Ezra Pound and William Carlos Williams and a whole generation of poets after Walt Whitman who had discovered that common ground of self and the dissolution of the self, common ground of this own mind and common ground of the city pavement he walked on with his fellow citizens" ("Allen Ginsberg" 350–351). In Ginsberg's more complimentary description of Pound as a poet of the "common" people, one hardly hears a condemnation like Shapiro's "the political simple-mindedness and viciousness of the great trio of Pound, Eliot and Yeats" (*Poetry Wreck* xv) or Rukeyser's "static" High Modernist verse.

Ginsberg's poem "Improvisation in Beijing" (937–939) reflects this phenomenon of embracing Whitman and somewhat less avidly aligning with Pound. The speaker enumerates the reasons why he writes poetry, structured using a Whitmanian anaphoric phrase: "I write poetry because." Whitman is mentioned more frequently than any other figure named as an inspiration (Williams, Pound, Mayakovsky and Yesenin, his father, being gay, Shelley, Confucius, and others). First, in the opening of the poem, Ginsberg writes, "I write poetry because Walt Whitman gave world permission to speak with candor / I write poetry because Walt Whitman opened up poetry's verse-line for unobstructed breath." Whitman then appears twice more, in the middle of the poem—"I write poetry to talk back to Whitman . . . to old aunts and uncles still living near Newark, New Jersey" (evoking the Jewish family from "Yiddishe Kopf")—and again, "I write poetry because Walt Whitman said 'Do I contradict myself? Very well then I contradict myself.'" The poem is a flagship in which to read Whitman in Ginsberg—poetically (the line/the breath), culturally (Jewish and American), and in relation to identity (able to contain contradiction). Whitman represents expansion, openness, freedom.

Pound, on the other hand, appears in the poem once, in a line that acknowledges his poetic significance but is critical of his worldview: "I write poetry because Ezra Pound saw an ivory tower, bet on one wrong horse, gave poets permission to write spoken vernacular idiom." This line signals how Ginsberg often writes of absorbing from Pound what he can poetically; yet there is a sense of resistance to aligning with Pound fully because of the elitism found in Pound ("the ivory tower"). One might ask: What is the "wrong horse" that Pound "bet on," according

94 CHAPTER THREE

to the poem? Fascism itself? In essence, Ginsberg's writing articulates a creative identification with Pound, but not a political or cultural one.

In addition to this concept of "poetic wisdom" that Ginsberg attributes to Whitman, Pound, and Williams, yet another poetic association emerges, which has to do with Ginsberg's explicit indebtedness to the poetics of Pound and Williams for being clear, concrete, and without decoration; as Ginsberg states, "[Poetry] has taught me not to indulge in abstract language which is undefined, but to try and nail down any generalization with a 'for instance.' You know, like 'give me a for instance.' . . . 'No ideas but in things,' as Williams says. Or 'The natural object is always the adequate symbol' says Pound" (Pacernick 148).[39] In addition to what Ginsberg writes of having absorbed from Pound and Williams, in the essay "Reznikoff's Poetics" (1984) (in fact a lecture series given by Ginsberg and later transcribed by Milton Hindus), Ginsberg expresses appreciation for a comparably clear poetic style in Reznikoff's Objectivist-style verse, which is likewise manifest in Ginsberg's poem "After Reznikoff & Whitman" (with the title itself obviously connected to Whitman).

In "Reznikoff's Poetics," Ginsberg praises Reznikoff's poetry for how it presents images to the reader in an exacting, direct manner, with an emphasis on Reznikoff's poetic technique of seeing or witnessing, as characteristic of Objectivist-style poetics; thereby, it is possible to see how Ginsberg's poetics are informed by this alliance to Reznikoff, whose poetry also reflects Jewish experiences for Ginsberg, with Whitman serving as a poetic intertext.[40] Ginsberg maintains that because of this mode by which Reznikoff's poetry displays a succinct rendering of figures, scenes, or experiences, his poetry should be taken as a useful model for doing so. Ginsberg states about Reznikoff's poetry, "There is the need to practice focusing clearly on what's happening around us and seeing clearly the fact of life . . . seeing the detailed facts and transcribing the sharpest, stickiest-to-the-mind details . . . telling it naturally as if you were telling a story" (140).[41] Ginsberg, moreover, signals an approval of Reznikoff's inclusion of images, even ones that might be unpleasant or off-putting to readers. For example, about a passage from "Sunday Walks in the Suburbs," which contains the lines by Reznikoff "a toothless woman opened her door / chewing a slice of bacon that hung from her mouth like a tongue," Ginsberg writes, "Because of the photographic accuracy and precision of detail, the whole somehow is more than the sum of its parts here" (142). In yet another complimentary assertion about Reznikoff's poetry, Ginsberg describes Reznikoff as "the least poetic of poets" because of this aptitude for distilling experiences:

The way he's done it is by simply being totally accurate to what stimulated the emotion in him, by observing so clearly or by being so *present* or by not trying to generalize it, but by trying to recall or reconstitute the sensation by gathering the data that caused the sensation. . . . By reconstituting the primary sensory data, Reznikoff has been able to transfer the emotional affective blood-gush into our bodies. (149)

Ginsberg also writes about this "affective blood gush" in a poem that is thematically quite Jewish: section 48 of "Uriel Accosta," which depicts a Jewish immigrant family living on the Lower East Side: "A pot of fish was boiling on the stove. Sometimes the water / bubbled over and hissed. The smell of the fish filled the / cellar" (149).

In the framework of Ginsberg's commentary on Reznikoff's poetry and Jewish poetry, there are intriguing similarities in Ginsberg's mode of writing about Whitman—intriguing because, again, Whitman's style and the Objectivist style seem so distinct. One may note passages from "Allen Ginsberg on Walt Whitman: Composed on the Tongue" (an essay in which Ginsberg writes about Whitman and explicates *Leaves of Grass*) whereby Ginsberg's descriptions of how Whitman observes and represents the "actual world" in his (Whitman's) poetry are analogous to the commentary about Reznikoff's mode of looking and clear representation. For example, Ginsberg remarks, "Well, [Whitman] recommended that everybody else look at the actual world around them rather than the abstract world they read about in the newspapers or saw as a pseudo-image/event" (334). Ginsberg also states that "[Whitman] has suffered a bit here, he does empathize with all the beggars, the monstrous convicts with sweat twitching on their lips, but his point here is that everybody so suffers, everybody is everybody else, in the sense of having experienced in imagination or in real life all of the non-respectable emotions of the elephants and the ants" (338). A third point that resonates with Ginsberg's analysis of Reznikoff appears near the end of the essay, in the context of Whitman's poem "I Sing the Body Electric": "He [Whitman] begins to describe his own body and other peoples' bodies in an intimate way, numbering all the parts, numbering all the emotions, and naming them and actually attempting to account, and give an accounting and itemization of all men" (339). Whitman's "looking at the real world," "empathizing" with everyone, "accounting for" (or cataloguing), are likewise features in Reznikoff's writing that Ginsberg admired.

96   CHAPTER THREE

In Ginsberg's poem "After Whitman & Reznikoff" in *Plutonian Ode*, these intersections of Whitman/Reznikoff appear very explicitly. The title marks Whitman and Reznikoff as dual poetic forefathers, demonstrating that the poets are associated for Ginsberg, and I would add that this association is manifest in terms of both poetic witnessing and precise representation. The first short section, with the subtitle "What Relief," begins with the probably sarcastic declaration "If my pen hand were snapped by a Broadway truck," it would be a welcome respite from having to write poetry and political letters, "disputing tyrants, war gossip, FBI" (732). Formalistically, the listing within these relatively short lines can be read as both Whitmanesque (for being repetitious) and Objectivist (for being terser in length relative to many of Ginsberg's poems). There is clarity in the depiction of the scene itself, as the speaker imagines that his poems might "gather dust in Kansas libraries," where only "adolescent farmboys [would be] opening book covers with ruddy hands." This idea is a gesture to Whitman as a gay predecessor and comrade, and although Whitman appears as a more overt poetic model in the first section, the legacies of both Whitman and Reznikoff are displayed in the lines.

In section 2, the speaker watches and describes an event involving "that round faced woman," at the same time run-of-the-mill and distressing. With a self-consciously Jewish sensibility, the poem takes place on Reznikoff's Lower East Side (and Whitman's Mannahatta):

Lower East Side

That round faced woman, she owns the street with her three big dogs,
screeches at me, waddling with her shopping bag across Avenue B.
Grabbing my crotch, "Why don't you talk to me?"
baring her teeth in a smile, voice loud like a taxi horn,

"Big Jerk . . . you think you're famous?"—reminds me of my mother.
April 29, 1980 (732)

The stanza, with a sarcastic turn, conveys Ginsberg's serious desire to be witness and to communicate—like Reznikoff and Whitman—what is "real." Ginsberg offers a list of unpleasant images: the woman waddles "with her shopping bag" in downtown Manhattan, grabs Ginsberg's "crotch," and snarls at him, "voice loud like a taxi horn," accusing him of being a "big jerk." Until the somewhat cynical interjection—"reminds me of my mother"—the poem contains stark details reminiscent of what Ginsberg points out about Reznikoff's

Objectivist style, with the poem also being a tribute to (or "after") Whitman. While Whitman's stylistic influence may not be as obvious as Reznikoff's, and though Ginsberg employs Whitman's style more overtly in other poems, like "Kaddish," "Howl,"[42] or "Yiddishe Kopf," with Ginsberg meditating on the association between Reznikoff and Whitman, the poem can be recognized as being informed by elements of both poets.

To apply this Modernist-Objectivist-Whitmanian-Jewish thread to another poem by Ginsberg—one that does not allude to Whitman or Reznikoff by name, but in which these dynamics are apparent—take "Waking in New York" from 1964. In this piece, in which Ginsberg's speaker enumerates what he sees, hears, and even smells upon waking up in the morning in New York City, the reader can detect a "photographic accuracy and precision of detail" (to go back to Ginsberg's statements about Reznikoff, as well as Whitman). The speaker describes a repugnant scene from within a presumably dilapidated apartment building (described as "sixth floor cold / March 5th Street old building plaster"; 347). And yet, the speaker writes of finding beauty and wonder in this scene, and thus the poem is also a more classically Whitmanesque celebration of the self (the "I") and New York, for instance, in these lines:

> I place my hand before my beard with awe
> and stare thru open-uncurtain window
> > rooftop rose-blue sky thru
> > which small dawn clouds ride
> > > rattle against the pane (347)

The speaker, with his hand in his beard, gazes through the window and describes the exact details he sees—the "rooftop rose-blue sky." The lines are at once Whitmanesque (with the "awe" of the self, the body, and New York) and typically Objectivist, with a series of shorter lines and images. These Whitmanian-Objectivist (and Modernist) features continue to be employed several lines later, where the speaker writes, "—our life together here / smoke of tenement chimney pots dawn haze / passing thru wind soar Sirs—" (347). Though optimism is probably the most dominant tone in the poem, the lines also communicate the speaker's sense of estrangement from his surroundings; for instance, in the morning, the speaker sings "my song" (naturally a Whitmanian song) and the song of his companions, but he does not know who, if anyone, hears them: "Morning, my song to Who listens, to / myself as I am" (348).

98 CHAPTER THREE

These "songs" are followed by another list of images of New York, whereby the beautiful is juxtaposed with the ugly: "Tenement streets' brick sagging cornices / baby white kites fluttering against giant / insect face gill Electric Mill / smokestacked blue & fumes drift up" (348). The scene is decrepit yet glorious and vivid, with the white kites in relief against the polluted corporate building. Descriptions such as these continue: "The giant stacks burn thick gray / smoke / Chrysler is lit with green [. . .] Oh fathers, how I am alone in this / vast human wilderness" (349). As he gazes, the speaker meditates further on the human condition: "Is somehow dying in all this stone building? / Child poking its black head out of the womb like a frightened eye?" (349). At the end of the poem, the act of looking, or witness, itself becomes explicit:

> I fail, book fails—a lassitude,
>
> > a fear—tho I'm alive
>
> and gaze over the descending—No!
> peer in the inky beauty of the roofs. (350)

In "the inky beauty of the roofs," one hears a Whitmanian "barbaric yawp over the roofs of the world" (78), except in this case, Ginsberg's speaker shouts to himself, gazing over New York, experiencing "lassitude," weakness, and "failure" all at the same time. Again, Reznikoff is present in the "sharpest, stickiest details" (again, Ginsberg's words), via Williams and Pound, with Whitman ever-present, from Ginsberg's first moment of "waking."

These essays and poems by Ginsberg therefore reveal how his adoption of Whitman is entwined with Reznikoff, as part of a dialogue with High Modernist poets like Williams and (somewhat) against Pound. Such a contextualization of Ginsberg's poetry of witness, and response to High Modernism, adds new dimensions to the narrative of Ginsberg and Whitman, two canonical American poets who are already recognized as being interconnected. This research identifies how Ginsberg's response to Whitman and Reznikoff is related to his being a Jewish American poet. In poems such as "Yiddishe Kopf," "After Whitman & Reznikoff," and "Waking in New York," in which the Whitman-Jewish-Objectivist influence is strong but more implicit, Ginsberg's connection to Whitman is filtered through Reznikoff. In the final section of this chapter, in the writing of Gerald Stern, one uncovers not only a poetics of witness but a hopefully now familiar conceit of being for and against Whitman (in Stern's case, even directly through Ginsberg). Though Stern was writing in one generation further from Pound and Williams than Ginsberg, in his poetry and essays are certain traces of this adoption of Whitman in response to Pound and some of the more conservative, discriminatory elements of High Modernism.

GERALD STERN

> I love Whitman. I don't love all of Whitman. There's a lot of
> Whitman that is repetitive, flat, excessive. But when he's on,
> there's no one like him.
>
> —GERALD STERN, "Ginsberg and I"

As with Allen Ginsberg, Walt Whitman's themes, poetic structures, and privileging of the "I" are pervasive in the writing of Gerald Stern.[43] Also like for Ginsberg, among the many influences identified as influences for Stern—the Bible, Shakespeare, Coleridge, Keats, Ralph Waldo Emerson, Emily Dickinson, W. H. Auden, Muriel Rukeyser, William Carlos Williams, W. B. Yeats, Grace Paley, Wallace Stevens, and Hart Crane—Whitman probably informs Stern's work most tangibly in poetic style and voice. As Jane Somerville writes on Stern and Whitman, "the Whitman persona is an imperative figure, magnified, heroized, and mythicized, as is Stern's spokesman" (13–14).[44] What remains to be fully recognized in Stern's case is the extent to which his affiliation with Whitman is entwined with Jewish American identity and that this affiliation is bound up with the lineage of Jewish American poets put forth in this book. In this chapter, Stern is positioned in a line of influence with Rukeyser and Ginsberg, to highlight a Whitmanian poetics of witness and shaping of poetry as a democratic form. Stern's long poem "Hot Dog," is a site in which these aspects of the Stern-Whitman-Jewish thread are visible, as the speaker narrates his experience of being a Jewish poet in America, a poet-of-witness, with Whitman featured as a main character that the Jewish speaker "follows through half of Camden." When investigated in this context, one sees that the (Jewish) Whitman is received by Stern through Ginsberg, and in the Modernist-Objectivist context of Pound and Williams.

Stern has noted significant indebtedness to Whitman, although his opinion of the American democratic poet vacillates between "love" and dismissal. On the one hand, Stern states that his poetic voice is a response to "beloved Walt's," for example, in the essay "What I Have to Defend, What I Can't Bear Losing":

100 CHAPTER THREE

> If there is a human voice behind, or a human voice engulfing, the poetic
> voice—the *persona*—it is that voice I am interested in. . . . It is the voice I
> listen to when I read Yeats or Chaucer. It is what the beloved Walt meant
> when he said, "Missing me one place search another." "Let us stand up,
> it is time to explain myself," he said. (319)

On the other hand, Stern conveys "resistance" to Whitman, for instance, in the essay "Ginsberg and I," where Stern distinguishes his own relationship to Whitman from that of Ginsberg: "We were both influenced by Whitman but [Ginsberg] claimed Whitman, he was a direct descendent, a continuation—I was more resistant" (266). Ginsberg embraced Whitman far less reservedly, in ways that Stern perhaps does not. It is possible to interpret Stern's remark about Whitman historically and culturally, whereby Stern, whose first collection of poetry, *Lucky Life*, was published in 1977 (with other major volumes of poetry including *The Red Coal* in 1981, *Bread Without Sugar* in 1992, and *American Sonnets* in 2002), after the peak of High Modernism.[45] One does not find Stern extensively disavowing Pound; in "The Red Coal," he relates with "affection" to a photograph of Pound and Williams: "I say it with vast affection, / wanting desperately to know what the two of them / talked about when they lived in Pennsylvania" (99). Still, there are hints in Stern of a reaction to prejudice by certain High Modernist figures, especially Pound and Eliot. In the essay "William Carlos Williams," Stern expresses liking Williams's language and the attentiveness to the details of humanity—what he calls "Williams's mystery" (366). Stern also remarks on reading Williams's poetry in the context of "the bomb," presumably Hiroshima in 1945, first implicating himself for not writing about the tragedies of World War I and World War II, and second offering an indictment of Pound's and Eliot's racist and antisemitic assertions:

> I was there in the early 1950s myself, writing "little aesthetic masterpieces"
> with no reference to the ugly 1930s and 40s. . . . The horror—in Europe,
> in Africa, in Asia may have been on Williams's mind—it was—but he
> chose to call it "the bomb." Eliot had already—years earlier—made his
> comment about how we cannot tolerate too many "secular free-thinking
> Jews," and expressed his regret over the death of the Confederacy, and
> Pound was still at it even to his late-late-self-serving insane comment
> (to Ginsberg) that he was guilty of what he called a "suburban prejudice"
> in his, Pound's hate-mongering. (365)

Despite this noting of Pound's "hate-mongering" to Ginsberg, I suggest that Stern's response to Whitman might not be as directly against Pound as is true for Reznikoff, Shapiro, Koch, or Rukeyser.

Regarding parallels between Stern and Whitman drawn by critics, Stern writes of taking issue with some of these comparisons, insisting that he does not embrace Whitman's poetics without reservation:

> I love Whitman. I don't love all of Whitman. There's a lot of Whitman that is repetitive, flat, excessive. But when he's on, there's no one like him. In "Song of Myself," he's elusive, he's a genius, he's brilliant, and he's smart. And I love that Whitman. I don't know how it happened that there are so many connections between him and me. . . . I find myself getting a little angry and resisting it. (119)

One of the reasons for Stern's resistance is what he perceives as Whitman's lack of engagement with Jewish people or Jewish culture (which, biographically speaking, was largely the case for Whitman). Stern writes of a quality or sensibility in Whitman that strikes him as distinctly non-Jewish:

> It's interesting about Whitman. He speaks very little about the Jews. I'm sure he loved the Jews. I'm sure he had a good nineteenth-century liberal vision of Judaism, if he thought about it. I don't think he thought about it a lot. Certainly he's an important element in Yiddish and Hebrew thinking. . . . But Whitman does not have a Jewish taste. There is humor in Whitman but it's a different kind of humor. I think that quality in me that is nervous, ironic, mean, even nasty, elusive in my way, derives from another place other than Whitman. . . . But I don't reject it, I'm just trying to elaborate on this. I'm not speaking against Whitman. God love Whitman. (120)

Stern thus acknowledges the impact Whitman has had on his Jewish writing, "Yiddish and Hebrew thinking," but for him, at least consciously, Whitman remains an Other—a poet with "a different kind of humor" than his own.[46] Ironically, this type of othering, or being an Other, is what defines Stern's speakers in many of his poems, which become relevant for this discussion about Stern, Whitman, and Jewish identity.

Stern's attitudes about Jewishness are as complicated as those toward Whitman. When asked if he considers himself a Jewish poet, Stern's response evokes Ginsberg's, as being referring to a culture and tradition that is intrinsic to his identity:

102 CHAPTER THREE

> The hardest question of all to answer. Of course I'm a Jewish poet. Some-
> times I'm consciously a Jewish poet, though rarely. . . . But one of the
> subjects that is very important to me is my Jewishness, and I'm interested
> in Judaism and have sentimental and loving as well as critical attitudes
> toward Jewishness. (Pacernick 111)

Like many secular Jewish writers, artists, and thinkers, including Rukeyser
and Ginsberg, Stern expresses skepticism toward traditional religious frameworks; yet Jewish themes, such as antisemitism, immigration, assimilation,
the Holocaust, Hebrew and Yiddish, and "old world" Jewish culture, populate
his writing, as expressed in the poems considered to be Stern's most "Jewish"
poems, "Behaving Like a Jew," "Lucky Life," and "Soap."[47] Multiple essays in
the collection *What I Can't Bear Losing: Notes from a Life* demonstrate Jewish experiences as well.[48] Stern was born in Pittsburgh, Pennsylvania, and
his parents (immigrants from Ukraine) spoke Yiddish around Stern, which
stayed with him, as is described in the essay "Sundays": "The lingua franca was
English, though there were some things that could be said only in Yiddish"
(1).[49] Taken together, Stern's poetry and prose display a deep engagement with
Jewish language, culture, and history, with attitudes toward Jewishness that
are both, to use his terms, "loving" and "critical" (very much like the attitudes
expressed by Stern about Whitman).[50]

The ambivalence with which Stern writes about his personal experience as
Jewish poet is echoed in the experience of outsiderness or "betweenness" that
informs the Sternian persona in poetry, as well as Stern's reading of Whitman.
Despite the elusive notion that Stern perceives Whitman to be non-Jewish,
Whitman is foregrounded in "Hot Dog," a seventeen-section poem from the
1995 collection *Odd Mercy* that explores race, class, and religion from a markedly Jewish and American perspective. The poem contains multiple motifs that
shift throughout the poem, including New York City, homelessness, Jewish
culture, America, the Holocaust, childhood, poverty, the treatment of animals,
nature in an urban environment, and existential questions of mortality. "Hot
Dog" is the name of the young homeless girl on the street. There is a distinct
listing or cataloguing of details in Stern's text, observed by the narrator from an
outsider position, with lines that recall a poetics of witness through Ginsberg
(and Reznikoff), High Modernist poetics, and Whitman.

Stern's Whitmanian poem opens on Avenue A in New York City. The speaker's
initial description of the scene is clear and rather bleak (reminding a reader of

WHITMAN'S POETICS OF WITNESS   103

Ginsberg evoking Reznikoff and Whitman in "After Whitman & Reznikoff"):
a solitary mushroom, a baby carriage without a baby, and a broken telephone:

> I.
> One white mushroom lying in the street across
> from Sappora East and one wicker baby carriage
> with dogs inside and one New York telephone
> with its mouth ripped off to go with my Augustine
> and one mini tulip and one black girl named Hot Dog
> sticking pins in her friends on Avenue A
> to go with my Whitman and one of her friends skating
> off the curb, Whitman and Augustine— (67)

The poem establishes the speaker as an outsider from, and witness to, the scene.
Peter Siedlecki has noted that both Stern and Whitman take up this position:
"Employing the first person as he does, Whitman not only charges his poetry
with the immediacy and energy that comes from eyewitness accounts; he also
establishes a situation that allows him to watch himself watching" (114). The
dual position of outsider/witness, which I believe is crucial, also reflects an
estrangement faced by Stern's speaker being an outsider as a Jewish American
poet. It is Whitman who comes to mitigate this estrangement; in the first section
of the poem, Stern refers to Whitman as a "friend" in New York:

> well, never seeing each other, though Whitman came later
> and he saw Augustine and maybe Whitman
> wander through Carthage; he would have been a goat
> and Augustine would have petted his bony head
> and stared into his eyes. I hate to do this
> but I am choosing one—you have to do it
> one way or another, you can't smile walking
> past the Japanese fruit store, you can't be
> benign forever—fuck that!—one is an enemy
> and one is a friend. (67)

The "friendship" with Whitman is described in contrast to that with Augustine; if Augustine is understood as a symbol of Christianity (an "enemy"),
then Whitman (the speaker's "friend") is another poet of the minority within
the majority (America). The speaker "hates" to choose between them but is
compelled to do so. The line "you have to do it / one way or another" further

104 CHAPTER THREE

emphasizes the speaker's sense of uncertainty toward his own Otherness. In the end, though, Stern's speaker is on Whitman's side and is what Whitman represents being a "goat" and outsider.

Whitman is alluded to again in section V, where the speaker, now seated in Tompkins Square in Lower Manhattan, "obsessing on death," imagines Whitman walking through a crowd of immigrants, past Sappora East, the Japanese fruit store mentioned in section I. The speaker muses about his own death and Whitman's philosophies of death, which leads into a passage expressing anguish over the death of Yiddish and the terrible endurance of antisemitism. Thus Whitman's "sweet," "exhilarating" idea of death is juxtaposed with Stern's despairing, perhaps more typically Jewish one:

> . . . though death itself
> was poisonous, [Whitman] was too brave there, he just whistled
> too much, he swaggered, north on First, as far
> as I know, past Sappora East, though sometimes
> he didn't swagger—I have to say that—death then
> was truer, I'll call it truer, he even called it
> exhilarating—it was his subject—sweet flag
> rising out of his breast, a plump bird
> singing dirges, a coffin half-floating past
> the gunny sacks of rice, voices moaning
> in Spanish and Korean, Yiddish driven
> into a corner onto some seats in back of
> a tiny theater on Second Avenue; I climbed
> the stage, we would have turned it into the language
> of feeling—we already did—we would have added
> more complexity and more profundity
> and borrowed less from the Russian and the English—
> and voices moaning in Polish and Ukrainian
> as one more coffin floated by: Forgive me,
> Jew, Jew; forgive me, kike; forgive me,
> you fucking turd; ah, where should we put the bell
> now that the goat his throat is slit? Ah Jew,
> fucking Jew. (75–76)

As Whitman "swaggers" through the immigrant milieu of "voices moaning" in Spanish and Korean, the absence of Yiddish-speaking people is evoked, with

Yiddish itself relegated or "driven" to the margins, "a tiny theater on Second Avenue." The Jewish speaker in New York mourns the disappearance of a language once spoken widely by the Jewish immigrant community (including by his own parents), which has all but vanished due to assimilation or genocide.

Stern then seems to introduce a second speaker, presumably the figure of an antisemite, who asks for "forgiveness" from the Jew, which is revealed to be disingenuous as the dialogue morphs into antisemitic slurring ("forgive me, kike") and an image of a coffin "floating by." The antisemitic speaker then asks who will be the "goat" (or scapegoat, in a Jewish context) if Jewish culture and language have already been destroyed or "killed": "ah, where should we put the bell / now that the goat his throat is slit?" These lines suggest that while aspects of Jewish culture have been lost, antisemitism persists. And though Whitman is not mentioned explicitly in this part of the poem, indirectly he is referenced through the symbol of the goat, since in section I, Stern refers to Whitman this way: "[Whitman] would have been a goat." There is a connection, therefore, between Whitman and Jewishness, with the disturbing image of the goat's throat being "slit," implying that Whitman, too, as a poet and Other, serves as a scapegoat in some form.[51]

Section VIII is centered on an imagining of Whitman's physical body, his house in Camden, New Jersey, his love of opera and the sea, and ideals of empathy and humanism that the speaker finds so pervasive in Whitman. The section begins with the speaker's pursuit of Whitman "through half of Camden":

I followed Whitman
through half of Camden, across on the ferry and back
to Water Street; I lay down on his bed
and pushed my hand against the wall to bring
the forces back into my arms; (85)

The pursuit is strongly symbolic, whereby, gesturing toward a shared misery touched by humor, the speaker "lay[s] down on his [Whitman's] bed," and thus the Jewish Sternian and non-Jewish Whitmanian personas are merged and unified. Some lines later, the speaker turns to the idea of Whitman's encompassing empathy (an idea Ginsberg mentioned in relation to both Williams and Whitman): "Walt Whitman loved / women, look how he grieved in the city dead-house alone with the poor dead prostitute" (87). Stern here alludes to the figures of "prostitutes" in Whitman's poems "The City Dead-House" (285–286) and "To a Common Prostitute" (299–300).[52] In the portrayal of

106 CHAPTER THREE

Whitman's witness of, and empathy for, the figures of these "prostitutes," who would so often be invisible to society, an approval of Whitman's humanistic empathy is signaled. The approval is further reinforced when Stern repeats the phrase, almost with a tone of awe, "and look how": "and look how he [Whitman] spoke to that other."

While I would suggest that Stern's notions of Jewishness are informed by this Whitmanian compassion toward the Other, in section XIII of "Hot Dog," one finds the speaker unable to replicate these Whitmanian ideals. For instance, when he envisions encountering the figure of Hot Dog herself, as well as the other people sleeping outside the Odessa Café, Stern's speaker writes of doubting that what he has to offer (money and poetry) is truly helpful or sufficient:

> ... both times I gave her
> money but it was matter-of-fact, there wasn't
> pity involved, or indignation, or self-righteousness; I waited for some
>   dark light
> to turn bright in front of the Odessa,
> I wanted to feel the light; I did it by stages,
> with one eye then the other, I almost threw
> myself down on their bed, there it was,
> their bluntness on that stone, their simplicity,
> their helplessness. (101)

The speaker never quite achieves Whitman's unmediated embrace of impoverished people but wishes he could have: "I almost threw myself down on their bed." Thus, the speaker is aware of not being entirely like the people who are forced to live on the margins of society, although the mention of the prototypically Jewish "Odessa" café is a reminder that he, too, as a Jewish poet in America, is a type of outsider.[53] Within the tradition of Jewish American poets before (and after) him, in the poem "Hot Dog," Stern invites Whitman to participate in the poetic experience of Jewishness in America, with Whitman serving as a lens through which these ideas are rethought, reconsidered, and redefined.

This triad of Muriel Rukeyser, Allen Ginsberg, and Gerald Stern together compose a branch of the Whitman-Jewish genealogy, whereby Whitman is employed as a mode of navigating Jewish identity in America, each poet adopting Whitman into their unique poetic project while responding through and to each other. Whitman is present for Rukeyser in her mission to shape

Jewishness and poetry as a mode of equality, and to distinguish her politically informed poetics from High Modernism; for Ginsberg, there is a Jewish-Whitmanesque-Modernist poetics in dialogue with Whitman through Reznikoff, Williams, and Pound; and finally, Stern, who challenges Whitman (at times), also portrays Whitman as a poetic comrade of the marginalized and receives Whitman through Williams, Pound, and Ginsberg (and Reznikoff). Across the twentieth century, Whitman is shaped into a spokesperson against exclusion and elitism, as a counterpoint to prejudicial strands within High Modernism, and into a symbol of humanistic poetics. These responses will come to inform Whitman's critical reception by later Jewish American poets, including the branch of Jewish American women poets investigated in chapter 4 (with Rukeyser's model of turning to Whitman as a Jewish American woman poet being instrumental).

CHAPTER FOUR

Jewish American Women Poets Respond to Walt Whitman: Adrienne Rich, Alicia Ostriker, and Marge Piercy

In Adrienne Rich's essay, "The Genesis of 'Yom Kippur 1984,'" she writes of a "considerable dialogue" (255) with the iconic American poet Walt Whitman and of how this "dialogue" comes into play in the process of composing her poem "Yom Kippur 1984"—which opens with a question about Jewishness: "What is a Jew in solitude?" This question can be taken as emblematic of, first, the complexities of the engagement with Jewishness and Americanness in Rich's writing; and second, the complexities of Rich's engagement with Whitman's poetics—intersecting realms explored later in this chapter. Aside from Rich herself, the Whitmanian-Jewish juncture in these texts can be taken to represent how Whitman's legacy has been carried forward by Jewish American poets from the mid- to late twentieth century and into the twenty-first. Finally, with Rich as a precursor of feminist, political poetry and criticism, her quote is an ideal way to open an examination of Whitman's role in the branch of the genealogy presented here—that of Jewish American women poets, including, in addition to Rich, Alicia Ostriker and Marge Piercy.

Muriel Rukeyser is a formative precursor for Rich, Ostriker, and Piercy, with Rukeyser having established the crucial groundwork of adopting Whitman into an oeuvre of humanistic and politically engaged poetry, in line with Whitman's prophetic *Leaves of Grass* project. Like Whitman, Rukeyser undertook a mission to shape an expansive, democratic Jewish American poetry, in response to injustices she observed occurring in America (and elsewhere in the world) and within the German Jewish Reform community in which she was raised.[1] Rich herself, in the essay "Beginners" (1993), refers to Rukeyser as "our twentieth-century Coleridge, our Neruda," with a legacy that ought to equal Whitman's and Dickinson's (15–16).[2]

With Rukeyser's mode of writing as a Jewish woman poet in dialogue with Whitman in mind, in this chapter, I explore arenas of Whitman, Jewishness, Americanness, politics, gender, and identity in poetry, essays, and interviews by Rich (1929–2012), Ostriker (b. 1937), and Piercy (b. 1936). Rich's first book, *A Change of World*, was published in 1951, somewhat earlier than Ostriker's *Songs: A Book of Poems* (1969) and Piercy's *Breaking Camp* (1968). As always, with respect to each poet's unique poetics and perceptions of Whitman, I argue that Whitman's poetic legacy is vital in the works of Rich, Ostriker, and Piercy. This chapter seeks to broaden scholarship on adoptions of Whitman by women writers; for example, Diane Middlebrook has written about the wider tradition of feminist poets turning to Whitman (including Rich and Susan Griffin): "Acknowledging Whitman as a model and precursor, feminist writers have identified an analogous need to free women from the literary culture long dominated by men as writers, critics, editors, and publishers" (15).[3] For these three Jewish women poets writing in and about America, in line with Rukeyser (along with other poets in this project, such as Ginsberg), Whitman is imagined as a poet of equality, inclusion, and political engagement, as well as the disappointments and disasters of America.

One aspect that sets these later twentieth-century women poets apart from previous generations of Jewish American poets responding to Whitman is the distance from High Modernism. Whitman's position within the American poetic canon was no longer under threat to the degree it was for, say, Charles Reznikoff and the Jewish Objectivists, Karl Shapiro, and Kenneth Koch, who had more direct ties to Ezra Pound and other High Modernist poets who (save for William Carlos Williams) were not entirely embracing of Whitman. There are some lingering points for Rich, Ostriker, and Piercy where Whitman is employed as a model against the attitudes of Pound; however, compared to a time in which Rukeyser was compelled to write of the "wretched and static condition" of the "New" group (*Life* 178) and Shapiro to ask, "What has happened to Whitman in the century since *Leaves of Grass* was published?" ("First White Aboriginal" 160), aligning with Whitman is a less radical and transgressive act.

110   CHAPTER FOUR

The contemporary Whitman is not without critics (Jewish and non-Jewish), who seek to call out—and I would claim justifiably—racist and discriminatory elements in Whitman's poetry and prose. Poet CAConrad points to a hypocrisy in Whitman in the essay "From Whitman to Walmart" (2015), claiming, "The fact that his egregious racist prose is so upsetting is because he is anything but obscure in America today." And in "Should Walt Whitman Be #Cancelled?" (2019), Lavelle Porter, who generally holds a more favorable attitude toward Whitman than CAConrad, asks what to "do" with Whitman in light of such rampant racism: "Whitman's racism was not limited to black people, but also extended to Native Americans, Hispanics, and Asians. . . . So, what do we do with old Uncle Walt now?" Porter's response is ultimately on the side of Whitman, as he states, "Reading the works of Black intellectuals on Whitman shows that confronting Whitman's racism is not about erasing Whitman." Even with certain contemporary critiques of Whitman, the critical reputation of Whitman is higher than at the beginning of the twentieth century—a phenomenon Scott MacPhail attributes to the post–World War II rise of American studies in the university, the valorization of the lyric form in New Criticism, and "the emergence of the United States as a superpower" (137–138).[4]

In addition to the general solidifying of Whitman's critical reception (to which the poets in this book have expressly contributed), the status of Jewish people in America continues to evolve since the early twentieth century, when Whitman is first employed in the context of Pound, Eliot, and the anti-Whitman and antisemitic attitudes common in that era. David Biale, Michael Galchinsky, and Susannah Heschel describe a "historical dualism" for modern Jewish people in America—on the one hand, the move toward assimilation, and on the other, the "desire" to retain a sense of Jewish selfhood:

> In contemporary America, this historical dualism has reached its greatest extremes. Never before have so few barriers existed to Jews' entering the corridors of political, cultural and economic power. Yet the path to integration has also created enormous contradictions in Jewish self-consciousness. Identification and integration with the majority stands at odds with the Jews' equal desire to preserve their identity as a minority. (5)

With these complexities, questions continue to arise around the "duality" or hyphenation of "Jewish" and "American." Though perhaps less "against" than for Jewish American poets of earlier generations, who were compelled to construct Whitman as a mode of claiming their identity as Jews, as well as resisting various experiences of exclusion, Whitman plays a no less substantive role in mediating hyphenated identity in the late twentieth and early twenty-first century. For Rich, Ostriker, and Piercy, Whitman continues to serve as a symbol through which to navigate radically complex identity positions and (in the spirit of Rukeyser) to promote a malleable, contemporary Jewishness, with aspirations for a more equitable America.

Thus, Whitman's presence in the work of these poets has evolved with historical and cultural phenomena, while remaining rooted in previous responses to Whitman by other Jewish American poets. Whitman as a figure is appropriated by Ostriker, Piercy, and Rich to navigate identity and often to challenge the status quo by arguing with certain ideas (and ideals) of America that Whitman promoted. As case studies of Whitman's role in Jewish American women's poetry, I examine Rich's essay "The Genesis of 'Yom Kippur 1984'" and the poems "Yom Kippur 1984" from *Your Native Land, Your Life* (1986) and "Tattered Kaddish" from *An Atlas of the Difficult World* (1991); Ostriker's essay "Loving Walt Whitman and the Problem of America" (2000), as well as the poems "Manahatta" and "Dry Hours: A Golden Shovel Exercise" from *Waiting for the Light* (2017) and "Elegy Before the War" from *No Heaven* (2005); and finally, Piercy's essay "How I Came to Walt Whitman and Found Myself" (1992), two prayer-poems from *The Art of Blessing the Day: Poems with a Jewish Theme* (1993), "The Art of Blessing the Day" and "Nishmat," and one last poem that I find displays the Jewish-American-Whitmanian thread, titled "Praise in Spite of It All" from *On the Way Out, Turn Off the Light* (2020).

ADRIENNE RICH'S WALT WHITMAN

The oeuvre of Adrienne Rich—poet, scholar, and intellectual—offers fertile territory in which to examine the juncture of Jewish American identity, political consciousness, and the role of Walt Whitman. Rich, recipient of two National Book Awards and a MacArthur Fellowship, is known for major contributions in poetry, such as *A Change of World* (1951), *Diving into the Wreck: Poems 1971–72* (1973), and *The Dream of a Common Language: Poems 1974–1977* (1978), and essays on writing, sexuality, and identity, like "When We Dead Awaken: Writing as Re-Vision" (1971), "Compulsory Heterosexuality and Lesbian Existence" (1980), and "Split at the Root: An Essay on Jewish Identity" (1982). The depth and breadth of Rich's engagement with Whitman is apparent, for example, in two essays by Rich, "The Genesis of 'Yom Kippur 1984'" and "Beginners." In the quote by Rich in the introduction, in "The Genesis of 'Yom Kippur 1984,'" about the process of composing a poem by that title, one encounters her description of a "considerable dialogue" with Whitman and the significance of Whitman as a poetic model. Rich goes on to state, "In the course of those months I was reading a lot in the Bible, and I was reading Whitman" (255). Here, I will argue that Rich incorporates Whitman as a poetic and political model and that Whitman informs her Jewish and American poetic sensibilities and uniquely the multiple or divided identities explored in Rich's poetry and prose (in terms of her Jewish and Southern Protestant upbringing, gender, and sexuality). Though Rich turns to Whitman in these ways, she writes of not always being in alignment due to certain inadequacies in Whitman, that is, ways in which Whitman represents America as a more tolerant, inclusive, democratic nation than is the case for those from minority groups.

Unlike Ostriker and Piercy, Rich does not pinpoint Whitman as a model for validating her own sense of identity (as Jewish American poet or otherwise); however, Whitman's poetic style does resonate in what Rich herself describes as a "looser mode" of poetics that she discovered in her work ("When" 175). Rich has conveyed in "When We Dead Awaken" how her formative mentors— many of whom were male—advocated for a more formalistic poetic style. She recalls that much of her early poetry was "formed by male poets: by the men I was reading as an undergraduate—Frost, Dylan Thomas, Auden, MacNiece, Stevens, Yeats" (171).[5] She adds that employing these more formalistic styles was a means of navigating challenging topics in her poems: "In those years formalism was part of the strategy—like asbestos gloves, it allowed me to handle materials I couldn't pick up bare-handed" (171).[6] Throughout Rich's collections, the development of this "looser," more anaphoric, Whitmanesque style can be detected, as evident in *Diving into the Wreck*, *The Dream of a Common Language*, *Time's Power* (1989), and *An Atlas of the Difficult World* and in poems that would become among her most well-known, like "Diving into the Wreck," "Yom Kippur 1984," "An Atlas of the Difficult World," and "Tattered Kaddish."

Scholars of Rich from different orientations, like Peter Erickson, Piotr Gwiazda, Nissa Parmar, Diane Middlebrook, and Maeera Y. Shreiber, have made crucial observations about Whitman's place in Rich's poetry. By and large, however, Rich's assessments of Whitman are examined outside the context of other Jewish American poets (save for Rukeyser, whose significance for Rich in terms of Whitman has been commented upon). In conversation with these and other critics, my reading augments the understanding of Rich's turn to Whitman, which is poetic, thematic, and ideological. In explorations of Whitman in essays such as "The Genesis of 'Yom Kippur 1984'" and the poems "Yom Kippur 1984" and "Tattered Kaddish," this project reveals how Rich distinctively, but in keeping with other poets in this genealogy, employs Whitman as a figure through which to negotiate Jewish identity in America. For instance, Rich (like Gerald Stern and Alicia Ostriker) does not simply embrace but criticizes Whitman, finding serious flaws in the vision of America that Whitman put forth. Moreover, Rich as a poet (like Rukeyser, Ostriker, and Piercy) wrote a great deal about occupying complicated identity positions, including in connection to Jewishness (Rich's father was Jewish, while her mother was of a Southern Protestant background), and Whitman's legacy is called upon to endorse a more progressive Jewishness in America and the world at large.

Again, the mode of inclusivity Rich sought from Whitman, I would argue, can be read in context with various identities she writes of navigating, in terms of Jewish and non-Jewish culture, sexual orientation, and having been raised in the South. Even the extent to which Rich is understood to be writing as a Jewish poet is a complicated issue; as Wendy Martin and Annalisa Zox-Weaver have noted, "Readers of Rich do not readily identify her as a Jewish poet, much less a religious writer" (418). These conflicted and "disconnected" identities are at the forefront of Rich's "Split at the Root": "Sometimes I feel I have seen too long from too many disconnected angles: white, Jewish, anti-Semite, racist, anti-racist, once-married, lesbian, middle-class, feminist, expatriate southerner, *split at the root*—that I will never bring them whole" (238). Rich goes on to declare her personal desire to investigate these identities as troubling, "dangerous," and "filled with shame and fear" (224). Nevertheless, Rich elaborates on her family history, writing about her father—Arnold Rich—a doctor whose parents were of Ashkenazi and Sephardic background,[7] and her mother, Helen Elizabeth (Jones), a "white, southern, Protestant woman, the gentile" (225).[8] Rich depicts a conflicting engagement with these cultures, aligning perhaps more closely to Jewishness, but all the while with an awareness that "according to Jewish law, I cannot count myself as a Jew" (225).[9] Thus, Rich writes of not identifying (or being identified by others) as completely Jewish or completely Christian.[10]

Rich also, in "Split at the Root," speaks to problematic expectations of heteronormativity in her family and society more broadly, exacerbating this condition of Otherness;[11] she states, "At different times in my life I have wanted to push

114 CHAPTER FOUR

away one or the other burden of inheritance, to say merely *I am a woman; I am a lesbian*" (226). It is these themes of divided identities that inform Rich's poetry and prose, around the experience of being Other (and Othered), raised with Jewish and Christian traditions in the American South, and with an awareness of her own sexuality being potentially objectionable. As Nissa Parmar notes, "Through [Rich's] status as a woman, lesbian, and Jew she viewed herself as a cultural outsider" (111). I would argue that these areas of "outsiderness" and difference, as expressed in her writing, also underlie the enfolding of Whitman's legacy into her own mission to offer inclusion to marginalized people, perhaps making Whitman's notions in Rich's writing all the more urgent.

Whitman in Rich's Poetry and Prose

Rich's long poem "An Atlas of the Difficult World" has probably received the most critical attention in terms of the role of Whitman.[12] In this section, I explore several texts that have received somewhat less consideration but in which Whitman features prominently: the essays "The Genesis of 'Yom Kippur 1984'" and "Beginners," as well as the poems "Yom Kippur 1984" and "Tattered Kaddish." These works represent the intersection of Jewish American identity and Whitman as imagined by Rich (with Rukeyser a prominent figure in Rich's discussion of Whitman). In "Beginners," where one finds Rich's description of Whitman as a poet central to the American canon, side-by-side with Dickinson and ultimately Rukeyser, whom Rich believes has been egregiously neglected due to the expansiveness of Rukeyser's project as a woman: "What happens when a woman, drawing on every political and social breakthrough gained by women since Dickinson's death in 1886, assumes the scope of her own living to be at least as large as Whitman's?" (16). Rich first discusses Whitman and Dickinson, designating them as the radical (in a positive sense) early inventors of American verse, "openers of new paths, those who take the first steps, who therefore can seem strange and 'dreadful' to their place and time" (12). Rich asserts later that Rukeyser's critical reception was harmed because she was viewed as too radical and "outside the grasp" of many of the leading poets of the time (who were predominantly male), including Pound, Eliot, and Williams:

> But in the history of poetry and ideas in the United States—always difficult to grasp because of narrow definitions, cultural ghettos, the politics of canon-makers—she has not been seriously considered, in the

way that, say, the group of politically conservative white Southern poets known as the Fugitives, or the generation of men thought to have shaped "modern poetry"—Ezra Pound, T. S. Eliot, William Carlos Williams, Wallace Stevens—have been considered. Her thought remains unintegrated into our understanding of the poetic currents, the architectonic shifts of the twentieth century. (17)

Such a statement is intriguing in the framework of a project on Whitman and High Modernist poets, setting into relief Rich's engagement with Whitman directly through Rukeyser's own, with vestiges of the problems of High Modernism and the male patriarchy that impacted Rich and Rukeyser. For Rich and Rukeyser, Whitman (though a white male poet, as Rich points out)[13] offered an alternative model of poetry, which Rich and Rukeyser have used for their respective, but similar, poetic and political agendas.

The essay "The Genesis of 'Yom Kippur 1984'" is an emblematic text that displays the intertwining of Whitman, Jewish and American identity, Rukeyser, and outsider identity, in which Rich unpacks the origins of one of her major Jewish-themed poems, "Yom Kippur 1984" (1989). As Rich reflects on how Whitman informed the writing of the poem, she presented him as a vital intertext.[14] The poem was composed around the time when, Rich writes, she had lost "roots, communities, ties," after moving to the West Coast. The poem interrogates the speaker's experience of isolation as a Jewish person in general and as a Jewish woman in particular: "Because I did feel very far off from my Jewish world, which had been gradually and in some ways painfully and very richly becoming more and more real to me over the past few years" (255). In lieu of this real-life community, the poem contains "dialogues" (255) with poets and textual traditions, namely Whitman, the Bible, and poet Robinson Jeffers.[15]

First, Rich meditates on how Whitman's long lines and the rhythms of the Bible came to inform her poem: "I looked at the line-lengths, which were fairly short, and broken up with blank spaces. . . . I realized that this technique, which I do use a lot, was altogether wrong for this poem. . . . It was that, it was also reading in the Hebrew Bible, the Old Testament. And certainly reading Whitman, with whom there turns out to be a considerable dialogue" (255).[16] Rich then turns to a discussion of Whitman's poem "When Lilacs Last in the Dooryard Bloom'd" and the notion of America that Whitman "imagined and believed in" (254–255). Rich states, "This dialogue with Whitman begins on the first page: 'something to bind me to this coast as lilacs in the dooryard

116   CHAPTER FOUR

once / bound me back there'" (255). This description of Whitman's lilacs being perpetually in bloom suggests a pleasant memory that connects Rich to her "roots" on the opposite coast. Rich's response to "Lilacs" thus begins rather favorably, with a focus less on Whitman's initial writing of the poem—an elegy meditating on Lincoln after the assassination and the reoccurrence of grief—and more on Whitman as a poetic and personal anchor. Later in the essay, the symbol of Whitman's "mockingbird" is likewise described as significant when Rich recalls a mockingbird outside the window: "the most wonderful series of songs, of compositions" (256).

On the other hand, the focus in Rich's essay also shifts to a troubling gap between the idealized America that Whitman "imagined and believed in," and the reality of Rich's own America—a place that she states can be "dangerous" for marginalized groups, among which she counts herself:

> Whitman depicts slavery, depicts hard labor, depicts prostitution, but although he names those things, his America is very different from the America of my poem. The America of the kinds of events my poem is talking about, that makes solitude dangerous for so many people, that can make it feel really dangerous to walk out beyond your own turn, your own protected area. (256)

In this contradictory version of Whitman, his poetry represents home, connection, and inclusion, with the vision being, to a large extent, an unfulfilled one.[17] In Whitman's America, Rich also finds a largely unrealized democratic experiment: "And did not feel like he had to deal with, despite his homoerotic poems. The America of violence" (256). In this context, Erickson has observed, "Rich is emphatic about asserting her historical distance from Whitman," and she undertakes "a forthright critique [of Whitman] fueled by an active principle of re-vision" (108).[18] I would contend that, yes, Rich undertakes such a "re-vision," adding that Rich's effort is majorly informed by the tension of occupying various outsider positions (and being Othered, as well), while writing within the idyllic America that Whitman, in the preface to the 1855 *Leaves of Grass*, described as "essentially the greatest poem" (*Whitman: Poetry and Prose* 5).

Rich's poem "Yom Kippur 1984" reflects Whitman being appropriated as a lens through which to explore these complicated, and at times contradictory, issues of Jewishness and notions of America.[19] The poem opens with the speaker asking about the experience of the Jewish outsider, then that same experience for other outsider groups and queer communities:

What is a Jew in solitude?

What would it mean not to feel lonely or afraid
far from your own or those you have called your own?
What is a woman in solitude: a queer woman or man? (633)

This emphasis on the speaker being "in solitude," alone, in search of dialogues written about in Rich's essay—including intertextual ones—asks what it would feel like not to experience alienation as a Jewish person. This searching for connection (and protection) leads unequivocally to Whitman, where the speaker recalls Whitman's "lilacs" as a healing or restorative symbol (mentioned precisely by Rich in the "Yom Kippur" essay):

Three thousand miles from what I once called home
I open a book searching for some lines I remember
about flowers, something to bind me to this coast as lilacs in the
                    dooryard once (633)

However, while Whitman's symbols in Rich's poem ("lilacs in the / dooryard once") evoke a pleasant memory for the speaker ("something to bind me to this coast"), this comfort is limited in scope, as the poem shifts to the very real danger of solitude for vulnerable people. Rich employs a Whitmanesque catalogue to enumerate these figures, targeted because of race, gender, and sexuality: "faggot kicked into the icy / river, woman dragged from her stalled car," and "young scholar shot at the university [. . .] nothing / availing his Blackness." A young Jewish woman is also among these figures, as Rich asks, "(did she die as queer or as Jew?)" (635).[20] The listing quality of these lines reflects the nuance of Rich overtly drawing on Whitman's forms to signal inclusion yet marking Whitman's concepts of America as, at the very least, deeply inadequate.

In the last section of the poem, where the core question of Rich's poem is restated—"What is a Jew in solitude? / What is a woman in solitude, a queer woman or man?"—a possible solution to the problem of "solitude" can also be seen as Whitmanian, evoking the joining or "merging" of selves from the 1855 version of "Song of Myself": "Who need be afraid of the merge?" Assuming a prophetic tone that recalls Whitman (and Rukeyser) as a poet-prophet, Rich's speaker describes a sort of apocalyptic reckoning, in which barriers between figures who are presumed to be not just different but perpetually in conflict are dissolved (like woman/man and Arab/Jew): "when our souls crashed together,

118   CHAPTER FOUR

Arab and Jew, howling our / loneliness within the tribes" (636). The solution to "solitude" for Rich (and Whitman and Rukeyser) is to reach away from "loneliness" and toward unity, "when center and edges are crashed together." Rich's poem thus seems to ask: If these boundaries between others and within ourselves are brought down ("crashed together"), can Whitman's notions of America actually come to fruition? As such, while recognizing Whitman's failures, Rich also imagines, through Whitman, the way (or a way) to a much less divisive and divided society.

The last poem I look at here, which embodies the dynamics of Whitman and Jewishness in Rich's poetry, is "Tattered Kaddish," a poem offering a re-imagining, and subversion of, the Mourner's Kaddish—a prayer recited after a death, traditionally recited by the eldest male relative for eleven months.[21] As Shreiber writes, "'Tattered Kaddish' is a powerful example of how a secularized text may at once evacuate and intensify the sacred narrative it takes as its precursor" ("'Where'" 315). Rich's poem re-appropriates the Mourner's Kaddish in two major ways. With respect to gender, the speaker is identified as female: the "Taurean reaper" and "messenger from earthmire." The poem is thus spoken (or recited) by a woman, expressly challenging the patriarchal element from within more traditionally Orthodox or religious branches of Judaism. With a woman speaking, there is a corresponding rethinking of the function of the prayer.[22] Moreover, Rich's Kaddish seeks to expand its relevance to those to have taken their own lives: "speak your tattered Kaddish for all suicides." The poem repeats "praise to life" and conveys empathy for the victim themselves: "how they loved it, when they could" (742).

I find Whitman's poetic heritage in "Tattered Kaddish" to be one contribution to Rich's reinvention of this Jewish prayer in a more progressive, secular American context. First, there is a Whitmanian repetition and anaphora of the phrase "Praise to life" in each of the five couplets of the poem; for example, the third stanza reads, "Praise to life though its windows blew shut / on the breathing-room of ones we knew and loved." This repetition of "praise" can be read as informed by liturgical structures and biblical verses, but Whitman's structures are also undeniable (and, as Rich wrote in the essay about "Yom Kippur 1984," she was reading the Bible and she was reading Whitman). The anaphoric structures are evidence of how this reshaping of a Jewish prayer alludes to Whitman. Moreover, Rich's poem calls to mind a Whitmanian notion of divinity in all beings, no matter how seemingly insignificant, marginalized, or oppressed, as in the lines from "Song of Myself" in which Whitman speaks to the idea of representing and honoring those who are cast aside: "Through me many long dumb voices, / Voices of the interminable generations of prisoners and slaves." One thus finds this Whitmanian notion brought by Rich, in the spirit of what Shreiber identifies as "transforming the personal into the collective" ("'Where'" 315). Rich's radical, feminist rethinking of a Jewish prayer is an important case of how Whitman inheres in a Jewish American text.

To sum up, Whitman is a complicated model for Rich but one that plays into Rich's politically engaged, Jewish and American poetry, which is informed by (and responding to) the poetics of Rukeyser as well as issues of gender, Otherness, and outsiderness. While this is a relatively brief study of Rich's responses to Whitman and there is potentially much more to investigate, taken together, the essays "Beginners" and "The Genesis of 'Yom Kippur 1984'" and the poems "Yom Kippur 1984" and "Tattered Kaddish" reveal Rich to be both for and against Whitman. There are commonalities in how Rich writes of viewing Whitman and how Ostriker and Piercy do so, discussed in this chapter, as well as with the poets in this book at large. A special correspondence, for example, exists between the appearance of Whitman in a Jewish prayer-poem like Rich's "Tattered Kaddish" and the Reconstructionist prayer-poems from Piercy's collection *The Art of Blessing the Day: Poems with a Jewish Theme*. For every Jewish American poet, including Rich, Ostriker, and Piercy, Whitman's function is found to be distinct, yet often with a goal, even beyond poetry, to create a more democratic society.

ALICIA OSTRIKER'S WALT WHITMAN

At its core, the work of Alicia Ostriker is political; she has claimed, "All art is political. Either it is political or it is wallpaper" (Pacernick 229). Ostriker is the recipient of a Guggenheim Foundation Fellowship in Poetry (1984–1985) and National Jewish Book Awards for *The Book of Seventy* (2009) and *Waiting for the Light* (2017), among other honors. Ostriker's poetry and scholarship, *Stealing the Language: The Emergence of Women's Poetry in America* (1987), *The Nakedness of the Fathers: Biblical Visions and Revisions* (1997), and *Dancing at the Devil's Party: Essays on Poetry, Politics, and the Erotic* (2000), often challenge various forms of oppression, whether societal, within religious frameworks, or in literary traditions. As Cynthia Hogue states, "Ostriker's art tracks one poet's struggle, the witnessing, the transmuting, the act of contemplative analysis

120   CHAPTER FOUR

that her poetry often entails: these are places where her poetics and ethics *fuse*" (108). In the poem "A Walker in the City," for example, from the collection *No Heaven*, the speaker bears witness to social inequities that pervade American society: "What you see is what you get, / An inventory of garbage lying loose—The poor are always with us, but the rich / Lurk behind one-way glass in limousines" (90).

Within Ostriker's oeuvre is an interplay of Jewish American identity and the legacy of Whitman, whose critical reception in Ostriker's poetry and essays is nuanced. She is not fully approving of Whitman (similar to Stern and Rich), especially the glorification of war and nationalist tone that Ostriker identifies in Whitman's *Drum-Taps*—but his influence is valuable, and grounded in what Ostriker calls an early "self-recognition" through Whitman, being a child of Jewish Russian immigrants raised in Brooklyn, New York ("Loving" 25–26). As for Adrienne Rich, Ostriker's views of Whitman possess a similar duality of both for and against.

In this way and in other ways, Ostriker's work can be understood as solidly rooted in the genealogy of Jewish American poets who look to Whitman, and more specifically, the Jewish American women poets, like Rukeyser, Rich, and Piercy, by whom Whitman has been appropriated as a poetic and political model. Ostriker has declared Whitman a poetic model and mediator, who appeals to women poets particularly, desiring to subvert accepted norms of poetry, religion, nation, culture, and gender: "Above all, Whitman speaks to us through his impulse to question boundaries—to prefer fluidity to fixity, experiment to status quo" ("Loving" 32).[23] Ostriker states that Whitman's poetry of inclusivity is useful to women, who are oftentimes themselves Othered: "The omnivorous empathy of [Whitman's] imagination wants to incorporate All and therefore refuses to represent anything as unavailably Other. So long as femaleness in our culture signifies Other, Walt's greed is our gain. In him we are free to be what we actually are . . . not negative pole to positive pole . . . but figures in an energetic dance" ("Loving" 36).

Ostriker also writes about Whitman's role as the iconic poet of America, writing, "[W]hen we turn, as poets, to the state of the nation and of our common life, the ghost of Whitman turns with us" ("Loving" 25). Amy Williams has characterized Ostriker as an American poet and part of this Whitman tradition: "Speaking in the tradition of Walt Whitman, [Ostriker] re-creates the American experience in each of her volumes" (239).[24] I suggest that Ostriker can be characterized as an American poet of the Whitman tradition, and even more accurately, a Jewish American poet of the Whitman tradition, who not only "re-creates" America but deconstructs and critiques the "American experience."[25] Ostriker's perception of Whitman is, therefore, engaged with issues of identity as an American poet, with a complicated stance toward the majority culture of America. Here, I will further uncover how Jewish American identity and Whitman are intertwined in Ostriker's writing, focusing on several major works by Ostriker in which Whitman is present, including the essay "Loving Walt Whitman and the Problem of America," as well as the poems "Manahatta" and "Dry Hours: A Golden Shovel Exercise," from the profoundly Whitman-informed 2017 collection *Waiting for the Light*, and the poem "Elegy Before the War" from an earlier collection, *No Heaven*.

Ostriker's Jewish and American Engagement with Whitman

In various sources, Ostriker has claimed an appreciation for and alignment with Whitman, declaring Whitman, together with William Carlos Williams and Allen Ginsberg, to be formative poetic influences; she states, "[A]s an American poet coming of age in the sixties and seventies, I was powerfully influenced by the Whitman, Williams, and Ginsberg line" (Pacernick 224–225). In "Loving Walt Whitman," Ostriker elaborates upon this Whitmanian influence, asking, "Why have I never before written about Whitman? I always identify myself to audiences as Whitmanic, and I have written about Blake and Ginsberg, who are important to me but surely not more important than Whitman" (25). Later in the essay, Ostriker writes about how an early encounter with Whitman, particularly "Song of Myself," resonated with her specifically as a child of Jewish immigrants in America. She found potential in Whitman—a creative or poetic freedom, "spirit," or "energy," which was available to pursue if she so wished:

> What I remember is reading ["Song of Myself"] straight through for the first time, when I was thirteen, outdoors amid some uncut grass. During the same year I decided Poe was mechanical, a puppet of a poet, all theatrical tricks, all indoors. This Whitman was a living creature, someone alive as I felt myself to be alive. The location was a meadow. I was a city girl sitting among grass and rocks in Manhattan's Central Park. . . . But the girl is mother of the woman; some portion of myself paused ecstatically at the moment when I (when it) encountered "Song of Myself" and elected thenceforth to celebrate itself and sing itself. . . .

> To read Whitman was to experience self-recognition. Here were the self's not-yet-articulated perceptions of reality, its not-yet-formulated ideological biases, which plainly inhabited me already because I was American. Or because I was a grandchild of Russian-Jewish immigrants? Or because I was young? The generosity of spirit meant that Whitman's energies could be mine if I chose. Like some improbably open-minded parent, he would permit everything. (25–26)

Whitman is thus imagined in this essay as a tangible figure, an urban, "living creature," whose themes and poetic forms bring about a sense of understanding and "self-recognition" in terms of the gendered self, the "not-yet-formulated" political self, the American self, and the third-generation Jewish American self. This passage represents among the most affirming portrayals of Whitman in Ostriker's writing—the Whitman who served as a vehicle for a celebrating of the self—to "sing the self," as per Ostriker's words, to embrace one's individuality, and eventually, to write poetry that is not defined by previous literary models (often male ones, like Poe's) but determined by one's own aesthetic choices, sensibilities, and values.

Though Whitman is of course a male poet, one also finds Ostriker conceptualizing Whitman as a model against strict patriarchal elements in society, religious frameworks, and spaces of practicing Judaism. In keeping with so many Jewish American poets, writers, thinkers, artists, and critics (definitely Rukeyser, Rich, and Piercy), a driving impetus in Ostriker's writing is to call out oppression and inequality of women and minority groups; for instance, in the essay "Secular and Sacred, Returning (to) the Repressed," where Ostriker interrogates boundaries between the sacred and secular in Jewish poetry, she claims that any organized religion, including Judaism, "gives us sexual repression, self-righteousness, ignorance, intolerance and war" (185). The type of Jewishness to which Ostriker relates is designated (by her) as distinctly "cultural"—as perhaps an offshoot of the "atheist socialist" culture in which she was raised:

> I was born and raised in America as a third-generation atheist socialist Jew. . . . My pride in being Jewish was always a cultural pride: Jews stood for learning, for cultural accomplishment, for the brotherhood of man, for tolerance and for justice, and against war, poverty, and injustice. . . . When I hear the phrase "speak truth to power," I think: Isaiah. Jeremiah. Amos. (186)

JEWISH AMERICAN WOMEN POETS RESPOND TO WHITMAN 123

The "cultural" pride conveyed by Ostriker shows in her work as a Jewish writer, a feminist writer, an anti-war writer, and an advocate for persons on the margins. Ostriker (in ways that resonate with Rich) speaks to an experience of being doubly marginalized: "never-included" as a woman, and only partially included as a Jewish woman:

> I am and am not a Jew. I am in the sense that every drop of blood in my veins is Jewish. . . . I am a Jew because my parents are. . . . So, naturally, is every thought in my head, my habits of thinking, my moral impulses and burden of chronic guilt, my sense of humor, if any, my confrontational and adversarial inclinations. . . . My laughter and tears are Jewish laughter and tears. . . . But I am not a Jew, I can't be a Jew, because Judaism repels me as a woman. . . . To the rest of world the Jew is marginal. But to Judaism I am marginal. ("Reflection" 541–542)

Ostriker describes an experience in this passage of being Jewish culturally, spiritually, and psychically—impacted by dual levels of rejection from Judaism as a woman and as a Jewish person from "the rest of the world," what she conveys elsewhere as being deprived of the "'vessel' of religious lineage and . . . spiritual participation in male-dominated Jewish ritual and intellectual life" (Williams, "Alicia Ostriker" 242).[26]

About Whitman, Ostriker writes that while the American poet is not "the man for all feminist purposes," and that his effort to identify with the Other has "reductive" aspects, Whitman does provide a useful "strength" for women poets. Ostriker claims, for example, "When a girl becomes a woman, and discovers her disadvantaged cultural status, Whitman's presence may strengthen her incalculably. Both for my own poetry and for the poetry of many other American women, Whitman has been the exemplary precursor, killer of the censor and clearer of ground" ("Loving" 31). This value for women poets stems also from a notion in Ostriker's essay that Whitman is not a poet who speaks for women, but instead, he grants a paradigm of "power without authority," which women poets can employ according to their own poetic and political agendas:

> [W]hat moves me, and I suspect other American women poets . . . [are] the gestures whereby Whitman enacts the crossing of gender categories in his own person. It is not his claim to be "of the woman" that speeds us on our way, but his capacity to be shamelessly receptive as well as

124 CHAPTER FOUR

> active, to be expansive on an epic scale without a shred of nostalgia for
> narratives of conquest, to invent a rhetoric of power without authority,
> without hierarchy, and without violence. ("Loving" 32)[27]

Ostriker alludes here to the frequency with which women poets in American (not just Jewish poets, of course) turn to Whitman, a male poet, due to a unique "crossing of gender categories." And yet, it is precisely her characterization of Whitman without "hierarchy" or "violence" that is troubling to Ostriker, because, in contrast to the idea of Whitman being a model of inclusion and fluidity, Ostriker identifies in Whitman a potentially dangerous form of nationalism, one she claims she "cannot forgive" ("Loving" 35).

The ways in which Ostriker characterizes Whitman's poetry as possessing "unforgivable" or inexcusable elements are connected to representations of war and violence in his Civil War poetry, especially in *Drum-Taps*. Ostriker has noted a correspondence between Whitman's war poetry and the historical moment in which she herself wrote the essay "Loving Walt Whitman": "during the first weeks of another war, the Gulf War of the winter of 1991, undertaken ostensibly to protect Kuwait from Iraqi imperialism, actually (of course) to protect the oil interests of the United States in the Middle East and to exhibit our military toys" (35). She suggests that Whitman portrays war "as pageantry, as tragic necessity," conveying "[a] taste for violence and self-destruction" (33). Thus, Whitman is for Ostriker at once a model of humanistic "fluidity" as well as a model of anti-humanistic "authority"—the binary is essentially a contradiction (this contradiction calls to mind Whitman's imperfections found by Rich). In fact, Ostriker expresses recognizing, and even reconciling, these contradictory views of "the panoramic, spectacular, dynamic America" with Whitman's "shallow, corrupt, material America." She asks, "Do we contradict ourselves? Very well then, we contradict ourselves" (37). Elsewhere, in an interview, Ostriker attributes this move of reconciliation back to Whitman's own:

> I want my readers to feel the kick of contradiction, the torsion of tension.
> Not only in myself but in themselves. Contradiction and tension are
> part of life. . . . And what's wrong with contradiction? You don't hear
> Whitman saying he wants to resolve his contradictions. Not at all. "Do I
> contradict myself? Very well then, I contradict myself. I am large, I contain multitudes." Life is like that. Face it. Denial is death. (Pacernick 231)

When exploring representations of Whitman in Jewish American poetry, this contradiction in Ostriker's conceptualization of Whitman becomes important, epitomizing how Whitman can hold several conflicting roles, even for the same poet at the same time, with Whitman seen both to substantiate Ostriker's outsider status as a Jewish woman poet in America and to symbolize the problematic history and policies of America.

Whitman in Ostriker's Jewish American Political Poems

These contradictory notions of Whitman, as revealed in Ostriker's essays and interviews, are manifest in poems from both earlier and later in her oeuvre and, most recently, in the collection *Waiting for the Light*, which explores many of Ostriker's major poetic concerns, including the beauty, diversity, possibility, and disappointment of America, embodied by a line from the last stanza of the penultimate poem, titled "Ghazal: America the Beautiful" (76–77), "Sometimes I still put my hand tenderly on my heart / somehow or other still carried away by America." The collection itself is strongly Whitman-oriented, with overt references to Whitman in poems like "Manahatta" and "Dry Hours: A Golden Shovel Exercise," as well as subtler, though no less significant, poetic and thematic echoes of Whitman in "A Walker in the City" and "Ghazal: America the Beautiful."[28] In "Manahatta" and "Dry Hours," a duality of Whitman Ostriker articulates is revealed, and one encounters the democratic Whitman on the one hand and the Whitman of America that has fallen short on the other.

The first poem, "Manahatta," represents the more embracing, democratic side of Whitman, the Whitman with a "generosity of spirit," as noted in Ostriker's "Loving Walt Whitman." The title of the poem is naturally a reference to Whitman's "Mannahatta," first appearing in the 1860 edition of *Leaves of Grass*, in which Whitman pays homage to the many different landscapes, waterways, citizens, and immigrants existing together in New York City: "A million people—manners free and superb—open voices—hospitality—the most courageous and friendly young men" (11). Ostriker's poem does not function as a critique of Whitman but, rather, as a reconceptualizing of Whitman's poem, with a mode of inclusion in Ostriker's own poetic style, reflecting engagement with Jewish and America themes and figures, including an allusion to Emma Lazarus's poem "The New Colossus." The poem opens by quoting the first line of Whitman's "Mannahatta," in which Whitman asks the city for something

126   CHAPTER FOUR

"specific and perfect," then goes on to describe Whitman, using the informal "Walt," and focusing particularly on Whitman's embrace of everyone in the city:

> *I was asking for something specific and perfect for my city*
> says Walt, lover of crowds, praiser of trades and occupations, celebrant
> of the daily tide of immigrants, and I too seek the perfect image of
>   you— (11)

In this description by Ostriker's speaker, this is the Whitman who wrote about the common people from different industries, backgrounds, and nations, a "lover of crowds." Some of Whitman's language in his "Mannahatta" about immigrants is also evoked, like the line "Immigrants arriving / fifteen or twenty thousand in a week." With this welcoming, inviting rendition of Whitman as a point of departure, the speaker in Ostriker's poem then indicates, adopting Whitman's ubiquitous phrase "I too," a similar desire for a "perfect," unflawed city, writing, "I too seek the perfect image of you—." There is a suggestion, in Ostriker's interpretation of "Manahatta," that this idyllic democracy does not really exist, but looking back and through Whitman, with a hope that has not been extinguished.

In the subsequent stanza of Ostriker's poem, one finds an enumeration of figures, of diverse backgrounds and walks of life, of this not always beautiful but always inclusive Whitmanian city:

> you mothering harbor, you royal sewer, you finger inside the sky,
> you dangling dream deferred, you queer hideout, you incubator of
>   Jewish jazz,
> you who exist as a landing field for helicopters, you whose laughter is
>   heartless, (11)

The city is imagined as an inviting, nurturing place for immigrants to arrive ("mothering harbor"), as well as a grotesque "sewer" these figures ideally all accepted, like in Whitman's "Mannahatta," where he writes, "City nested in bays! my city!" (361). In addition to Whitman, the poem alludes to other poets who endorse a democratic vision of New York and America, like Langston Hughes's poem "I, Too" (Ostriker's "dangling dream deferred"), as well as Lazarus's "The New Colossus."[29] The reference to Lazarus's democratic poetry in Ostriker's Whitmanian poem is quite salient in the context of this project, as Lazarus's poem endorses this notion of the Whitmanian city, with outsiders and minorities, including Black, Jewish, and queer people, all part of this flawless democracy in America. "Manahatta" ends with an amusing anecdote, whereby the speaker is in a store buying a "toaster," and one shopkeeper tells the speaker that the other shopkeeper "went skinny dipping" in the Harlem River: "B says, *I have to let my bad girl out sometime.*" In a Whitmanian way, Ostriker's poem honors these people and daily encounters—and Whitman, who envisions this type of city.

In the poem "Dry Hours: A Golden Shovel Exercise," one finds an allusion to the more radically problematic side of Whitman, according to Ostriker.[30] This poem is primarily an imagined conversation with Gwendolyn Brooks and opens with an address to Brooks herself, remarking that while "Gwen, you are from Chicago" and "my [the speaker's] family is from New York," the two experienced many shared historical events that took place in the US, like the Great Depression, the New Deal, and World War II (19). The poem has both personal and political elements, with the speaker describing Brooks's hair as "going grey" after becoming disillusioned with the direction of America itself. In the middle of the poem, after "the war with the Nazis is won," the allusion to Whitman appears, reflecting on what might have been Whitman's similar disappointment in the "dream" of America, after the Civil War:

> It worked, we won. The greyed-
> out newsreels of the forties, the blackouts in
> our cities, who can forget? And
> you were already turning grey,
> like Whitman after the Civil War wondering if the "dream"
> was going to come true, or if capitalism makes
> every dream finally turn rancid

While the war itself is won, and the Nazis are defeated, there are frequent "blackouts" and America's continuous privileging of capitalism. This Whitman is dismayed in the aftermath of the Civil War, with the *Leaves of Grass* project that had likely failed to unite the nation. Though no additional references to Whitman appear in the rest of the poem, it turns from "Whitman's wondering" into a meditation about systemic racism in America, presenting a disturbing image of a lynching: "No sound / from the beaten bodies and not / a sound from the strong / oak limbs where the bodies hung like / hams in a butcher shop." Such a line cannot help but recall the symbol of the "live-oak" in Whitman's poem "I Saw in Louisiana a Live-Oak Growing" (105). Racism, slavery, Whitman, and disenchantment with America: all appear together in this poem by Ostriker.

128 CHAPTER FOUR

The speaker envisions a Whitman mired in that disillusionment—the "dream" that does not come to fruition—much like Whitman's failure to achieve the dream of America that is communicated by Rich.

If "Manahatta" contains a more positive interpretation of Whitman and "Dry Hours" a more negative one, then the poem "Elegy Before the War" from Ostriker's collection *No Heaven* can be said to embody the Whitman of Ostriker's contradictions. "Elegy," originally published in the "Beat Bush Issue" of the journal *Long Shot*, features a juxtaposition of private and public motifs, as is characteristic of Ostriker's work. The poem displays intertwining narratives of the speaker's mother's death ("my mother is dead two weeks"), with a mourning for the promise of America and peace more widely, referencing "tanks roaming in Ramallah and Nablus" (118). Whitman's poetic style can be detected throughout the poem; for example, in section 2, bespeaking the impact of the mother's death and the speaker's outrage at actions undertaken by the Israeli military in Ramallah and Nablus (from an American, thus inherently distant, perspective):[31]

> And we burned her and flew to Arizona
> And the tanks roamed Ramallah and Nablus

The anaphora creates a relationship between these ostensibly different events—the "burning" of the mother and the war and "tanks roaming."[32] Whitman's rhetorical style about America is appropriated by Ostriker into an "elegy" for a parent, for Israel, and for America in the Bush era. Whitman's "and" and cataloguing thus demarcate the speaker as an American Jewish poet vis-à-vis America and an American Jewish poet vis-à-vis Israel.[33]

Elsewhere in section 2, Whitman's themes from "Song of Myself" arise when Ostriker's speaker introduces the idea of collective empathy through a Whitmanian exchange of breath and "molecules" of oxygen, suggesting a possible solution to this personal and political turmoil:

> The air I breathe you breathe.
> Just now a molecule breathed by Buddha
> Might have entered your lungs. (118)

The sharing of "air" and "molecules" in "Elegy" echoes the very exchange of "atoms" between Whitman and his readers in "Song of Myself": "And what I assume, you shall assume, / For every atom belonging to me as good belongs to you" (29). This interrelationship that Whitman creates between the speaker and the addressee ("you") represents the antithesis of the conflict that the poem condemns.[34] This section of "Elegy" thus falls in the category of the optimal version of Whitman as imagined by Ostriker, whereby the "I" and the "you" are in dialogue with each other.[35]

In addition to these more general formal and thematic allusions to Whitman, there are two overt references to Whitman in "Elegy," both of which represent complex, and conflicting, versions of Ostriker's Whitman, as a figure of humanism and compassion on one hand and an emblem of violence and the severe flaws of America on the other. The same section contains a series of questions as to where the poets are—first Blake's "Exuberance is beauty," then Whitman, then Ginsberg's "kindness":

> "Exuberance is beauty," and where is Walt Whitman
> And where is Ginsberg, genius of kindness?
> I beg my mother come back sometime. (119)

These poets (Blake, Whitman, and Ginsberg) are seemingly inaccessible to the speaker but hold some type of cure to the speaker's condition of grief. Together, they are imagined as serving as a guide for the speaker, although evoking them does not solve the internal and external conflicts within herself, or America, with any finality.

The second reference to Whitman (found in section 5) again expresses a criticism of America, juxtaposed with optimism and "peace" for America, dually through Whitman and Blake:

> Friday night getting smashed in America.

> Ignorant violence that stuns the intelligence.
> Dear animal inside us whom in other respects
> We cherish, is it you?

> Whitman and Blake inside of us, celebrants of war equally with peace, is
> it you? (122)

Here, the America of "ignorant violence" and "war" inheres within Whitman and Blake;[36] yet the poets are likewise presented as a symbol of "peace" and of more hopeful interactions between human beings, or at least the potential for them. Together with Ostriker's other writing, in "Loving Walt Whitman and the Problem of America," "Manahatta," and "Dry Hours: A Golden Shovel Exercise" one finds Whitman serving as a model that Ostriker engages with

130   CHAPTER FOUR

from the juncture of being a Jewish poet, an American, and a woman poet. In these significant ways, in poetry and prose, Ostriker at the same time embraces and subverts Whitman (in alignment with Rukeyser, Rich, and Piercy), enacting a search for "liberty / And justice for all," the very notion advocated by the speaker's mother in "Elegy" and evident in Ostriker's project in its totality.

MARGE PIERCY'S WALT WHITMAN

In the title poem of the collection *To Be of Use* (1973), Marge Piercy recognizes those who contribute to an active, equitable world: "The people I love the best / jump into work head first / without dallying in the shallows" (106).[37] This commitment to "being of use" is a tenet that permeates Piercy's nearly twenty collections of poems, among them *Breaking Camp* (1968), *Stone, Paper, Knife* (1983), and *What Are Big Girls Made Of* (1997). For her poetry, Piercy has received prestigious awards, such as a National Endowment for the Arts Award (1978) and the Sarton Award (1991). Piercy has also published noted novels, science fiction, and memoirs, like *Woman on the Edge of Time* (1985), *He, She, and It* (1993), and *Sleeping with Cats: A Memoir* (2002).[38] Like Muriel Rukeyser, Adrienne Rich, and Alicia Ostriker, Piercy has been engaged in a lifetime of political activism, informed by her own belief "to be of use."

As with these other three women poets, Whitman functions in Piercy's work in realms of poetry and identity, as exemplified by Piercy's essay, "How I Came to Walt Whitman and Found Myself," in which she claims, "[W]hat I derived from Whitman was permission to be where I was and who I was" (99). Piercy's collection of poetry *The Art of Blessing the Day: Poems with a Jewish Theme* (1993), in which one encounters Jewish motifs (as the title indicates)—among them identity, Hebrew language, Jewish holidays and practices, liturgy, history, and the Holocaust—is a focal point of this chapter. Poems within it embody the extent to which Whitman's poetics inform Piercy's Jewish American poetics, particularly her Jewish prayer-poems, which emerge within the unique context of Reconstructionist Judaism. I will also explore what I find to be dynamics of Jewishness, Whitman, and liturgy in the poem "Praise in Spite of It All," from Piercy's *On the Way Out, Turn Off the Light* (2020). Again, in the case of Piercy, Whitman (a non-Jewish, nineteenth-century poet) is brought into the poetry of a Jewish American woman poet to shape a more open, progressive Jewishness in America.

Jewish identity is portrayed in Piercy's writing as complicated (similarly to Rich and Ostriker); as articulated in Piercy's poem "The Ram's Horn Sounding," the speaker speaks to a richness in Judaism (evoking Rukeyser's "gift" of Judaism in "To Be a Jew"), as well as its more vexing "contradictions": "A woman and a Jew, sometimes more / of a contradiction than I can sweat out, / yet finally the intersection that is both collision and fusion, stone and seed" (*Art* 174). Piercy was born and raised in Detroit, with her mother (Bert Bunnin Piercy) of Jewish heritage and her father (Robert Piercy) of non-Jewish heritage (Bickford 1).[39] Piercy has described the significance of her participation within the Reconstructionist movement of Judaism, with its promotion of more flexible Jewish practices, inclusion, and equality:[40]

> I am a Reconstructionist Jew myself; that's the movement of Judaism I feel most at home with. There's a lot of tradition, but there is also sexual equality. Reconstructionists were the first to ordain lesbians and gay men. The basis of the Reconstructionist movement is that you must re-experience every aspect of Judaism that you accept. You have to make it meaningful to you. For some Reconstructionists God is a very important concept; for others, not. (Lyons, "Interview" 332)

With Piercy identifying with the Reconstructionist movement, and her poems "being of use" there, here I point to the role of Whitman in Piercy's progressive Jewish American poetics related to a branch of Judaism that emphasizes self-determination and inclusiveness. In other words, Whitman features in the act of what Piercy refers to as "making meaning" in a Jewish and poetic context.

This notion of Whitman and "meaning" is displayed in "How I Came to Walt Whitman and Found Myself," published in the 1992 issue of the *Massachusetts Review*, an issue devoted to "A Celebration of Walt Whitman."[41] There Piercy depicts Whitman as an early model for an acceptance of the "self" as a poet and a Jewish woman poet. Strikingly echoing Ostriker's description of her early encounters with Whitman as related to "self-recognition" in "Loving Walt Whitman" (25–26), Piercy writes of her experience of reading Whitman as one of "light and heat and identity":

> I came to Walt Whitman early, in High School. In those days we actually read poems in English class. I believe it was my sophomore year, but it might have been my junior year. Certainly the textbook we were using

132   CHAPTER FOUR

contained some poems of Whitman's. I read them aloud again and again and experienced inebriation and an intense loosening, a revelation of light and heat and identity. (98)

Similar also to Ostriker's reading of Whitman is Piercy's assertion that Whitman and Ginsberg were freeing, "liberating" poets, who offered American poetic paradigms through which she was able to express a sense of individuality:

Whitman's long flowing line and American exuberance, the sense of being rooted in his own body and this landscape, this reality, liberated me to deal with my feeling and my experiences. I link the influence that hearing Ginsberg had on me in 1959 with reading Whitman in 1950 or 1951, because both of them said to me that to write authentically from yourself, no matter how queer or outside the mainstream society seemed to regard you, was inherently valuable if you wrote well. (98–99)

Later in the essay, Piercy reiterates how Whitman was a lens through which to legitimize her sense of outsider identity, as a woman with "a body," as a political person, and implicitly as a Jewish woman in America:

[W]hat I derived from Whitman was permission to be where I was and who I was: to be American, to have a body, which was loud and demanding and altogether wrong, to feel politically, to think that my life, my place and my time were worthy of poetry. (99)

The "permission" Piercy notes here, again, can be seen as specifically corresponding to Ostriker's claim about first encountering Whitman: "Like some improbably open-minded parent, he would permit everything." Piercy, too, writes that Whitman's poetry is a paradigm of inclusion of the Other—a model of acceptance of the Jewish self and female self.

Moreover, as a Jewish poet, Piercy states that Whitman "confirmed" her Jewish poetics in relation to a liturgical style in Whitman, which she notes recalled "earlier rhythms" of Jewish songs, prayers, and texts that she had absorbed "naturally," in other words, perhaps more subconsciously:

I found in Whitman a confirmation of earlier rhythms from Jewish liturgy and the Torah and the Psalms, rhythms that were not those of most poetry I had been taught in school, but rhythms that came more naturally to me. Later I would learn many other lines and work steadfastly on what I wanted to do with line length and line breaks and sound qualities, but early in my apprenticeship as a writer Whitman directed me to the oral power of verse. His poetry was written as notation for reciting it. He used many familiar structures, as many of the poets I had read before him used rime. His ways were more useful to me and I began to study them. (99)

These "earlier rhythms" found in Whitman, I would argue, as well as the "Jewish liturgy and the Torah and the Psalms," can be traced to prayer-poems by Piercy in *The Art of Blessing the Day*. Whitman, notably, is described as "useful" to Piercy (or "of use," to use Piercy's own notion) in this way. With this association between Whitman and texts that are markedly Jewish, yet another instance comes to light of a Jewish American poet engaging with Jewish tradition through the American poet.[42]

Whitman in Piercy's Jewish Prayer-Poems

Each section of *The Art of Blessing the Day: Poems with a Jewish Theme* represents a facet of Jewish-related experiences and life-cycle events: *Mishpocheh* (Family), *The Chuppah* (Marriage), *Tikkun Olan* (Repair of the World), *Toldot Midrashim* (Of History and Interpretation), *Teffilah* (Prayer), and *Ha-Shanah* (The Year). According to Piercy's dedication to the collection, the poems can be interpreted and adopted individually by each reader: "For all who may find here poems that speak to their identity, their history, their desire for ritual— ritual that may work for them—these poems are yours as well as mine" (1). This notion is an invitation to participate in Judaism but to uniquely shape it. Indeed, the very dedication bespeaks a Whitmanian direct address to the reader, being, in Piercy's words, "yours as well as mine." With this inviting dedication as a point of departure, I turn to ways in which Piercy's engagement with Whitman in the essay "How I Came to Walt Whitman"—in terms of self-determination, the body, poetic rhythms, and liturgy—appear to manifest in the title poem of the collection, "The Art of Blessing the Day," as well as in the poem "Nishmat."[43] Both poems are composed with a liturgical role in mind, display Whitmanian themes such as nature and the body, and contain a style of recitative verse that calls to mind Piercy's associations of Whitman and those "earlier rhythms from Jewish liturgy and the Torah and the Psalms." Finally, I contend that these poems are informed by the "permission" Piercy took from Whitman to "feel politically," signaling how Whitman is adapted

134 CHAPTER FOUR

not only into poetry but into practices within non-traditionally religious contemporary American Judaism.

At its core, the poem "The Art of Blessing the Day" conveys gratitude for life, a "blessing" of the world in a more secularized context, composed with Whitmanian motifs and structures. For example, throughout the poem, the extended repetitions evoke psalm-like, Whitmanian forms, with lists of nature imagery characteristic of both Whitman and Piercy, such as in the opening stanza:

> This is the blessing for sun after long rain:
> Now everything shakes itself free and rises.
> The trees are bright as pushcart ices.
> Every last lily opens its satin thighs.
> The bees dance and roll in pollen
> and the cardinal at the top of the pine
> sings at full throttle, fountaining. (3)

Piercy's speaker's list of symbols for which to be grateful ("sun," "trees," "lily," "bees," "pine") quite clearly echo Whitman, and in particular, Whitman's manner of elevating nature to the realm of the divine, like in some of the first lines of "Song of Myself," where Whitman writes, "And limitless are leaves stiff or drooping in the fields, / And brown ants in the little wells beneath them" (32). In Piercy, and for Whitman, nature can be a mode of universalizing the "blessing," because ideally, readers of different persuasions and backgrounds would find meaning in a poem that is a blessing of the natural world. Moreover, reflecting the spirit of Piercy's engagement with Reconstructionist Judaism, the poem does not explicitly reference God, or any higher power or authority, suggesting that this blessing poem can be read, interpreted, and "used" outside of a specifically Jewish, or even traditional religious, framework.

This mode is not only used for cataloguing symbols of nature. In the fifth stanza, for instance, the focus of "The Art of Blessing the Day" becomes more explicitly political—"a blessing for a political victory"—and I would point to the reverberation of Whitman here as well:

> This is the blessing for a political victory;
> Although I shall not forget that things
> work in increments and epicycles and sometime
> leaps that half the time fall back down,
> let's not relinquish dancing while the music

JEWISH AMERICAN WOMEN POETS RESPOND TO WHITMAN   135

fits into our hips and bounces our heels.
We must never forget, pleasure is real as pain. (4)

To "bless" the "political victory" is likewise a blessing of a Whitmanian influence; the "we" of the poem is a Whitmanian, collective, humanistic "we," which widens the poem to include "all"; thus, one once again discovers a weaving of Whitman into a Jewish American liturgical poem to promote more egalitarian Jewishness. The humanistic core of the text is further developed in stanza 7, which contains an expansion of the liturgical, Whitmanian cataloguing of blessings (for a family pet, friends, money, nourishment), as well as a condemnation of the potential "oppression" within a patriarchal strand of traditional Judaism:

> The blessing for the return of a favorite cat,
> the blessing for love returned, for friends'
> return, for money received unexpected,
> the blessing for the rising of the bread,
> the sun, the oppressed. I am not sentimental
> about old men mumbling the Hebrew by rote
> with no more feeling than one says gesundheit. (4)

Again, the repetition of Piercy's verse relies on Whitman's poetic structures of repetition to mock or ridicule the conservative attitudes of Judaism that Piercy is working against—attitudes represented by "old men mumbling the Hebrew by rote," that is, from memory, without questioning or critiquing. The alternative provided to the figures of the "old men" in Piercy's poem is that Whitmanian freedom to define one's own culture, gender roles, and religious engagement. These structures demonstrate that in this essential poem in Piercy's collection, Whitman is integrated into a Jewish liturgical style and is a figure through which Piercy, as per the Poundian phrase at the end of the poem, "get[s] ready to make it new."

In analogous ways, Piercy's "Nishmat" in the *Teffilah* (Prayer) section of the collection is a re-envisioning of the Jewish Nishmat Kol Hai prayer. The original prayer, recited during Shabbat services and the Passover seder, serves to express joy and appreciation for God and God's creation of all beings in the world.[44] Piercy's poem contains some language and rhetoric from the English translation of the Nishmat Kol Hai prayer, and Whitman's psalm-style poetics are also detectable, like in this passage:

136 CHAPTER FOUR

When the night slides under the last dimming star
and the red sky lightens between the trees,
and the heron glides tipping heavy wings in the river,
when crows stir and cry out their harsh joy,
and swift creatures of the night run toward their burrows,
and the deer raises her head and sniffs the freshening air,
and the shadows grow more distinct and then shorten

then we rise into the day still clean as new snow. (129)

Anaphoric forms are of course found in the Jewish Nishmat prayer, but Piercy's version is closer to Whitman's holiness of nature and the repetition of natural symbols (also displayed in "The Art of Blessing the Day"), like the rejoicing of nature ("red sky," "heron," "deer," and "new snow"). These elements of nature do not feature in the same way in the original Nishmat Kol Hai prayer, so Piercy's poem is bestowed with a more universal sense of spirituality. Also, as in the case of "The Art of Blessing the Day," the "Nishmat" poem by Piercy expresses thanks for the blessings of life yet omits the act of giving thanks to, or sanctifying, a religious figure or authority, such as God, akin to Whitman's more spiritual model.

Furthermore, in Piercy's poem, one comes upon a Whitmanian notion of appreciation and holiness in the human body. This motif does appear in the original Nishmat prayer, in a thanks to God for creating each body part, but one cannot overlook Piercy's more Whitmanesque interpretation of this celebration of the body, separate from God:

We are lent for a time these minerals in water
and a morning every day, a morning to wake up,
rejoice and praise life in our spines, our throats,
our knees, our genitals, our brains, our tongues. (130)

This enumeration of body parts in the last two lines of the stanza recalls other lines from "Song of Myself": "My respiration and inspiration . . . the beating of my heart . . . the passing of blood and air through my lungs" (30). The speaker in Piercy's poem attributes an acceptance of the body to Whitman, and this acceptance is an important tenet of Piercy's poem: to serve as a more universal version of Nishmat Kol Hai, appealing perhaps to all readers, not just those readers with Jewish cultural or religious connections. Thus, while Piercy's "Nishmat" is a re-imagining of a Jewish prayer, it is marked as American by virtue of this engagement with the non-Jewish Whitman in the context of Piercy's contributions to the liturgy of Reconstructionist Judaism.

The dynamics of Whitman in Piercy's Jewish American prayer-poems (or prayer-like poems) is not a phenomenon limited to *The Art of Blessing the Day* collection, and in fact it continues to reverberate in a poem titled "Praise in Spite of It All," from Piercy's *On the Way Out, Turn Off the Light*. Resembling *The Art of Blessing the Day, On the Way Out, Turn Off the Light* is divided into sections that reflect key themes of Piercy's oeuvre of poetry, including language, family and romantic relationships, Jewishness, and America, such as "Language Has Shaped My Life," "Love Is No Accident," "A Jew in America Now," and "Mishpocheh = Family." Like the other poems by Piercy discussed here ("The Art of Blessing the Day" and "Nishmat"), "Praise in Spite of It All," at least parts of the poem, conveys appreciation to the world for the pleasurable aspects of the human experience and, I would argue, with allusions to Whitman similar to the ones discussed in earlier poems, in terms of listing and nature imagery; the poem begins, "I thank the cool night that let me sleep. / I thank the bright morning that wakes me."

The added context of this poem, and what sets it apart from the previous texts, is that presumably it responds to the political and historical events occurring in the US around the time of the poem's publication, closely following the election of the forty-fifth US president.[45] Accordingly, displaying the speaker's dismay with these events, the poem contains stanzas to those whom the speaker deems worthy of praise ("I praise") and those she does not ("I do not praise"). A variation on this dual phrasing appears with the repetition of "I thank" and "I do not thank." In terms of the latter, with Whitmanian, liturgical-style repetitions, the speaker also avidly condemns those selfish, "greedy idiots" working against a democratic vision of the world, enacting harm to nature ("the sea, the air"), and behaving unjustly toward anyone deemed by society to be "less human":

> I do not praise greedy idiots who poison
> the sea, the air, food, bees and us. I do
> not praise those who stand on the bodies
> of those they consider less human. (40)

These same Whitmanian poetic structures can be found in the speaker's mode of "thanking" the world for the wonder and "beauty" of life, which can still be found, despite the "greedy idiots," in connection, friendship, and "love":

138   CHAPTER FOUR

> I thank what I can as I age toward
> the end. So much is beautiful, friends
> are kind, I have loved many and
> some even have loved me. Amein. (41)

The last word of the last line of the poem, "Amein"—"Amen" with a Yiddish-sounding inflection—signals that the poem can, in fact, be understood as a prayer-poem, and possibly a prayer-poem with Jewish sensibilities. All of these works by Piercy together promote this widely encompassing, humanistic vision, often intersecting with liturgical poetic forms, within a Jewish American framework, involving turns to Whitman's "light, heat, and identity." Bringing Whitman into these poems can be read as a version of the Poundian idea of "making it new" that is reconceptualized in the last line of "The Art of Blessing the Day": "get ready to make it new."

Adrienne Rich, Alicia Ostriker, and Marge Piercy, with Muriel Rukeyser as an instrumental precursor, imagine Walt Whitman in various poetic and political modes. With Whitman woven by these poets into texts such as "Yom Kippur 1984" and "Tattered Kaddish" by Rich, Ostriker's "Manahatta" and "Dry Hours: A Golden Shovel Exercise," and poems "of use" for the Reconstructionist movement by Piercy, such as "The Art of Blessing the Day," "Nishmat," and "Praise in Spite of It All," all three imagine Whitman as a democratic model, at times with suggestions of being against Pound (Rich), in regard to outsider identity (with Rich being "split at the root), and in the context of gender (Ostriker and Piercy). These poets also find profound contradictions in Whitman's legacy—on the one hand embracing Whitman and yet criticizing him for an America that does not reflect a more idealized democratic vision (Rich and Ostriker). Finally, they also adopt Whitman into Jewish American liturgy and prayer-poems (Rich and Piercy). Taken together, these poets represent Whitman as ingrained in the navigation of multiple forms of Jewishness in America. This chapter has sought to show that, collectively and individually, the poets advocate for a more democratic Jewishness and a more democratic America, to construct (like Rukeyser via Whitman) a more democratic world.

CONCLUSION

The Enduring Jewish American Walt Whitman

To trace interpretations of the American poet Walt Whitman in the nineteenth-century poetry of Emma Lazarus and Adah Isaacs Menken, through English- and Yiddish-language poets of the twentieth century, and into contemporary poetry of the twenty-first century is to encounter Whitman's poetics and ideology powerfully embedded in the Jewish American poetic tradition. For Charles Reznikoff, and to an extent the other members of the Jewish Objectivist group, Louis Zukofsky, Carl Rakosi, and George Oppen, Whitman was adopted consistently, but more subtly, with their proximity to Ezra Pound and High Modernism—a culture in which anti-Whitman, and anti-Jewish, sentiments, were expressed. The writing of Karl Shapiro and Kenneth Koch displays a far more overt alignment with Whitman, with their respective attacks against High Modernism and High Modernist figures like Ezra Pound, W. B. Yeats, and T. S. Eliot. Muriel Rukeyser, Allen Ginsberg, and Gerald Stern display an engagement with Whitman as a democratic American figure, in relation to dynamics of High Modernism, and a Whitmanian poetics of witness, while being in dialogue with other Jewish American poets (such as Ginsberg with Reznikoff and Stern with Ginsberg). And finally, with Rukeyser serving as an imperative precursor, Adrienne Rich, Alicia Ostriker, and Marge Piercy are found to draw upon, as well as disagree with, Whitman around complicated realms of Jewish and American identity, politics, gender, and liturgy. This study reveals that Whitman's role relates to poetics and politics, often in response to an exclusionary atmosphere within High Modernism that

140 CONCLUSION

was generated by prominent literary figures, such as Pound and—as established by Anthony Julius—Eliot.[1]

Notwithstanding the diversity of these poets in terms of period and aesthetics, one finds a uniting strategy of appropriating the poetics of Whitman as Jewish poets in America. The broad import of Whitman for these poets, over more than a century, is evidence that the Jewish American poetic appropriation of Whitman goes beyond—although certainly includes—Ginsberg, whose connection to Whitman is re-positioned and re-contextualized here. These enlistments of Whitman also go beyond—though include—the significance of Whitman's psalmic-verse, although this element, too, is relevant for poets such as Ginsberg, Rich, and Piercy. Effectively, this book demonstrates that for Jewish American poets during and after the High Modernist period, Whitman's texts, and in several cases (such as for Rukeyser and Stern) even Whitman's imagined physical body, are a site through which poets negotiate experiences of being Jewish in America.[2]

In keeping with shifting aesthetic, cultural, and historical concerns, Whitman is thus recruited into the construction of hyphenated Jewish and American identity. This recruitment is precisely "[a] unique contribution of Jewish American writing to the evolution of a transnational, multicultural American literary history" (*Call It English* xii), as Hana Wirth-Nesher has articulated. The paradox inherent in this recruitment of a non-Jewish poet should not be overlooked, whereby Whitman—"form'd from this soil" (America), as he writes in "Song of Myself"—is employed by Jewish poets to establish themselves not only as Americans but as Jewish. To an extent, this employment of Whitman determines the kinds of Judaism that will be shaped, or brought to the fore, and excludes others. The Jewish dialogue with Whitman privileges and perpetuates an American, more secularized Judaism (as per Rich's "Tattered Kaddish" and Piercy's liturgical poems), with the right to choose to appropriate Whitman itself a deeply American notion.

Far from being a comprehensive record of Whitman's influence on Jewish American poetry and culture, this book puts forward a narrative in which other Jewish American affiliations to Whitman (poetic or otherwise) can be interpreted, as established in the introduction. One example of a poet whose work is not discussed in this book but whose work would greatly contribute to this genealogy is Jerome Rothenberg (b. 1931). Rothenberg has stated that he appreciates poets whom the New Critics held with "suspicion," such as Whitman (*Pre-faces* 22). Such a claim reflects those by many other poets in this

CONCLUSION   141

book (among them Rukeyser, Shapiro, and Koch). Also, in the introduction to *New Selected Poems: 1970–1985*, Rothenberg refers to Whitman as a paradigm of "open," encompassing poetry:

> I have no desire to work in isolation & I don't. Everything & everyone around here are welcome to come into the poem—in particular what has been hidden for so long that the poem has almost to create it (or to seem to do so) to make it visible again. This is the open invitation of our poetry since Whitman. We come to it in whatever ways we can. (viii)

Rothenberg's reference to "our" poetry might refer to American poetry; however, as a poet highly aware of Jewish identity, he might also intend for the reference to be read in connection to Jewishness.

Another example of a contemporary Jewish American poet in conversation with Whitman is Charles Bernstein (b. 1950); for instance, consider Whitman's multiple selves and enumerations of the "I" featured in Bernstein's poem titled "Solidarity Is the Name We Give to What We Cannot Hold" (1999):

> I am a nude formalist poet, a sprung
> syntax poet, a multitrack poet, a
> wondering poet, a social expressionist
> poet, a Baroque poet, a constructivist poet,
> and ideological poet. I am a New York poet in
> California, a San Francisco poet on
> the Lower East Side, an Objectivist poet
> in Royaumont, a surrealist poet in Jersey,
> a Dada poet in Harvard square,
> a zaum poet in Brooklyn, a merz poet
> in Iowa, a cubo-futurist poet in Central Park. (223)

In his embrace of multiple poetic identities ("nude formalist," "constructivist," "Dada poet"), Bernstein resonates with Whitman's assuming of identities, as in Whitman's poem "The Sleepers": "I am the actor, the actress, the voter, the politician" (326).

Finally, C. K. Williams (1936–2015), in the collection of essays that explores Whitman's poetics titled *On Whitman* (2010), does not examine Whitman through a Jewish lens;[3] and yet, Williams's description of Whitman's overwhelming "inspiration" echoes views of Whitman by other Jewish American poets, such as Rukeyser, Stern, Ostriker, and Piercy:

142   CONCLUSION

> Whitman's inspiration, and his enactment of that inspiration, is inimitable and seemingly inexhaustible. For me, the only other poet with whom he can compare this way is Shakespeare. . . . With both, but particularly with Whitman, I need a respite, surcease, so as not to be overwhelmed, obliterated. This is more raw than Bloom's "anxiety of influence," more primitive: there's no question of influence here, it's more a colonization, an evaporation, the fear that if I give myself over too completely to him, my own poet will be annihilated, that I'll become a mere acolyte, a follower, an appendage—a terrible nightmare, from which Whitman's poems themselves thank goodness awaken me yet again. (x)

Just as Rukeyser writes of the "folly" of trying to emulate Whitman and Ostriker describes having "paused ecstatically" when she read Whitman, Williams conveys a fear of being "overwhelmed" and "obliterated" by Whitman. These Jewish poets, whether feminist, Dadaist, or L=A=N=G=U=A=G=E in inclination, all respond to Whitman.[4] As this book has tried to establish, the allusions themselves merely begin to touch upon a myriad of adjacent questions about poetic agenda, political affiliation, mode of engagement with Jewish and American identity, responses to Whitman, and other intertextual associations. The framework of this book seeks to provide a foundation for exploring such questions as Whitman's critical reception evolves further.

As these and other Jewish American poets continue to appropriate Whitman in poetry and criticism, Whitman will likely continue to be adopted elsewhere in Jewish American culture and practices. One case of this adoption is the prayer book used by Congregation Beit Simchat Torah in New York City, *Siddur B'Chol L'vav'cha: With All Your Heart*, which contains Whitman's poem "O Captain! My Captain!," as well as a passage from "Song of Myself" ("letters dropped by God"). The stated mission of the Beit Simchat Torah congregation is to embrace anyone who might be excluded from other (typically more conservative) Jewish communities: "Founded in 1973, CBST attracts and welcomes gay men, lesbians, bisexuals, transgender, non-binary, queer and straight individuals and families who share common values."[5] Putting aside analysis of Whitman's poems chosen for the prayer book, the selection of Whitman, a non-Jewish poet, is both surprising and unsurprising, given the perception(s) by Jewish American poets of Whitman as a democratic poet (albeit an imperfect one), with an ideology of inclusivity, in terms of not only Jewishness but race, religion, gender, and sexuality more broadly.

The ways in which Whitman's ideologies continue to be employed as a foundation for Jewish American poets, and within Jewish American cultural and religious institutions, will have a lasting impact on how Whitman is received among future readers, not only within the United States but likely traversing nations, cultures, and religions. This book has attempted to elucidate how Whitman has been perceived by Jewish poets as both a poet of the American majority and a poet of the Jewish minority, marking him as a malleable and largely liminal figure. As an outsider and insider—a figure of the in-between—Whitman is almost imagined to be Jewish himself (in the spirit of Karl Shapiro). Thus, the Jewish turn to Whitman is a means not only by which Jewish poets have made themselves Jewish, and by which Jewish poets have made themselves American, but by which Walt Whitman the poet is made Jewish and American.

ACKNOWLEDGMENTS

Books are so often the work of not a single person but a community. That is the case here. Endless appreciation is due to the entire community of scholars, colleagues, family, and friends who have helped bring this project to fruition.

Ed Folsom at the University of Iowa—mentor and friend—has supported this project from its infancy, when it was but a grain of an idea for a research topic. Without Ed's unfailing encouragement, not to mention inimitable qualities as a scholar, lecturer, editor, and kind companion on a walk through Jerusalem, this book simply would not exist.

Hana Wirth-Nesher and Karen Alkalay-Gut—my advisors at Tel Aviv University—are not only extraordinary scholars but sharp readers and generous with their time. I am grateful for how they helped shape this project and for our many chats about poetry, writing, and life. I was also fortunate that Hana agreed to serve as an early reader of this manuscript in book form, including the book proposal and new chapters.

I have been fortunate to have the support of colleagues in the Department of English and American Studies at Tel Aviv University. Milette Shamir and Yael Sternhell helped arrange funding for a research assistant (Ella Kay). To Nir Evron, Sonia Weiner, Jonathan Stavsky, Shirley Zisser, Anna Kissin-Shechter, Elana Gomel, Noam Reisner, Louise Hyatt, Spencer Morrison, Tamar Gerstenhaber, Maya Klein, and Meital Galili, I cannot overstate the extent to which our camaraderie, and occasional commiseration, have made this book possible.

To those in my new(ish) home at Tel Aviv University—the Division of Languages—a sincere thank you for the time and patience you afforded me,

146 ACKNOWLEDGMENTS

especially as I worked to put some of the last revisions into the manuscript. To dear Rosalie Sitman—scholar, friend, who helped me carve a new path at TAU—to Elana Spector-Cohen, Mónica Broido, Dorin Amzalag, Hava Stern, Michal Yaary, Riva Mane, and every other teacher and administrator in the Division, I could not be more grateful for your support and well wishes along this road.

I am appreciative of Meredith Stabel, acquisitions editor at the University of Iowa Press, for our correspondence over the past few years. I always looked forward to Meredith's gracious, informative messages. And to the rest of the fantastic team at Iowa, in particular Tegan Daly, Suzanne Glémot, Susan Hill Newton, and Margaret Yapp, from day one I have felt myself lucky to have been working with you. Barbie Halaby meticulously and brilliantly served as copyeditor for the manuscript. It was also an honor to have Matt Miller from Yeshiva University as the reviewer of this project. The expert insights and comprehensive reader's report have strengthened this book in innumerable ways.

Scholars whose insights and feedback have been important to this project at earlier stages are Julian Levinson at the University of Michigan and Maeera Y. Shreiber at the University of Utah. I wish also to thank Kinneret Lahad at Tel Aviv University for generosity as a scholar and friend. My thanks are likewise due to Kenneth M. Price from the University of Nebraska and Ranen Omer-Sherman at the University of Louisville, who have dedicated time to this project.

Other scholars, poets, and translators that I wish to thank for their encouragement, from near and far, are Rachel Tzvia Back, Yosefa Raz, Annie Kantar, Sabine Huynh, and Diana Marie Delgado.

Since most of this research was conducted at Tel Aviv University, I wish to convey thanks to the stellar library staff at the Sourasky Central Library for obtaining books, essays, and interlibrary loans in an efficient, timely way. Itai Burstein from Sourasky has generously shared his knowledge of the technicalities of research databases with me, as well as with my students. And I thank my students in my courses for the many fun and interesting conversations about Whitman's writing.

To Ella Kay, who served as the research assistant for this project, I wish to express endless gratitude for her dedication, but more specifically for organizational abilities, speed with finding obscure sources, and good spirit, all within a pandemic. Ella's work was essential to the production of this book, as well as other articles and conference papers. I am in awe of the many talents

ACKNOWLEDGMENTS   147

possessed by Ella. In uniquely challenging circumstances, our meetings in Webb (or, when necessary, on Zoom) were a constant bright spot.

I wish to express appreciation to my family and friends, who have supported me tirelessly in so many endeavors. For their love and concern, I thank my father Michael Barnat for giving everything he could (may his memory be a blessing), my grandmother, Lee Katz, PhD (may her memory be a blessing), Rhonda Barnat, Jeremy Barnat, Stuart and Suzanne Katz, and the Katz cousins —Rachel, Alex, and Harrison—and their partners and children. To Sari, Danielle, Sara, Ashley, Mira, Nicole, and Ariel, thank you for being there, dear friends, through thick and thin.

To all the Tartakovskys—Nira, Netta and Freddy, Boris and Mirit and Tom— the best family in Israel (or anywhere) that I could ask for. I am profoundly grateful for our visits, outings, and meals together. The care for me and our small family on Zeitlin Street, and especially Max, not only means the world to me but has provided the time necessary to complete this book.

And to Roi Tartakovsky—my partner in work and life for nearly twenty years, my first reader since we were graduate students, now a loving, attentive dad to Max and caretaker to Lily, the dog. Thank you for what you have done to make this book possible. Truly the list is infinite, from reading drafts of this manuscript, to shopping, to everything in between. With my thanks, this book is dedicated to you and to Max, who is growing by leaps and bounds before our eyes.

NOTES

INTRODUCTION: WALT WHITMAN
AND AMERICAN JEWRY

1. Unless otherwise indicated, lines and passages from poems by Whitman are taken from the last (what is sometimes referred to as the deathbed) edition of *Leaves of Grass* (1891–1892), which is found at the Walt Whitman Archive. Quotes from other editions of *Leaves of Grass* are likewise found at the Walt Whitman Archive, such as the 1860–1861 edition. Finally, yet other quotes by Whitman, including from the preface to the 1855 *Leaves of Grass*, are from *Whitman: Poetry and Prose*, edited by Justin Kaplan. All the editions of *Leaves of Grass* can be found at the Walt Whitman Archive: https://whitmanarchive.org.

2. About this passage, Allen Ginsberg in fact comments somewhat facetiously about Whitman's claim to being an American: "[Y]ou can't accuse him of being un-American, he's 4th, 5th, 6th generation so he can say whatever he wants, on his own soil, on his own land, nobody can intimidate him" ("On Walt Whitman" 333).

3. The full lines from "Salut a Monde!" are as follows: "You Jew journeying in your old age through every risk to stand once on Syrian ground / You other Jews waiting in all lands for your Messiah!" (119). And from the "Song of the Answerer," the lines read as such: "A Jew to the Jew he seems, a Russ to the Russ, usual and near, removed from none" (136). In this context of Whitman's encounters with Jewish culture and practices in America, Leonard Prager has observed that Jewish people are often represented by Whitman as mythical figures, rather than his "friends and neighbors in Camden" (22).

4. According to the website for Congregation Shearith Israel, the Crosby Street Synagogue in which Whitman did his reporting was built in Lower Manhattan in 1834: https://shearithisrael.org/content/crosby-street-synagogue.

5. This notion of a reductive Jewishness is in keeping with what Anita Norich has deemed a "mythic view" of Jewish people: a view that "imagines a world in which Jews were ghettoized—literally or figuratively—but were also more autonomous, somehow purer, less tainted by the assimilation and acculturation that are often believed to have begun in the Enlightenment and culminated in American suburbs" (3).

6. This simultaneous embrace of and argument with Whitman is by no means limited to Jewish American poets or writers; as Ed Folsom has accurately observed about the breadth of poets responding to Whitman, "most American poets after Whitman have directly taken him on—to argue with him, agree with him, revise, question, reject or accept him—in an essay or poem" ("Talking" 22). I will say, however, that Jewish American poets can be seen to do so for reasons that are specifically related to the Jewish American experience.

7. For further material on the link of Stein to Whitman, see Couser; and Matt Miller, "Makings of Americans."

8. In particular, the interviews conducted by Gary Pacernick with poets Ginsberg, Gerald Stern, and Alicia Ostriker have been valuable to this book. Looking at Pacernick's poetry for a Whitmanian turn would also be rewarding, as Pacernick writes in the introduction to the collection, "Then I read *Leaves of Grass* and couldn't put down the book, for it offered hope, optimism, and energy" (3).

9. See Edward Hirsch's poem, "Whitman Leaves the Boardwalk," published in the journal *TriQuarterly*, which begins, "I am so small walking on the beach at night under the widening sky" (185).

10. For other sources in which Whitman is discussed by Ben Lerner, see Clune, as well as Lerner, "On Disliking Poetry."

11. For example, refer to Joy Ladin's critical essay on Whitman "'What I Assume,'" as well as the personal/critical piece "Ours for the Making," where Ladin discusses Whitman in the context of poetry and transgender identity: "For example, though I wanted to write sensual, overflowing, Walt-Whitman-having-a-one-night-stand-with-Pablo-Neruda poems, I couldn't. When I lived as a male, I rarely felt that I had a body, so I drew a blank when I tried to evoke the sounds and smells, colors and shapes and textures."

12. In a review of Rosebud Ben-Oni's book *turnaround, BRXGHT XYXS*, Anthony Frame notes a Whitmanian feature in Ben-Oni's collection, "a book-length love poem to the self that would make Whitman both proud and blush."

13. Yosefa Raz explores how the poet Rob Halpern both "condemns Whitman for his embrace of the pathos of war, and he echoes and critiques Whitman's *Drum-Taps* in his 2012 *Music for Porn*" (2). Adopting Whitman in this contradictory way is like so many poets in this project, like Ostriker (also aptly noted by Raz), Rich, and Stern.

14. This list of poets is extremely partial. Other active English-language poets include Jane Medved, Annie Kantar, Joanna Chen, Lonnie Monka, Rachel Neve Midbar, and Michael Dekel. For additional perspective on the development of English-language poetry in Israel, see Karen Alkalay-Gut's essay, "The Poem and the Place."

15. Here I would align with Hana Wirth-Nesher and Michael P. Kramer, who state in the introduction to *The Cambridge Companion to Jewish American Literature*, "If the American difference gives coherence to Jewish American literary history, it is a very incoherent coherence indeed. In fact, it may make more sense to talk about many Jewish American literatures" (4). Likewise, in the case of this project, I might speak of Jewish American "poetries."

16. Sincere gratitude is due to Julian Levinson for his comments on this project in an earlier version and calling my attention to the connection between Whitman and Adah Isaacs Menken. This study draws on Levinson's work, expanding the territory by focusing on Whitman within Jewish American poetry.

17. Along these lines, Jonathan N. Barron and Eric Selinger have observed that Emerson, Whitman, and Transcendentalism should be considered "to understand the origins and shaping tensions of Jewish American poetry" (5).

18. The quote by Emerson reads, "Dear Sir: I am not blind to the worth of the wonderful gift of Leaves of Grass" (https://whitmanarchive.org/published/LG/1856/poems/34).

19. Roger Asselineau has also discussed aspects of the complexities of Whitman and the Transcendentalist movement, claiming, "Actually, whether Emerson was the direct source of Whitman's ideas or not, the fact remains that there are striking similarities between the main themes of *Leaves of Grass* and the basic tenets of New England transcendentalism" (737).

20. Herbert Levine has noted that Whitman's writing reflects ideas, such as a juxtaposition of the sacred and the secular, of Reconstructionist Judaism.

21. Roland Barthes's earlier theorization that every text is "a tissue of past citations" (39) complicates the possibility of employing intertextuality as a practical tool of criticism. However, as Chana Kronfeld argues, if every text exists as no more than an infinite network of previous texts, it would be impossible to critically address intertextual manifestations like quotation, parody, allusion, or pastiche ("Intertextual Agency" 2). I align with critics such as Kronfeld, who have theorized notions of influence, showing how the concept of intertextuality—while not a perfect paradigm—is preferable to the concept of "influence," because the very term "influence" suggests reader-centered criticism, which can raise problematic questions of privilege, biography, and authorial intention (*On the Margins* 2). Ziva Ben-Porat, also, in her seminal work on allusion, has explored devices that fall within the category of

intertextuality. In this analysis of how Whitman has been conceptualized and perceived by Jewish American poets, I employ a variety of terms that fall within these theoretical concepts of intertextuality and allusion, like appropriation, allusion, response, echo, or adoption, depending upon the textual case.

22. In the context of Jewish American poetry, Maeera Y. Shreiber has written about the seeming binary of "formal aesthetic practices" and "ethnic/religious/cultural orientation" ("Jewish American Poetry" 159).

23. In *Walt Whitman & the World*, Gay Wilson Allen and Ed Folsom amass essays on Whitman's transnational reception, including by V. K. Chari (India), Sigurdur A. Magnússon (Iceland), Walter Grünzweig (Germany), and Ezra Greenspan (Israel). Greenspan states that in Israel, Whitman has been "embraced by the poles of modern Israeli society, from the socialist Left to the nationalist Right, from the secular to the religious, from the academic to the journalistic" (394). The question of the reception of Whitman by Jewish poets in American is quite distinct from that of Hebrew-language Jewish authors in Israel, with radically different historical, national, cultural, and linguistic issues at stake.

24. See Perlman et al.'s *Walt Whitman: The Measure of His Song* for various literary responses to Whitman and a bibliography of Whitman-related writings. For a perspective on "internationalist writing," see also Walter Grünzweig's article, "'For America—For All the Earth.'"

25. Xilao Li has stated about these intertextual relationships, "The relationship between Whitman and ethnic writers can be described as a kinship between a father and his daughters and sons" (109).

26. In a similar vein, George Hutchinson writes about Whitman's favorable reputation among Black writers like Alain Locke, James Weldon Johnson, and Jean Toomer: "We know more today about Walt Whitman among the French, the Russians, the Irish, the Japanese, the Germans, and the Argentineans than about Whitman among the African American modernist movement . . . [yet] Whitman contributed crucially to some of the most fruitful developments in black writing of the twentieth century" (201).

27. Kenneth M. Price, who has investigated responses to Whitman in the work of Gloria Naylor, Ishmael Reed, and William Least Heat-Moon, writes that Reed "battles him" (90).

28. See Levinson, "Seventh Angel" (148).

29. Renee M. Sentilles describes how in the 1850s Menken married Alexander Isaac Menken, a Jewish man, and subsequently claimed her own Jewish identity, promoting herself as a Jewish poet, and that her Jewish identity was likely self-selected (133). As Sentilles also points out, Menken is named a "Jewish poet" in contemporary Jewish publications and archives (123).

NOTES TO PAGES 14–18   153

30. Levinson notes the "prophetic mode" in Menken's work, with influences from the Bible and Romanticism, as well as the Whitman connection ("Seventh Angel" 148).

31. Such a connection has been suggested by Aaron Kramer: "Two American poets greeted the waves of Jews who began fleeing Eastern Europe after the pogroms of 1881: Walt Whitman and Emma Lazarus" (15).

32. "Commentary: Horace Traubel," Walt Whitman Archive, https://whitmanarchive.org/criticism/disciples/traubel/WWWiC/2/med.00002.87.html.

33. "Commentary: Horace Traubel," Walt Whitman Archive, 459, https://whitmanarchive.org/criticism/disciples/traubel/WWWiC/2/med.00002.88.html.

34. These poems appear in *J19*, where Zachary Turpin states that it is "time we accept Lazarus as a queer poet" (421). I am very much in agreement with this excellent reading of Lazarus. Turpin also states that Lazarus chooses "not to exceed the limits of traditional form, as Walt Whitman" (419). From this claim about Whitman and Lazarus I depart, with poems such as "By the Waters of Babylon" displaying a more Whitman-inspired free verse.

35. Other critics have identified Whitmanesque features in Lazarus's writing, such as Kramer, who states that Lazarus's poems "The New Colossus" and "By the Waters of Babylon" embody Whitman's poetic rhythms and embrace of the immigrant masses (15).

36. Another Whitman connection in Lazarus is noted by Dan Vogel, who identifies that the poem "Idyl" is in dialogue with Whitman's poem "Out of the Cradle Endlessly Rocking" (74).

37. It is also valuable to read Whitman and Lazarus in the context of Ranen Omer-Sherman, who considers Lazarus to be "the harbinger of the modern American *ethnic* Jew" ("Emma Lazarus" 170).

38. See Albert Waldinger's essay "Stopping by the Woods: Classic American Poems in Yiddish" for further discussion of Yiddish translations of Whitman, including by I. Leyeles, Malka Heifetz Tussman, and Louis Miller. About Miller's translation of Whitman's "Starting from Paumanok," Waldinger notes a correlation between Whitman's phrase "marches humanitarian" as "*mentshheyts marsh,*" which Waldinger finds to evoke "the Jewish/Yiddish value of *mentshlekhkeyt* or 'humanity'" (164).

39. As Levinson states, the Yiddish Cooperative Book League of the Yiddish International Workers Order has published the most substantial collection of Whitman's poetry and prose to appear to date in Yiddish translation, "complete with a biographical sketch, photographs, and an appended monograph" (*Exiles* 121).

40. Many thanks here to the scholar Matt Miller, a generous reader of this manuscript, for calling my attention to the figures Louis Miller (1866–1927) and Louis Miller (1889–1967), both seminal figures in the history of Whitman's place in

154 NOTES TO PAGES 18–27

Yiddish-language writing. Also, as Miller has pointed out to me, the first essay in Yiddish on Whitman was probably written by Josheph Bovshover—a member of Di Yunge—and that Whitman-related material is found in Yiddish as early as 1897.

41. I. J. Schwartz was yet another important translator of Whitman's poetry into Yiddish, as noted in the *Jewish American Literature: A Norton Anthology* (Chametsky et al. 224). The opening lines from Schwartz's "Kentucky" are: "The broad fields of Kentucky— / Even now I feel the tender breezes; / The same sun casts its light on me, / And its trees shelter me" (225).

42. Prager has also explored Whitman and Yiddish writing, stating that "Jews writing in a quintessential Jewish language, Yiddish, especially in New York City, have been much involved with Whitman" (23). He traces "Whitman-consciousness" in the essays, poems, and translations of Joseph Bovshover, Morris Rosenfeld, A. Eysen, and L. Miler.

43. Here I acknowledge the University of California Press for granting permission to include this translation of H. Leyvik's poem by Benjamin Harshav and Barbara Harshav.

44. Regarding Whitman within Jewish American prose, in *To Walt Whitman, America*, Price has identified echoes of Whitman in Bernard Malamud's short story "The German Refugee" from *Idiots First* (1963). M. A. Quayum has also examined Saul Bellow's notions of Whitman in "Transcendentalism and Bellow's 'Henderson the Rain King.'"

45. Though this book deals with Jewish American poetry, in regard to the juncture of Jewish and American "identity," I would align with Wirth-Nesher when she claims in the introduction to *What Is Jewish Literature?*, "I have aimed to undermine any one essentialist view of Jewish culture, while at the same time tracing the distinctive features of the act of self-definition in recent Jewish literary history. Each one of these definitions is an invention that answers specific needs of time and place. What *is* Jewish literature? Why do you want to know? Who said such a thing exists anyway? And why not ask?" ("Defining" 11–12).

46. Ginsberg's appropriation of Whitman has received a significant amount of critical attention (as discussed in chapter 3), and quite recently by Ostriker. For example, in a Jewish (and American) context, Ostriker writes, "From America Allen takes Whitman. The manly love of comrades, the open road, the democratic vistas stretching to eternity, and also the eyes of America taking a fall, which he plants, later, in his mother's head. America will always be, for him, infinite hope and infinite disappointment. That's very Jewish" ("Poet as Jew" 118). Indeed, Ostriker's reading of Ginsberg's reading of Whitman marks how Ginsberg interprets Whitman, and how Ginsberg's reading of Whitman has influenced Ostriker herself—a turn to Whitman explored in chapter 4.

NOTES TO PAGES 29-34 155

47. Such critics include Peter Erickson, Piotr Gwiazda, Nissa Parmar, Diane Middlebrook, and Maeera Y. Shreiber.

48. As Marge Piercy states, "I am a Reconstructionist Jew myself; that's the movement of Judaism I feel most at home with" (Lyons, "Interview" 332).

CHAPTER 1: CHARLES REZNIKOFF, THE JEWISH OBJECTIVIST POETS, AND WALT WHITMAN

1. This chapter joins scholars of Charles Reznikoff, including Robert Alter, Milton Hindus, Anne Stevenson, Stephen Fredman, and Ranen Omer-Sherman, who have identified Whitman's voice in individual poems by Reznikoff, as well as in certain aspects of Reznikoff's project as a whole. By demonstrating how Reznikoff's appropriation of Whitman is inextricable from Ezra Pound and the culture of High Modernism, I hope to enrich this critical conversation.

2. This poem is found in a section of Reznikoff's *Complete Poems* that contains incomplete and unpublished poems by Reznikoff. These texts were collected posthumously by editor Seamus Cooney (200).

3. The Permissions Company, LLC, has granted approval to reprint the poems by Reznikoff that are featured in this chapter.

4. For example, David Barnes has written about Pound's engagement with fascist figures in Italy in the 1930s and how Pound wrote and published articles with blatantly antisemitic titles, such as "Jewish Infection" (28).

5. However, several scholars have demonstrated that Whitman did serve as an influence on their poetry, both directly and through French poets and writers, such as Baudelaire. See, for example, the chapter on "Ezra Pound's Cantos" in James Miller's *American Quest* and Betsy Erkkila's *Walt Whitman Among the French*. Lorelei Cederstrom has also noted poetic correlations between Whitman and Imagist poets, including John Gould Fletcher, Richard Aldington, F. S. Flint, and Amy Lowell.

6. Amy Lowell, for instance, quite detested Whitman; Cederstrom claims, "She found him guilty of 'inversion . . . clichés . . . wrong use of foreign words,' and that catch-all of modern disparagement, 'bad taste'" (205–206).

7. As one finds in Stephen Tapscott, Pound, too, though publicly rebuffing Whitman, was in significant ways also "working towards an image of Whitman that can fit his own modernist ambitions" (23).

8. As Norman Finkelstein states in *Not One of Them in Place*, "modernist poetry makes sense to the original Objectivists: the children or grandchildren of immigrants, on intimate terms with historical upheaval, they see in it a literature that acknowledges that history is accelerating to the breaking point" (20).

156   NOTES TO PAGES 34-36

9. Notably, outside of Pound's more direct circle, Jewish American poets in that period were writing in a more explicitly Whitmanesque style, like Edgar Lee Masters, Vachel Lindsay, and Carl Sandburg, who formed the Chicago-based "hub of a new, Whitmanian strain of letters" (Fredman, *Menorah* 10). In the essay "1916: Sandburg Anoints Pound," Sandburg praises Pound, albeit reservedly: "If I were driven to name one individual who, in the English language, by means of his own examples of creative art in poetry, has done most of living men to incite new impulses in poetry, the chances are I would name Ezra Pound. This statement is made reservedly, out of knowing the work of Pound and being somewhat close to it for three years or so" (249). The grounds for Sandburg's complex position toward Pound—"somewhat close"—may mirror Reznikoff's own reservations about Pound. Yet Reznikoff and the other Jewish Objectivist poets were bound more conceptually, and concretely, to Pound than Sandburg was.

10. The relation between Pound and Zukofsky was so intimate, as Fredman notes, that in their letters the play of "Yiddish accents and Jewish stereotypes between a Jewish poet and his anti-Semitic mentor can become quite dizzying" (*Menorah* 130). For another study of the relationship between Zukofsky and Pound, see chapter 3 of Finkelstein's *Not One of Them in Place*. This "dyad" of Jew and antisemite, as Finkelstein aptly observes, "cannot be neglected in any narrative of modernism" (42).

11. Louis Zukofsky argues in the essay "Sincerity and Objectification" that Reznikoff's poetics were an ideal example of the Objectivist mode: "The verbal qualities of Reznikoff's shorter poems do not form mere pretty bits (American poetry, circa 1913), but suggest . . . entire aspects of thought: economics, beliefs, literary analytics, etc. The entire matter involves the process of active literary omission and a discussion of method finding its way in the acceptance of two criteria: sincerity and objectification" (273).

12. Other poets who became connected to the Objectivist group were Basil Bunting and Lorine Niedecker.

13. Notably—although outside the scope of this chapter—Whitmanian structures are evident in poems by Zukofsky, such as "A." For other textual and ideological influences traced in Zukofsky, including Trotsky and Marx, see Ruth Jennison's article, "Combining Uneven Developments."

14. The Cooney edition of *The Complete Poems of Charles Reznikoff* is divided into two sections: poems from 1918–1936 and poems from 1937–1975. In this chapter, I will refer to the former section as "vol. 1" and the latter section as "vol. 2."

15. Reznikoff composed the poem in 1944 as a tribute to the thirteenth year of the *Menorah Journal*.

16. Fredman has observed that this strategy of returning to history is

NOTES TO PAGES 36–44   157

characteristic of Reznikoff: "Over and over during the course of his career, Reznikoff returned to major events in Jewish history in the way that a midrashic commentator recurs to passages of Scripture, hoping to weave an identity for modern Jews by knotting present events—especially calamities—to earlier moments" (*Menorah* 105–106).

17. Fredman has noted the connection between Reznikoff and Whitman and suggests that Reznikoff "borrows [Whitman's] litany of prepositional phrases to intone the sights of Jewish disaster" (*Menorah* 104). This mode of invoking Whitman's catalogues as a memorial appears in another poem by another Jewish American poet: Irving Feldman. In the poem "The Pripet Marshes," the litany of names serves as a memorial for Jews who perished in the Holocaust: "Maury is there," "And Frank," "And blond Lottie" (Feldman 24–27). Whitman's poetics are thus shown to be adaptable to the act of ritual naming in a Jewish context.

18. Reznikoff has been questioned, and even attacked, for this in-between position; one critic who does so is Harold Bloom, in "The Sorrows of American-Jewish Poetry," where Bloom asks, "Why attempt to translate Yehudah Halevi into the idiom of Pound and William Carlos Williams? Is the form of this in any way appropriate to its burden?" Another is Paul Auster, who writes of Reznikoff being neither fully Jewish nor fully American: "Neither fully assimilated nor fully unassimilated, Reznikoff occupies the unstable middle ground between two worlds and is never able to claim either one as his own" (156–157).

19. The poem most frequently cited as an embodiment of Reznikoff's outsider identity is section 40 of *Inscriptions: 1944–1956*, where he compares his English name "Charles" to his Hebrew name "Ezekiel." The poem conveys tension experienced by Reznikoff for having been renamed, putting forth a clear division between Reznikoff's Jewish and American "self."

20. Here it is also possible to hear echoes of Wordsworth's poem "Splendour in the Grass."

21. Reznikoff also draws associations between the Jewish American experience and "grass" at the end of the first section of *In Memoriam: 1933* (which would have been several decades earlier): "we Jews are as the dew, / on every blade of grass, / trodden under foot today / and here tomorrow morning" (vol. 1, 141).

22. This anonymous review states that, like Spinoza, Whitman enveloped every facet of humanity into his poetry, "holding the mirror up to the universe at large" (Walt Whitman Archive, https://whitmanarchive.org/criticism/reviews/leaves1860/anc.00241.html).

23. Spinoza was also recognized to be an important figure for Zukofsky in terms of secular Judaism; as Joshua Schuster states, "they take part in a long tradition of Jewish secularism that *uses Judaism to get out of Judaism*" (130). I suggest that

158   NOTES TO PAGES 47–48

the presence of Spinoza in Zukofsky's work can probably be read in the context of Whitman as well.

24. See Linda Simon, who states about the idea of witness in Reznikoff, "Whether Reznikoff sets his poems in Biblical or medieval times, turn-of-the-century America, or in his contemporary New York, his themes remain consistent. He bears witness" (235).

25. Reznikoff has, in fact, been criticized for exaggerating his objectivity and therefore displaying a lack of empathy for the subjects in his poems. Regarding Reznikoff's long poem *Testimony*, Robert Alter states, "The poems are disturbing . . . less for what they reveal about American history and the program of genocide . . . than for what they reveal about the state of the poet's mind" (131). I would suggest that a seeming lack of feeling in Reznikoff's poetry can be read differently through the prism of Whitman, where Reznikoff, enacting Whitman's mode of seeing and elevating the smallest creatures, evokes a more empathetic stance, as found in the 1855 preface to *Leaves of Grass*: "The greatest poet hardly knows pettiness or triviality. If he breathes into any thing that was before thought small it dilates with the grandeur and life of the universe" (*Whitman: Poetry and Prose* 10).

26. Here, I concur with a point made by Finkelstein, who writes that Reznikoff's engagement with the Other and his "testimony" are based in the Jewish idea of "personal responsibility in the determination and judgment of truth" (*Not One* 21).

27. Occasionally, in the work of other Jewish Objectivists, this position of witness can be found; for example, section 25 of Oppen's "Of Being Numerous" is reminiscent of Reznikoff: "Strange that the youngest people I know / Live in the oldest buildings // Scattered about the city / In the dark rooms / Of the past—and the immigrants, // The black / Rectangular buildings / Of the immigrants" (164).

28. The Whitman-Reznikoff connection in terms of poetic witnessing has been remarked on by Anne Stevenson and Michael Farley, who state, "In so far as [Reznikoff] was an American, he wrote in the tradition of Whitman—the Whitman of the 'lists.' In so far as he was a Jew, his method was that of The Old Testament. An amasser of details, both a poet and a scribe, his way was not to preach but to tell" (180). Stevenson and Farley furthermore claim that Reznikoff's effort to poetically represent "truth" is a distillment of the same effort in Whitman, which they call the "historical/ prophetic tradition": "[Reznikoff] had only to pick up the threads of Whitman's images and 'facts,' and discard his rhetoric" (183). I am generally in agreement with these points; one additional idea I would offer is that reading Whitman in Reznikoff as an American is inseparable from reading Whitman in Reznikoff as a Jewish poet. It is precisely Reznikoff's "sacred duty" to "bear witness" that is rooted in Reznikoff's experience of being Jewish and American with Whitman.

29. Such imagery recalls Whitman's poem about New York "A Broadway Pageant," in which Whitman gazes at and embraces everyone, especially the masses

of immigrants, who could so easily have been ignored and excluded: "The countries there with their populations, the millions en-masse are curiously here" (194–195).

30. Certain other intertexts that resonate here are "special providence in the death of a sparrow" (*Hamlet*, act 5, sc. 2, lines 215–216), as well as the famous 1905 gospel hymn "The Eye Is on the Sparrow," in which the sparrow itself symbolizes one's belief in God.

31. Allen Ginsberg will later remark about this poem, "This is such a horrible picture you know it is poetry!" ("Reznikoff's Poetics" 142). Such a declaration by Ginsberg about Reznikoff's poetics is emblematic of how Reznikoff is in fact an instrumental precursor for Ginsberg's own reaching back to Whitman, as discussed further in chapter 3.

CHAPTER 2: WHITMAN VERSUS HIGH MODERNISTS

1. I am grateful to the *Walt Whitman Quarterly Review* for publishing an article on Shapiro and Whitman, from which the section of this book is adapted: "'Beyond Religions and Even Beyond Mankind': Karl Shapiro's Jewish Walt Whitman" (2014).

2. For instance, about Shapiro being a prototypical American poet, Louis D. Rubin claimed, "[Shapiro's] strength as a poet had come from his ability to invest the objects and emotions of middle-class American experience with the language and dignity of poetry. His first mature collection had taken for subject matter such things as new cars, drugstores, barbershops, row houses, railway stations . . . [and] transformed them into poems that imaged them with a clarity and even a literary radiance that they had not hitherto received" ("Karl Shapiro" 109).

3. Images of American youth culture and iconic symbols of sports, jazz, and Coca-Cola populate Shapiro's poems, such as "Drug Store": "Youth comes to jingle nickels and crack wise; / The baseball scores are his, the magazines / devoted to lust, the jazz, the Coca-Cola, / The lending library of love's latest. / He is the customer; he is heroized" (*Collected Poems* 11).

4. For a discussion of Shapiro's tenure as chief editor of *Poetry*, which he served from 1950 to 1955, see Oostdijk.

5. For a broad investigation of these writers on the political left, see Wald.

6. Shapiro's poem "University" is yet another text that depicts issues of not only religious but racial and ethnic discrimination, for example in the lines, "To hurt the Negro and avoid the Jew / Is the curriculum" (*Collected Poems* 10). Shapiro's condemnation of institutions that exclude minorities ("Negros" and "Jews") is especially notable.

7. Regarding influences on Shapiro (in addition to Whitman), see *Start with the Sun*, which contains essays about William Carlos Williams and Henry Miller. See

160   NOTES TO PAGES 58–67

also Shapiro's *The Poetry Wreck* for essays on Williams, Auden, Jarrell, and others.

8. The rhetoric of Shapiro's statements is in keeping with what Robert W. Daniel describes as "[The] belligerent, iconoclastic, exasperating/stimulating style [that] seems to keep [Shapiro] ever in an adversary relationship with something or somebody" (xc).

9. Shapiro defines this concept of "cosmic consciousness" as "[a] sense of identification with the universe, and intellectual enlightenment or illumination which may last only briefly . . . but which places the individual on a new plane of existence" ("Cosmic Consciousness" 31).

10. Flanzbaum has observed about this introduction that Shapiro "thrusts Jewishness into the world of metaphor" (269).

11. Karl Malkoff has noted about Shapiro's view here that the Jew becomes for Shapiro "a terrible symbol of the Holocaust, of man brought face to face with annihilation" (214).

12. Several years after the publication of the collection *Poems of a Jew*, Shapiro qualified these claims made in the introduction, especially the notion of universalizing Jewish suffering. In "The American-Jewish-Writer," he states, "What my collection of poems tried to illustrate was my belief that the Jew is absolutely committed to the world, and it is the commitment which also makes him, when he is here, so intensely American" (8).

13. Koch does chide Whitman for undertaking so many revisions of *Leaves of Grass*—"corrections"—that according to Koch are "almost always terrible" ("The Art of Poetry," 2). However, in "Whitman's Words," Koch's essay explicating Whitman's verse and philosophies, Whitman's contribution to promoting equality and ideological inclusion is laid bare: "There are no privileged characters in Whitman and no privileged words. And so 'as good belongs to you,' folksy though it is, is just fine for a philosophical statement. What's easiest and most natural is what's truest; profundity's in plain talk and not in fancy academic or poetical speech" (36–37).

14. Koch, in the essay "Educating the Imagination," also credits Williams and Whitman as offering an alternative to fixed verse, and thus "to escape from rhyme and meter" (158), a poetic style he perceived as limiting.

15. Though these five poets are widely considered to be the main poets of the New York School, these delineations are debated by critics, like Terence Diggory, Stephen Paul Miller, David Lehman, and Sara Lundquist. One feature of the group that is widely agreed upon is their rich creative and intellectual collaboration—what Diggory calls "a mode of 'belonging'" ("Community" 15).

16. As David Chinitz writes, "Despite the significant and influential body of work Koch has produced . . . academic criticism . . . has largely ignored him" (312). Lehman also argues that despite Koch's long career publishing poetry, and being the recipient of prestigious poetry prizes, including the Bollingen Prize (1995), Koch's

humoristic tone is one cause of "critical neglect" (204–205).

17. See, for example, Lundquist on recent critics of the New York School describing the group as "a kind of guy gang" (12), therefore minimizing Barbara Guest's key role in the group's development.

18. See Schneiderman for a further account of the correspondence between O'Hara and Koch around the matter of Roskolenko's poetry review (351–357).

19. Another important point of connection for O'Hara turning to Whitman as a poetic father is in the arena of sexuality; as David Eberly writes, "Both gay, they explored their sexuality and the 'city of orgies, walks and joys'—Manhattan—which nourished and protected it" (69).

20. In "A Note on Frank O'Hara in the Early Fifties," Koch recalls a Whitmanian influence on O'Hara's poem "Easter," "a wonderful, energetic, and rather obscene poem of four or five pages. . . . It was like Lorca or Whitman in some ways, but very original" (21).

21. For more on Koch's critical reception, see Pelton, "Kenneth Koch's Poetics."

22. Also, rather uncannily like for Shapiro, the period that Koch spent teaching in academic institutions (like the New School and Columbia) has been described as "stormy" (Gray 228).

23. All poems quoted by Kenneth Koch are from *The Collected Poems of Kenneth Koch*, unless otherwise stated.

24. This poem from Koch's collection *New Addresses* contains a series of apostrophe poems narrated in first person, with each poem addressing a task, experience, or life event, like "To Driving" and "To My Fifties."

25. The speaker describes being "kept out of the Harvard clubs," due to his Jewish background, presumably.

26. Another mention of the Koch-Whitman connection appears by David Spurr: "If parody and buoyant flippancy have characterized many of his poems, these qualities have always been accompanied by an earnest desire to record the simple pleasures of being alive, as if Walt Whitman had a sense of humor" (345).

27. Lehman, too, has remarked on the Whitmanian-style listing: "Koch is enamored of the list as an organizing principle for, I suspect, the same reasons that attracted Whitman: Lists record the simultaneity of experience, they are antiheirarchical, and they enable the poet to be as inclusive as possible" (226).

CHAPTER 3: WHITMAN'S POETICS OF WITNESS

1. I gratefully acknowledge *Studies in American Jewish Literature* for publishing an article on Rukeyser and Whitman, from which parts of this section are drawn: "'Women and Poets See the Truth Arrive': Muriel Rukeyser and Walt Whitman" (2015).

162   NOTES TO PAGES 78–79

2. Unless otherwise stated, all selections of poems by Muriel Rukeyser are taken from *The Collected Poems of Muriel Rukeyser*.

3. Kertesz 1.

4. Kertesz 42.

5. Herzog.

6. Gardinier 90.

7. Flynn 270.

8. Virginia Terris relates more extensively to Rukeyser's engagement with the Whitman-Transcendentalist tradition: "[Rukeyser's] highly personal contemporary voice . . . project[s] her into our era which, with its radical departures from traditional Transcendentalism, is yet a reaffirmation of it" (410).

9. Such writers who express admiration for Rukeyser include Erica Jong, Alice Walker, Sharon Olds, Denise Levertov, Gerald Stern, Marge Piercy, Adrienne Rich, and Alicia Ostriker. Anne Sexton's affection for Rukeyser is expressed in a letter (dated November 1, 1967), where Sexton praises Rukeyser's book *The Speed of Darkness*, stating that the book "glistens here like the first washed flowers in spring." Sexton then writes, "I just want to tell you again, beautiful Muriel, mother of everyone, how I cherish your words, as well as the memory of your good face" (322). Maxine Kumin also refers to Rukeyser as the "mother of everyone" in a poem by that title in the collection *The Long Marriage*.

10. As Kate Daniels points out, Rukeyser had been regarded as "the best woman writer of her generation, the best of recent Yale Younger Poets, the best of the young 'revolutionist' poets," but also attacked vehemently in "Grandeur and Misery of a Poster Girl," a series of articles in *The Partisan Review* that "condemned her entire poetic behavior and called into question her personal and poetic motives" (248). Along these lines, Alicia Ostriker observes that Rukeyser has been spurned both by New Critics for "excessive interest in politics and sexuality" and by the Left for "excessive formal experimentation and an impudent refusal to toe a correct proletarian line" ("Foreword" xiv).

11. Elsewhere, in an article from *Studies in American Jewish Literature*, I have written more extensively about poetry and the body through Whitman for Rukeyser. The body clearly informs Rukeyser's thinking about her own poetics and Whitman's. In the 1974 "Craft Interview," Rukeyser conveys how the rhythms of her body and breath shape the rhythms of her work: "a physical binding, like the recurrence of the heartbeat and the breathing and all the involuntary motions as well. But in a poet I care very much about physical reinforcement, the structure in recurrence. And I love it myself" (163). This description of the physicality in Rukeyser's poetic forms strikingly corresponds to a description of Whitman's poetry and the body in Rukeyser's *The Life of Poetry*: "Out of his own body, and its

relation to itself and the sea, [Whitman] drew his basic rhythms. They are not the rhythm, as has been asserted, of work and love-making; but rather of the relation of our breathing to our heartbeat, and these measured against an ideal of water at the shore, not beginning nor ending, but endlessly drawing in, making forever its forms of massing and falling among the breakers, seething in the white recessions of its surf, never finishing, always making a meeting place" (80).

12. In the introduction to *The Life of Poetry*, Rukeyser writes about her experience traveling to Spain during the Spanish Civil War and the "responsibility" to bear witness that she took seriously: "They had seen how, as foreigners, we were deprived; how we were kept from, and wanted, above all things one: our responsibility. This was a stroke of insight: it was true. 'Now you have your responsibility,' the voice said, deep, prophetic, direct, 'go home: tell your peoples what you have seen'" (xv).

13. Like the epigraph to this chapter, Rukeyser states in *The Life of Poetry* that her major influences were Blake, Keats, Donne, and the Bible, but "[a]nybody coming too close to the method of Whitman falls into a pit" (155).

14. Rukeyser is certainly not the only Jewish writer mentioned in this collection of "Under Forty" essays to relate part of their Jewish identity to non-Jewish (and American) culture and texts. Among these writers who responded to the question of whether they "formed a conscious attitude toward his heritage or merely [reflected] it in a passive, haphazard, and largely unconscious fashion" (3) was Alfred Kazin. Kazin writes that he experienced being Jewish without "any meaningful Jewish life or culture" and that he fashioned his own "culture" out of Blake, Transcendentalist writers such as Melville and Emerson, and "the seventeenth-century English religious poets, and the Russian novelists" ("Under Forty" 11). Rukeyser herself would probably not say she experienced no meaningful Jewish life or culture, but both Rukeyser and Kazin engaged with major American writers, like Melville, Emerson, and Whitman.

15. As Rukeyser wrote in her contribution to the famous "Under Forty" collection, "My themes and the use I have made of them have depended on my life as a poet, as a woman, as an American and as a Jew" (8).

16. See Selma C. Berrol's article on the culture of German Jews in America, "In Their Image: German Jews and the Americanization of the *Ost Juden* in New York City."

17. Despite Rukeyser's perception of lacking Jewish culture in her family, she did receive an extensive Reform Jewish education, and she writes of being taught Jewish history, the Bible, and a "smattering of prayer book Hebrew" ("Under Forty" 5).

18. Another scholar who discusses the connection between Rukeyser's politics and Jewish identity is Robert Shulman, who observes that Rukeyser's Jewish identity is "inseparable from her political radicalism" (34).

19. When Rukeyser was nineteen years old, her political activism took her to Alabama, where she wrote about the Scottsboro Boys trial. She later traveled to West Virginia to document the death of mining workers from silicosis (the focus of her long series of poems *The Book of the Dead*, discussed here) and covered the 1936 anti-fascist Olympics in Barcelona, where she formed an intimate relationship with another anti-fascist activist, Otto Boch, who was killed in the war. Later in life, she traveled to South Korea as president of the American PEN organization to protest for the release of Kim Chi-Ha.

20. One of Rukeyser's most well-known poems about Jewish American identity, "To Be a Jew," embodies her criticism of such assimilation: "To be a Jew in the twentieth century / Is to be offered a gift. If you refuse, / Wishing to be invisible, you choose / Death of the spirit, the stone insanity. / Accepting, take full life" (243). The poem equates assimilation with absolving oneself of social responsibility: "But the accepting wish, / The whole and fertile spirit as guarantee / For every human freedom, suffering to be free."

21. Walt Whitman Archive, https://whitmanarchive.org/published/LG/1860/whole.html.

22. This poem also evokes Adrienne Rich's poem "Diving into the Wreck," where Rich takes a camera and goes diving "to explore the wreck." Rich has articulated in the essay "Beginners" how Rukeyser was a crucial inspiration for her own vision.

23. Whitman is also, therefore, central in what Walter Kalaidjian calls Rukeyser's "metaphor of the photographic eye . . . to explore the ideological powers of scenic representation" (72).

24. To accurately represent these workers in her poetic account, Rukeyser frequently integrates journalistic records, congressional hearings, personal interviews, letters, doctors' reports, stock market statistics, and other official documents. In "The Disease," Rukeyser uses a transcript from a court case in which a doctor is being questioned about silicosis: "There is difficulty in breathing. / Yes. / And a painful cough? / Yes. / Does silicosis cause death? / Yes, sir" (86–87).

25. Photography also appears as a symbol in *Theory of Flight*, like in "Poem Out of Childhood": "Ratat a drum upon the armistice, / Kodak As You Go : photo : they danced late / and we were a generation of grim children" (5).

26. Leslie Ann Minot writes that Rukeyser's use of photography is "crucially linked to various forms of bearing witness . . . and Rukeyser is not afraid to see the terrible truths it may show us" (266).

27. Shoshana Wechsler has discussed how Rukeyser's mode of poetic witnessing in *The Book of the Dead* places her in dialogue with Ezra Pound's Modernist poetics, as well as the Objectivist usage of "facts" to document historical events (226).

28. The dichotomy of light as connoting positivity and dark connoting negativity

NOTES TO PAGES 89–92   165

can be traced to the Old Testament; see for example Isaiah 9:2.

29. Unless otherwise indicated, quotes of poems by Allen Ginsberg are from *Allen Ginsberg: Collected Poems 1947–1980*.

30. In one example of negative criticism that Ginsberg received, M. L. Rosenthal claimed in 1967 that Ginsberg held a "consciously Whitman-like inclusiveness" (96). Rosenthal also referred to Ginsberg as an "exhibitionist" and argued that his style had "lost its way" (112).

31. I present this interpretation of "Yiddishe Kopf" as "Yiddish Brain" in consultation with scholar Hana Wirth-Nesher. Craig Svonkin offers the translation "Yiddish Head," "with its idea of an essentialist, inescapable 'head,' or personality, and with its Yiddish title's implication of an essential Jewish spirit, often referred to with the term '*Yiddishkeit*'" (185).

32. Michael Schumacher notes, "Ginsberg's interest in Russia dated back to his boyhood, when his mother [. . .] told Allen and Eugene [his brother] harrowing tales of the persecution of Jews in rural Russia . . . including stories of the pogroms" (*Iron Curtain* 167).

33. Here I find Allen Grossman's idea of America being foreign for Ginsberg to apply; Grossman states, "[T]he national image in Whitman is a stable symbol of an ideal form of the self," whereas "Ginsberg's reference to America is an effort to naturalize a fundamentally alien and precariously grounded consciousness" (156).

34. These poetic themes manifest in poems from his earliest work throughout the collections later in his life. Poems with Whitman at the center include "Love Poem on Theme by Whitman," "A Supermarket in California," "After Whitman & Reznikoff," "I Love Old Whitman So," and "Whitmanic Poem." In addition, there are poems with more minor references to Whitman, such as "Death to Van Gogh," "Siesta in Xbalba," and "Ode to Failure," as well as epigraphs from Whitman's collections, such as in the first edition of *Howl* from "Song of Myself" ("Unscrew the locks from the doors! / Unscrew the doors themselves from their jams!") (809), and a section of "Democratic Vistas" for *The Fall of America (1965–1971)* (811). Many of Ginsberg's poems do not mention Whitman outright but are blatantly Whitmanian in form, such as "Howl," "Kaddish," and "America."

35. The themes of Jewish identity in the poem parallel sentiments from an interview where Ginsberg declares, "My whole family is Jewish and that's just the whole thing in my bones" (Pacernick 144).

36. This poem was composed as an elegy for William Carlos Williams after his death.

37. Brian Jackson has written about Ginsberg searching for Williams's approval of his poetry, which Williams granted after Ginsberg sent poems that were more Modernistic in style, clearer and more "concrete" (300–301).

166   NOTES TO PAGES 93–102

38. As mentioned in chapter 1, David Barnes has written about Pound's dialogue with fascist entities in Italy in the 1930s, writing articles that were profoundly antisemitic in nature.

39. Jackson has observed as well how Ginsberg received a "Modernist poetics of looking" from Pound and Williams (298).

40. I explore more in depth Reznikoff, Ginsberg, Whitman, and Ginsberg's views of Whitman through Reznikoff in an essay titled "Walt Whitman and Jewish American Poetry: Charles Reznikoff and Allen Ginsberg," forthcoming in *The Oxford Handbook of Walt Whitman*, edited by Kenneth M. Price and Stefan Schöberlein. I am very grateful to the editors, Price and Schöberlein, for their invitation to contribute to this volume, as well as the invaluable feedback they provided throughout the process of developing the essay, as a project adjacent to my wider research on Whitman and Jewish American poetry.

41. Svonkin also mentions Reznikoff as a potential type of Jewish patrilineal figure for Ginsberg: "Ginsberg was searching for a Jewish poetic father, perhaps to serve as a Jewish, Modernist substitute of sorts for the anti-Semitic Pound" (186).

42. Though outside the scope of this chapter, I would argue that "Howl" and "Kaddish," of course two of Ginsberg's most famous poems, can both be interpreted through this notion of witnessing; for example, "Howl" begins "I saw the best minds of my generation destroyed by madness." "Kaddish" also has references to walking and looking: "I go out and walk the street, look back over my shoulder, Seventh Avenue." In retrospect, these poems can be understood through this idea of poetic witnessing.

43. A version of this section on Stern appears in "'I Followed Whitman Through Half of Camden': Gerald Stern, Walt Whitman, and Jewish American Identity," *Insane Devotion: On the Writing of Gerald Stern*, edited by Mihaela Moscaliuc (Trinity UP, 2016). Tremendous thanks go to the editor of the volume and the press.

44. Gary Pacernick has also compared Stern's tone to Whitman's "praise and exaltation for the people, places, and things that he affirms. Like Whitman, [Stern] is mesmerized by the life around him and often writes in long catalogues" (109).

45. Jane Somerville has explored the foundations of Pound and Eliot for Stern, ultimately finding the models of Wallace Stevens, Williams, and Whitman more prominent in Stern's writing (17).

46. In fact, humor is an aspect that Stern associates with his Jewish writing: "Is the Judaism I speak of in the forgiveness, in the justice, in the relentlessness, in the affection, in the humor?" (*What I Can't* xi).

47. Seeds of Stern's engagement with Jewish identity are also evident in his earlier work; for instance, in the collection *Rejoicings* (1973). In "The Poem of Life," the speaker describes sitting with a Jewish friend named Bob Summers (an underdog

NOTES TO PAGES 102–109   167

character that appears also in "Bob Summers' Body" and "Bob Summers: The Final Poem"), ruminating about "the poem of life." At the end of the poem, Stern references the Holocaust and the experience of American Jews in suburbia: the "brutal memories" of "two delectable Jews, / spending our happy and cunning lives / in the honeysuckles" (*This Time* 24).

48. In "The Day Without the Jews," for example, Stern writes about his encounter with antisemitism and denial of the Holocaust. In "The Sabbath," he considers the nature of the Christian Sabbath versus the Jewish "Shabbos."

49. Stern has spoken elsewhere about not only Yiddish but Hebrew liturgy as an influence on his poetic style: "I think there is an interesting rhythmic influence from the Hebrew prayers, which are memory to me, a manner of repetition, of modification that is the Hebrew way of organizing poetry, which I think is a big influence on me" (Pacernick 113).

50. Sanford Pinsker observes that Jewishness in Stern's writing is conveyed through "sadness, a deep sense of one's mortality and of history" ("Weeping" 188).

51. In section V of the poem, Stern writes of Whitman successfully being able to transform the ugliness of death into beauty: Whitman knew "how the foul liquid and meat / turned into melons and apricots and roses." In the Ginsberg tradition of Whitman (again through Reznikoff), Stern's speaker insists on finding beauty in a landscape that might otherwise be only horrid and tragic.

52. In the former poem, "The City Dead-House," Whitman writes compassionately of encountering "a poor dead prostitute": "The divine woman, her body—I see the Body—I look on it alone" (284).

53. Pinsker has claimed that while Stern employs Whitman's poetic "litanies," Stern is more "rooted in a cultural past" ("Weeping" 194) than Whitman, to which I largely concur, adding that in "Hot Dog," Stern in fact invites Whitman into his own Jewish past and present.

CHAPTER 4: JEWISH AMERICAN WOMEN POETS RESPOND TO WALT WHITMAN

1. In the essay "Under Forty," Rukeyser describes these four core facets of her identity: "My themes and the use I have made of them have depended on my life as a poet, as a woman, as an American and as a Jew" (8).

2. Adrienne Rich also asks, rather pointedly, about Rukeyser's critical reputation, "Had a man of her class and background put forth this kind of lifework in scholarship and theory along with poetry, would it be so difficult to embrace his achievement, to reach him?" ("Beginners" 18).

3. The feminist interest in Whitman is not limited to the contemporary period, or

168   NOTES TO PAGES 110–113

even the twentieth century. As Harold Aspiz writes, the nineteenth-century feminist figure Eliza W. Farmham, author of *Woman and Her Era* (1864), quotes Whitman (408).

4. Notably, Scott MacPhail cites Ginsberg, Rukeyser, Ostriker, Piercy, and Rich as examples of writers who perceive Whitman as a symbol of personal and national identity, "the vehicle for transforming an inner identification into a public, national one" (134). MacPhail also mentions June Jordan and Gary Schmidgall, who "find in Whitman the means of making the marginal also the national" (152).

5. Albert Gelpi writes that Rich's poetics is one fundamentally of "change," a term that "stitches Adrienne Rich's poetry into a continuity" (138), and that idea of transformation would come to be central to Rich's later poetry.

6. Rich goes on to write about the relief of discovering a "freedom of mind" around the late 1950s in the essay "When We Dead Awaken," which focuses on "Aunt Jennifer's Tigers"—a poem from Rich's first collection that often appears in anthologies but does not necessarily reflect most of Rich's oeuvre, in terms of fixed rhyme and meter: "Aunt Jennifer's tigers, prance across a screen, / Bright topaz denizens of a world of green" (171).

7. Rich's father's father, as she writes, was from "Birmingham, Alabama," and his father's mother, Hattie Rice, was "a Sephardic Jew from Vicksburg, Mississippi" ("Split" 225).

8. In "Motherhood and Daughterhood," Rich describes the personal and sociological history of her relationship to her mother and describes her mother wishing to be a pianist and composer but eventually being compelled to take on domestic duties, like Rich herself. Rich also writes of an erased history of women intellectuals on her mother's side, with her mother and grandmother "a lost writer and a lost composer between them" ("Split" 225).

9. Rich is referring to a traditional law in Judaism (*halacha*), whereby Jewishness is passed through the matrilineal line, not through the patrilineal one, thus representing another level of outsiderness for Rich.

10. Rich also describes becoming increasingly aware of antisemitic encounters in her life and, in retrospect, also her father's life. Rich writes, "I believe that my father's Jewishness profoundly shaped my own identity and our family existence. They were shaped both by external antisemitism and my father's self-hatred, and his Jewish pride" ("Split" 232). Interestingly, Rich states that she reflected on her father's experience of having been Jewish years later, only after discovering the poem by Karl Shapiro that contains the lines, "To hurt the Negro and avoid the Jew / Is the curriculum" (225) (a poem mentioned in chapter 2).

11. In regard to these heteronormative expectations, Rich states, "There was the inveterate romantic heterosexual fantasy, the mother telling the daughter

NOTES TO PAGES 114–116   169

how to attract men (my mother often used the word 'fascinate')" ("Compulsory Heterosexuality" 225).

12. "An Atlas" is rife with Whitman allusions; for example, the very end of Rich's poem, "I know you are reading this poem because there is nothing else / left to read / there where you have landed, stripped as you are" (728), strongly echoes the final verse of "Song of Myself": "Missing me one place, search another, I stop somewhere waiting for you" (79). For further reading on Rich's integrating of Whitman into "Atlas," see Piotr Gwiazda, who writes about Rich incorporating Whitman's poem of America that "functions as both geography and history, offering a panoramic view of 1980s and early 1990s" (165). Also, see Maeera Y. Shreiber, who locates the poem in the context of being a lament of America itself: "Writing in response to the Gulf War crisis, a moment which requires that she question her conviction in 'nation' as a way of configuring community, Rich longs to convey what she knows to be true: that poetry can be a powerful, socially constitutive force" ("'Where'" 309). In section 5, "Atlas" also references Rukeyser's poem "The Book of the Dead" (718).

13. Whitman and Dickinson are likewise described by Rich as representing a type of racial and economic privilege: "Whitman and Dickinson shared this problematic status of being white poets in a century of slavery, wars against the Indians, westward expansion, the Civil War, and the creation of the United States as an Imperial power" ("Beginners" 13). Thus, Whitman and Dickinson are not, according to Rich, without a complicated status themselves, which is another example of how Rich disagrees with Whitman.

14. Rich also recalls "Yom Kippur 1984" as being a departure from the intellectual training in New Criticism that she received in the 1950s, in which a poetic text would be considered "an aesthetic object unrelated to life and history and social circumstances" ("Genesis" 253). For Rich, poetry does not represent this type of detachment from biography, but neither is a poem "a biographical anecdote" (253). In this context, Rich suggests the first line from "Out of Childhood," in Rukeyser's first collection of poems, *Theory of Flight*—"Breathe in experience, breathe out poetry" (253)—as a type of ideal combination.

15. In addition to Whitman, Wordsworth's poem "I Wandered Lonely as a Cloud" also makes an appearance in Rich's seeking out "dialogue" ("Genesis" 256).

16. A few times, Rich compliments Whitman's efforts at inclusion through cataloguing, mentioning this effort as an inspiration for lines in the poem: "That series in my poem—'faggot kicked into the icy river, woman dragged from her stalled car,' and so on—is a kind of Whitmanesque catalogue, naming and evoking the different kinds of people that make up the American landscape, the American city" ("Genesis" 257).

17. Refer to Nissa Parmar for additional insight into how Rich's project is rooted

170   NOTES TO PAGES 116–120

in Whitman's poetry in an effort to "revise" America itself (112). Parmar points out ways in which Rich differs from Whitman, stating that Rich "does not clearly present herself as the hero of her epic" (113). I largely agree with Parmar but would add that Rich was invested in the idea of reshaping Jewishness as well.

18. This idea of Rich's parallel celebration of Whitman's vision while simultaneously recognizing its limits has been noted by other critics, such as Gwiazda, about "An Atlas of the Difficult World": "Like Whitman, whose characteristic technique of catalogue and anecdote she borrows in her poem, Rich recognizes the great promise of America, but also acknowledges its negative elements" (165). Shreiber also states about that poem, "Seeking to write a 'song of the times,' Rich is obliged to both acknowledge a debt and to address his limits" ("'Where'" 314). Finally, Parmar writes that Rich "drew on Whitman's democratic multiculturalism, but she re-visioned the poet and his poetic as, in her words, 'a paradigm of "New" "World" masculinity'" (110).

19. All poems quoted by Adrienne Rich are from *Collected Poems: 1950–2012* unless otherwise stated.

20. As Wendy Martin and Annalisa Zox-Weaver have observed, "[Rich] would face the given world through poetry and social action, through poetry *as* social action" (410). One can extend this notion to Rich's engagement with poetry as political action in a Jewish context, in line with the projects of the women poets Rukeyser, Ostriker, and Rich, as well as other poets, such as Reznikoff, whose Jewish Objectivist poetics was informed strongly by a Whitmanesque seeing of the Other, as described in chapter 1.

21. The poem was composed to honor the suicide of Alfred Conrad, Rich's former husband (cited in Shreiber, "'Where'" 315).

22. In Rich's own notes for *An Atlas of the Difficult World*, there is one for "Tattered Kaddish," in which Rich quotes a main figure of Kabbalistic thought, Moses Cordovero. This quote provided by Rich seems to point to a creative link between femininity, Torah, and renewal and perhaps an inspiration for "Tattered Kaddish": "Malkhut is called the Apple Field, and She grows sprouts of secrets and new meanings of Torah. Those who constantly create new interpretations of Torah are the ones who reap Her" (Cordovero, Or ha-Hammah on Zohar III, 106a, qtd. in *Collected Poems* 1134). I would add that one way by which Rich "reaps" new meanings in her Jewish-themed poems is also though Whitman.

23. Ostriker states elsewhere that Whitman is an example, with William Blake, of a breakdown in the duality of male and female: "[T]he mind-body dichotomy [the masculine/feminine dichotomy] is stupid. It's old, it's philosophically enshrined, but it's stupid. Mind and reason aren't superior to emotion and the body. Read Blake, who was the first poet in the English language to say this in poetic form. Read

Whitman. And men are not in fact particularly rational, nor are women in fact particularly emotional. These are myths" (Pacernick 227).

24. Occasionally, statements by critics about Ostriker's poetry and ideology indirectly call Whitman to mind, such as with Martha Nell Smith, who claims, "Alicia is all about connectedness, connectedness to the world and each and every one of us" ("Introduction" 3).

25. Often the speakers in Ostriker's poem report from the position of outsider-witness, exemplified in the poem "Fix": "The puzzled ones, the Americans, go through their lives / Buying what they are told to buy, / Pursuing their love affairs with the automobile" (*No Heaven* 108–109). Here, the third-person pronoun "they" refers to an "Other"—Americans—meaning the speaker herself is not one of them. The speaker only references a collective American "us" when she writes about the white self among "immigrant faces" and the "blacks, whose faces are hurt and proud" (109).

26. For other critical responses to Ostriker, see Costello; Dame; Jelen; Kirkpatrick; Smith and Enszer; and Zierler.

27. See chapter 5 of *Stealing the Language* for another discussion by Ostriker of how women's poetry is "most indebted to Whitman" ("Loving" 37).

28. For example, though "Walker in the City" mentions poets such as Blake, Lorca, and Leroy Jones, and not Whitman, Ostriker's "Walker" can also be seen as in dialogue with Jewish poets and writers, like Alfred Kazin, Charles Reznikoff, and Allen Ginsberg.

29. Emma Lazarus's ubiquitous lines from "The New Colossus" are: "Here at our sea-washed, sunset gates / shall stand a mighty woman with a torch, whose flame / Is the imprisoned lightning, and her name / Mother of Exiles" (58).

30. Ostriker indicates that this poem is written in a form invented by the poet Terence Hayes, in which the last word of each line follows an original poem or line of poetry, in that same order (*Waiting* 81). Ostriker indeed is following the words of the epigraph by Gwendolyn Brooks: "We are things of dry hours and the involuntary plan. / Greyed in a grey. 'Dream' makes a giddy sound, not strong / Like feeding a husband, satisfying a man" (19).

31. Israel is assumed to be the perpetrator of the violence described in the lines, though it is never named explicitly.

32. Though there is an allusion to cremation, which is prohibited in all streams of Judaism, the mother is identified as Jewish in section 7 of the poem: "What drove her crazy, what wasted her beauty and intellect, was it America, / The *goldene medina* just a joke" (134).

33. One encounters a similar Whitmanesque catalogue later in section 2, as the speaker describes attempting to survive the grief or "extended drought" brought on

172 NOTES TO PAGES 129–131

by the confluence of these individual and collective traumas: "I want my language to be like / The desert. My words and phrases to be like ocotillo, yucca, saguaro. / Prickly. Thorny" (118). Ostriker's "grammar" of the American desert plants calls to mind Whitman's language in "Passage to India": "I cross the Laramie plains, I note the rocks in grotesque shapes, the buttes, / I see the plentiful larkspur and wild onions, the barren, colorless, sage-deserts" (317).

34. Ostriker herself has written about "Song of Myself" as being a poem about interrelationships: "Whitman's poetic method at its best. . . . Describing (inventing) a scene (or fantasy) of masturbation, or of lovemaking with another person, or of mystical communication—it is impossible to tell which, the point is that such scenes are interchangeable and equivalent, just as 'I' and 'the other I am' and 'you' stand in poised balance" ("Loving" 27).

35. In this context of interrelationships, Ostriker also cites Coleridge in a passage from *Biographia Literaria*: "The primary IMAGINATION I hold to be the living Power and prime Agent of human perception, and as a repetition in the finite mind of the eternal act of creation in the infinite I AM" ("Loving" 37).

36. Section 2 of "Elegy" also seems to echo "Beat! Beat! Drums!" from *Drum-Taps*, where Whitman famously begins, "Beat! beat! drums!—blow! bugles! blow!" (222). In turn, Ostriker's poem reads, "Beat on our membranes hard / And let us be drums. Artillery / Will always outshout us, testosterone explosions / Are more thrilling than anything" (119). The adoption by Ostriker of Whitman in this context (with an ironic "thrilling") can be read as a subtle critique of Whitman's nineteenth-century poems that seem to celebrate war in America.

37. The poems quoted in this chapter by Marge Piercy are from *Circles on the Water: Selected Poems of Marge Piercy*, unless otherwise indicated.

38. See discussions of Piercy's feminist work, such as Anolik and Booker.

39. In 2015, I had the distinct pleasure to interview Piercy for *The Rumpus*, following the publication of Piercy's 2015 collection, *Made in Detroit*. As Piercy states about growing up Jewish in Detroit, "Detroit formed me in many ways. Everything was visible, the concentric rings starting with poverty going out to the fancy houses of the wealthy. I was not white as a child. Jews were not white then. After the first couple of years in the old Jewish neighborhood where we shared an apartment with another couple where the husband was also out of work, my father was rehired by Westinghouse and bought a house (asbestos siding, very small but with a yard that had one of those huge beautiful elms that had been planted all over Detroit then) at auction from a bank that had foreclosed on it in a neighborhood that was white or black by blocks. Anti-Semitism, racism, enmities between nationalities, all were out in the open and blatant" (Barnat, "Rumpus").

40. Piercy's employment of Whitman can absolutely be read through

what Deborah Dash Moore and Andrew Bush claim about the appeal of Reconstructionist Judaism in America: "Reconstructionism's easy egalitarianism, participatory congregations, and openness to experimentation often attracted American Jews who were disaffected with Jewish life" (149). Whitman would then represent both an "openness and experimentation" in Piercy's Jewish American poetics.

41. The issue included contributions about Whitman by a diverse group of poets, such as A. R. Ammons, Allen Ginsberg, Yusef Komunyakaa, Mary Oliver, and Stanley Plumly. Ginsberg includes the poem "I Love Old Whitman So."

42. Though I focus on the particularities of Whitman in Piercy's prayer-poems, Whitmanesque long lines, catalogues, and a prominent first-person speaker are found in other collections by Piercy, like *Breaking Camp* (1968), *Hard Loving* (1969), *To Be of Use* (1973), *Made in Detroit* (2020), and *On the Way Out, Turn Off the Light* (2020). "Without Whitman," Piercy states, "I would not have had a strong foundation on which to build my later practice" ("How I Came" 99).

43. Other poems in the *Teffilah* section are revisions of already existing Jewish prayers, such as "S'hema" and "Kaddish" (more along the lines of Rich's "Tattered Kaddish").

44. The English translation of the Jewish "Nishmat Kol Hai" prayer, in translation by Rabbi Zalman Schachter-Shalomi, begins as follows: "All breathing life / adores Your Name / Yah, our God— / All flesh alive / is raised to ecstasy / each time we become aware of you!" The version of the full Nishmat Kol Hai prayer appears in *The Open Siddur Project* (https://opensiddur.org).

45. The poem "Praise in Spite of It All" was first published in *LIPS* (spring 2017).

CONCLUSION: THE ENDURING JEWISH AMERICAN WALT WHITMAN

1. As Anthony Julius elucidates, antisemitic sentiments are pervasive in the poetry and prose of T. S. Eliot. Julius reveals how Eliot "is able to place his anti-Semitism in service of his art" (11) and writes of the enmeshment of Modernism and antisemitism in the context of Eliot's poem "Sweeney Among the Nightingales" and other texts.

2. Karen Alkalay-Gut has stated that Jewish American poets perceive "English language and/or American culture as a tool to be used and examined, rather than an absolute or automatic lens through which to observe the world" ("Jewish American Poetry" 1168). In line with Alkalay-Gut, I would claim that Whitman's poetics (a mode of language) is thereby one of these "tools" that Jewish American poets employ to engage with English language and American culture.

3. Much of C. K. Williams's poetic oeuvre is not predominantly Jewish themed; however, there are exceptions, like the poems "A Day for Anne Frank," "Spit," "Bialystock, or Lvov," "Jews," and "After Auschwitz." An engagement with Jewishness is a central (and often poignant) theme of Williams's memoir *Misgivings: My Mother, My Father, Myself.*

4. See also a new book by Reagan M. Sova, *Wildcat Dreams in the Death Light*, in which the main speaker and protagonist references Whitman and *Leaves of Grass.*

5. The mission statement for Congregation Beit Simchat Torah appears on the website: https://cbst.org/About/Mission.

WORKS CITED

Alexie, Sherman. "Defending Walt Whitman." *Beloit Poetry Journal*, vol. 66, no. 3–4, 2016, pp. 30–31.

Alkalay-Gut, Karen. "Jewish American Poetry." *The Greenwood Encyclopedia of American Multiethnic Literature*, edited by Emanuel S. Nelson, Greenwood Press, 2005, pp. 1168–1174.

———. "The Poem and the Place: How Poetry in the Alien Language of English Exists in Israel." *Lyre*, forthcoming 2023.

Allen, Gay Wilson, and Ed Folsom, editors. *Walt Whitman & the World*. U of Iowa P, 1995.

Alter, Robert. *Defenses of the Imagination: Jewish Writers and Modern Historical Crisis*. Jewish Publication Society of America, 1977.

Anolik, Ruth Bienstock. "Appropriating the Golem: Female Retellings of Jewish Tales." *Modern Language Studies*, vol. 3, no. 2, 2001, 39–55.

Aspiz, Harold. "An Early Feminist Tribute to Whitman." *American Literature*, vol. 51, no. 3, 1979, pp. 404–409.

Asselineau, Roger. "Transcendentalism." *Walt Whitman: An Encyclopedia*, edited by J. R. Lemaster and Donald D. Kummings, Garland Publishing, 1998, pp. 737–739.

Auster, Paul. "The Decisive Moment." *Charles Reznikoff: Man and Poet*, edited by Milton Hindus, National Poetry Foundation, 1984, pp. 151–165.

Axelrod, Steven G. "The Middle Generation and WWII: Jarrell, Shapiro, Brooks, Bishop, Lowell." *War, Literature, and the Arts*, vol. 11, no. 1, 1999, pp. 1–41.

Barnat, Dara. "'Beyond Religions and Even Beyond Mankind': Karl Shapiro's Jewish Walt Whitman." *Walt Whitman Quarterly Review*, vol. 31, 2014, pp. 107–122.

———. "'I Followed Whitman Through Half of Camden': Gerald Stern, Walt Whitman, and Jewish American Identity." *Insane Devotion: On the Writing of*

Gerald Stern, edited by Mihaela Moscaliuc, Trinity UP, 2016, pp. 74–83.

———. "The Rumpus Interview with Marge Piercy." *The Rumpus*, June 2, 2015, https://therumpus.net/2015/06/the-rumpus-interview-with-marge-piercy/.

———. "Walt Whitman and Jewish American Poetry: Charles Reznikoff and Allen Ginsberg." *The Oxford Handbook of Walt Whitman*, edited by Kenneth M. Price and Stefan Schöberlein, Oxford UP, forthcoming.

———. "'Women and Poets See the Truth Arrive': Muriel Rukeyser and Walt Whitman." *Studies in American Jewish Literature*, vol. 34, no. 1, 2015, pp. 94–116, https://doi.org/10.5325/studamerjewilite.34.1.0094.

Barnes, David. "Fascist Aesthetics: Ezra Pound's Cultural Negotiations in 1930s Italy." *Journal of Modern Literature*, vol. 34, no. 1, 2010, pp. 19–35.

Barron, Jonathan N., and Eric M. Selinger, editors. *Jewish American Poetry: Poems, Commentary, and Reflections*. Brandeis UP, 2000.

Barthes, Roland. "Theory of the Text." *Untying the Text: A Poststructuralist Reader*, edited by Robert Young, Routledge & Kegan Paul, 1981, pp. 31–47.

Ben-Porat, Ziva. "The Poetics of Literary Allusion." *PTL*, vol. 1, no. 1, 1976, pp. 105–128.

Bernstein, Charles. *A Poetics*. Harvard UP, 1992.

———. "Solidarity Is the Name We Give to What We Cannot Hold." *All the Whiskey in Heaven: Selected Poems*, Farrar, Straus and Giroux, 2010, pp. 223–225.

Berrol, Selma C. "In Their Image: German Jews and the Americanization of the *Ost Juden* in New York City." *New York History*, vol. 63, no. 4, 1982, pp. 417–422.

Biale, David, Michael Galchinsky, and Susannah Heschel, editors. *Insider/Outsider: American Jews and Multiculturalism*. U of California P, 1998.

Bickford, Donna M. *Understanding Marge Piercy*. U of South Carolina P, 2019.

Bloom, Harold. "The Sorrows of American-Jewish Poetry." *Commentary Magazine*, vol. 53, no. 3, 1972, https://www.commentary.org/articles/commentary-bk/the -sorrows-of-american-jewish-poetry/.

———. "Walt Whitman as Center of the American Canon." *The Western Canon: The Book and School of the Ages*, Harcourt Brace & Company, 1994, pp. 264–290.

Booker, M. Keith. "Woman on the Edge of a Genre: The Feminist Dystopias of Marge Piercy." *Science Fiction Studies*, vol. 21, no. 3, 1994, pp. 337–350.

Breslin, James. "Whitman and the Development of Early William Carlos Williams." *PMLA*, vol. 82, no. 7, 1967, pp. 613–621.

Burt, Stephanie. "Song." *New Literary History*, vol. 50, no. 3, 2019, pp. 339–344.

CAConrad. "From Whitman to Walmart." Poetry Foundation, June 8, 2015, www.poetryfoundation.org/harriet-books/2015/06/from-whitman-to-walmart.

Carruth, Hayden. "A Salute in Time." *Seriously Meeting Karl Shapiro*, edited by Sue B. Walker, Negative Capability Press, 1993, pp. 3–5.

WORKS CITED 177

Cederstrom, Lorelei. "Walt Whitman and the Imagists." *Walt Whitman of Mickle Street*, edited by Geoffrey M. Sill, U of Tennessee P, 1994, pp. 205–223.

Chametsky, Jules, John Felstiner, Hilene Flanzbaum, and Kathryn Hellerstein, editors. *Jewish American Literature: A Norton Anthology*. W. W. Norton & Company, 2001.

Chari, V. K. "Whitman Criticism in the Light of Indian Poetics." *Whitman: The Centennial Essays*, edited by Ed Folsom, U of Iowa P, 1994, pp. 240–250.

Chari, V. K. "Whitman in India." *Walt Whitman & the World*, edited by Gay Wilson Allen and Ed Folsom, U of Iowa P, 1995, pp. 396–405.

Chinitz, David. "'Arm the Paper Arm': Kenneth Koch's Postmodern Comedy." *The Scene of My Selves: New Work on New School Poets*, edited by Terence Diggory and Stephen P. Miller, National Poetry Foundation, 2001, pp. 311–326.

Clune, Michael. "The Hatred of Poetry: An Interview with Ben Lerner." *Paris Review*, June 2016, www.theparisreview.org/blog/2016/06/30/the-hatred-of -poetry-an-interview-with-ben-lerner/.

Costello, Bonnie. "Response to Alicia Ostriker." *Contemporary Literature*, vol. 30, no. 3, 1989, pp. 465–469.

Couser, G. Thomas. "Of Time and Identity: Walt Whitman and Gertrude Stein as Autobiographers." *Texas Studies in Literature and Language*, vol. 17, no. 5, 1976, pp. 787–804.

Dame, Enid. "A Paradoxical Prophet: Women Poets Re-Imagine Miriam." *Bridges*, vol. 12, no. 1, 2007, pp. 4–14.

Daniel, Robert W. "Paleface and Redskin." *Sewanee Review*, vol. 84, no. 3, 1976, xc– xcii.

Daniels, Kate. "Muriel Rukeyser and Her Literary Critics." *Gendered Modernisms: American Women Poets and Their Readers*, edited by Margaret Dickie and Thomas Travisano, U of Pennsylvania P, 1996, pp. 247–263.

Dayton, Tim. *Muriel Rukeyser's "The Book of the Dead."* U of Missouri P, 2003.

Dembo, L. S., and Charles Reznikoff. "Charles Reznikoff." *Contemporary Literature*, vol. 10, no. 2, 1969, pp. 193–202.

Diggory, Terrence. "Community 'Intimate' or 'Inoperative': New York School Poets and Politics from Paul Goodman to Jean-Luc Nancy." *The Scene of My Selves: New Work on New School Poets*, edited by Terence Diggory and Stephen P. Miller, National Poetry Foundation, 2001, pp. 13–32.

Diggory, Terence, and Stephen P. Miller, editors. *The Scene of My Selves: New Work on New School Poets*. National Poetry Foundation, 2001.

Duckworth, Alistair M. "Karl Shapiro's 'University' and the Ideology of Place." *Seriously Meeting Karl Shapiro*, edited by Sue B. Walker, Negative Capability Press, 1993, pp. 10–27.

WORKS CITED

DuPlessis, Rachel Blau. *Genders, Races and Religious Cultures in Modern American Poetry*. Cambridge UP, 2001.

DuPlessis, Rachel Blau, and Peter Quartermain, editors. *The Objectivist Nexus: Essays in Cultural Poetics*. U of Alabama P, 1999.

Eberly, David. "A Serpent in the Grass: Reading Walt Whitman and Frank O'Hara." *The Continuing Presence of Walt Whitman: The Life After the Life*, edited by Robert K. Martin, U of Iowa P, 1992, pp. 69–81.

Emerson, Ralph Waldo. "The Poet." *Poetry*, 1844, www.poetryfoundation.org/articles/69389/from-the-poet.

Erickson, Peter. "Singing America: From Walt Whitman to Adrienne Rich." *Kenyon Review*, vol. 17, no. 1, 1995, pp. 103–119.

Erkkila, Betsy. "'To Paris with My Love': *Walt Whitman Among the French* Revisited." *Celebrating Walt Whitman: Leaves of Grass 1855–2005*, special issue of *Revue française d'études américaines*, vol. 108, 2006, pp. 7–22.

———. *Walt Whitman Among the French*. Princeton UP, 1980.

Feldman, Irving. *Collected Poems: 1954–2004*. Schocken Books, 2004.

Fiedler, Leslie A. *An End to Innocence*. Stein and Day, 1971.

Finkelstein, Norman. *Not One of Them in Place: Modern Poetry and Jewish American Identity*. SUNY P, 2001.

———. "Tradition and Modernity, Judaism and Objectivism: The Poetry of Charles Reznikoff." *The Objectivist Nexus: Essays in Cultural Poetics*, edited by Rachel Blau DuPlessis and Peter Quartermain, U of Alabama P, 1999, pp. 191–209.

Flanzbaum, Hilene. "The Imaginary Jew and the American Poet." *ELH*, vol. 65, no. 1, 1998, 259–275.

Flynn, Richard. "'The Buried Life and the Body of Waking': Muriel Rukeyser and the Politics of Literary History." *Gendered Modernisms: American Women Poets and Their Readers*, edited by Margaret Dickie and Thomas Travisano, U of Pennsylvania P, 1996, pp. 264–279.

Folsom, Ed. "Talking Back to Walt Whitman: An Introduction." *Walt Whitman: The Measure of His Song*, 2nd ed., edited by Jim Perlman, Ed Folsom, and Dan Campion, Holy Cow! Press, 2014, pp. 21–75.

———. *Walt Whitman's Native Representations*. Cambridge UP, 1994.

———, editor. *Whitman: The Centennial Essays*. U of Iowa P, 1994.

Folsom, Ed, and Gay Wilson Allen. "Introduction: 'Salut au Monde!'" *Walt Whitman & the World*, edited by Gay Wilson Allen and Ed Folsom, U of Iowa P, 1995, 1–10.

Frame, Anthony. "10 Great Poetry Collections You Might Have Missed." *Chicago Review of Books*, December 2019, https://chireviewofbooks.com/2019/12/04/10-great-poetry-collections-you-might-have-missed/.

Fredman, Stephen. "'And All Now Is War': George Oppen, Charles Olson, and the Problem of Literary Generations." *The Objectivist Nexus: Essays in Cultural*

Poetics, edited by Rachel Blau DuPlessis and Peter Quartermain, U of Alabama P, 1999, pp. 286–293.

———. *A Menorah for Athena: Charles Reznikoff and the Jewish Dilemmas of Objectivist Poetry*. U of Chicago P, 2001.

Gardinier, Suzanne. "'A World That Will Hold All the People': On Muriel Rukeyser." *Kenyon Review*, vol. 14, no. 3, 1992, pp. 88–105.

Gelpi, Albert. *American Poetry After Modernism: The Power of the Word*. Cambridge UP, 2015.

Ginsberg, Allen. *Allen Ginsberg: Collected Poems 1947–1980*. Penguin Books, 1987.

———. "Allen Ginsberg on Walt Whitman: Composed on the Tongue." *Walt Whitman: The Measure of His Song*, 2nd ed., edited by Jim Perlman, Ed Folsom, and Dan Campion, Holy Cow! Press, 2014, pp. 329–352.

———. *Iron Curtain Journals: January–May 1965*. Edited by Michael Schumacher, U of Minnesota P, 2018.

———. "Reznikoff's Poetics." *Charles Reznikoff: Man and Poet*, edited by Milton Hindus, National Poetry Foundation, 1984, pp. 139–150.

Gold, Michael. *Jews Without Money*. *Jewish American Literature: A Norton Anthology*, edited by Jules Chametzky, John Felstiner, Hilene Flanzbaum, and Kathryn Hellerstein, W. W. Norton & Company, 2001, pp. 357–362.

———. "Ode to Walt Whitman." *Walt Whitman: The Measure of His Song*, 2nd ed., edited by Jim Perlman, Ed Folsom, and Dan Campion, Holy Cow! Press, 2014, pp. 168–171.

Gray, Timothy. "Fun City: Kenneth Koch Among Schoolchildren." *Texas Studies in Literature and Language*, vol. 51, no. 2, 2009, pp. 223–262.

Greenblatt, Stephen, and Giles Gunn, editors. *Redrawing the Boundaries: The Transformation of English and American Literary Studies*. Modern Language Association, 1992.

Greenspan, Ezra. "Whitman in Israel." *Walt Whitman & the World*, edited by Gay Wilson Allen and Ed Folsom, U of Iowa P, 1995, pp. 386–395.

Grossman, Allen. "The Jew as an American Poet: The Instance of Ginsberg." *The Long Schoolroom: Lessons in the Bitter Logic of the Poetic Principle*, U of Michigan P, 1997, pp. 150–167.

Grünzweig, Walter. *Constructing the German Walt Whitman*. U of Iowa P, 1994.

———. "'For America—For All the Earth': Walt Whitman as an International(ist) Poet." *Breaking Bounds: Whitman and American Cultural Studies*, edited by Betsy Erkkila and Jay Grossman, Oxford UP, 1996, pp. 238–250.

———. "'Inundated by This Mississippi of Poetry': Walt Whitman and German Expressionism." *Walt Whitman of Mickle Street*, edited by Geoffrey M. Sill, U of Tennessee P, 1994, pp. 224–256.

180 WORKS CITED

——. "'Teach Me Your Rhythm': The Poetics of German Lyrical Responses to Whitman." *Walt Whitman: The Centennial Essays*, edited by Ed Folsom, U of Iowa P, 1994, pp. 226–239.

Gwiazda, Piotr. "'Nothing Else Left to Read': Poetry and Audience in Adrienne Rich's 'An Atlas of a Difficult World.'" *Journal of Modern Literature*, vol. 28, no. 2, 2005, pp. 165–188.

Harshav, Benjamin, and Barbara Harshav. *American Yiddish Poetry: A Bilingual Anthology*. U of California P, 1986.

Heller, Michael. *Exigent Futures: New and Selected Poems*. Salt Publishing, 2003.

Herzog, Anne F. "'Anything Away from Anything': Muriel Rukeyser's Relational Poetics." *"How Shall We Tell Each Other of the Poet?": The Life and Writing of Muriel Rukeyser*, edited by Anne F. Herzog and Janet E. Kaufman, St. Martin's Press, 1999, pp. 32–44.

Herzog, Anne F., and Janet E. Kaufman, editors. *"How Shall We Tell Each Other of the Poet?": The Life and Writing of Muriel Rukeyser*. St. Martin's Press, 1999.

Hindus, Milton. *Charles Reznikoff: A Critical Essay*. Black Sparrow Press, 1977.

——, editor. *Charles Reznikoff: Man and Poet*. National Poetry Foundation, 1984.

Hirsch, Edward. "Whitman Leaves the Boardwalk." *TriQuarterly*, vol. 114, 2002, p. 185.

Hogue, Cynthia. "On Ethical Poetics: The Example of Alicia Ostriker." *Everywoman Her Own Theology: On the Poetry of Alicia Suskin Ostriker*, edited by Martha Nell Smith and Julie R. Enszer, U of Michigan P, 2018, pp. 106–116.

Hollander, John, editor. *Emma Lazarus: Selected Poems*. Library of America, 2005.

——. "The Question of American Jewish Poetry." *What Is Jewish Literature?*, edited by Hana Wirth-Nesher, Jewish Publication Society, 1994, pp. 36–52.

Hutchinson, George. "The Whitman Legacy and the Harlem Renaissance." *Whitman: The Centennial Essays*, edited by Ed Folsom, U of Iowa P, 1994, pp. 201–216.

Jackson, Brian. "Modernist Looking: Surreal Impressions in the Poetry of Allen Ginsberg." *Texas Studies in Literature and Language*, vol. 52, no. 3, 2010, pp. 298–323.

Jelen, Sheila E. "Reading and Writing Women: Minority Discourse in Feminist Jewish Literary Studies." *Prooftexts*, vol. 25, no. 1–2, 2005, pp. 195–209.

Jennison, Ruth. "Combining Uneven Developments: Louis Zukofsky and the Political Economy of Revolutionary Modernism." *Cultural Critique*, vol. 77, 2011, pp. 146–179.

Jordan, June. "For the Sake of People's Poetry: Walt Whitman and the Rest of Us." Poetry Foundation, Aug. 15, 2006, www.poetryfoundation.org/journal/article .html?id=178489.

WORKS CITED 181

Julius, Anthony. *T. S. Eliot, Anti-Semitism, and Literary Form.* Cambridge UP, 1995.

Kalaidjian, Walter. "Muriel Rukeyser and the Poetics of Specific Critique: Rereading 'The Book of the Dead.'" *Cultural Critique*, vol. 20, 1991, pp. 65–88.

Katz, Wendy. "Untying the Immigrant Tongue: Whitman and the Americanization of Anzia Yezierska." *Walt Whitman Quarterly Review*, vol. 21, 2004, pp. 155–165.

Kaufman, Janet. "'But Not the Study': Writing as Jew." *"How Shall We Tell Each Other of the Poet?": The Life and Writing of Muriel Rukeyser*, edited by Anne F. Herzog and Janet E. Kaufman, St. Martin's Press, 1999, pp. 45–61.

Kazin, Alfred. "Under Forty." *Contemporary Jewish Record*, vol. 7, no. 1, 1944, pp. 9–12.

Kertesz, Louise. *The Poetic Vision of Muriel Rukeyser.* Louisiana State UP, 1980.

Kirkpatrick, Kathryn J. "Poetry Matters." *NWSA Journal*, vol. 14, no. 1, 2002, pp. 185–195.

Koch, Kenneth. "The Art of Poetry." *The Art of Poetry: Poems, Parodies, Interviews, Essays, and Other Work*, edited by David Lehman, U of Michigan P, 1996, pp. 1–15.

———. *The Collected Poems of Kenneth Koch.* Alfred A. Knopf, 2005.

———. "Educating the Imagination." *The Art of Poetry: Poems, Parodies, Interviews, Essays, and Other Work*, edited by David Lehman, U of Michigan P, 1996, pp. 153–167.

———. "An Interview with Jordan Davis." *The Art of Poetry: Poems, Parodies, Interviews, Essays, and Other Work*, edited by David Lehman, U of Michigan P, 1996, pp. 187–214.

———. "A Note on Frank O'Hara in the Early Fifties." *The Art of Poetry: Poems, Parodies, Interviews, Essays, and Other Work*, edited by David Lehman, U of Michigan P, 1996, pp. 19–22.

———. "Whitman's Words." *The Teachers and Writers Guide to Walt Whitman*, edited by Ron Padgett, Teachers and Writers Collaborative, 1991, pp. 36–39.

———. "Writing for the Stage—An Interview with Allen Ginsberg." *The Art of Poetry: Poems, Parodies, Interviews, Essays, and Other Work*, edited by David Lehman, U of Michigan P, 1996, pp. 176–185.

Kohler, Dayton. "Karl Shapiro: Poet in Uniform." *College English*, vol. 7, no. 5, 1946, pp. 243–249.

Kramer, Aaron. "1881: Whitman's Impact on American Jewish Poetry." *Paumanok Rising: An Anthology of Eastern Long Island Aesthetics*, edited by Vince Clemente and Graham Everett, Street Press, 1981, pp. 15–20.

Kronfeld, Chana. "Intertextual Agency, Translation, and the Construction of Poetic Subjectivity." Conference in Honor of Ziva Ben-Porat, Tel Aviv University, May 2006, Tel Aviv, Israel, Conference Presentation.

—— . *On the Margins of Modernism*. U of California P, 1993.

Kumin, Maxine. *The Long Marriage: Poems*. W. W. Norton & Company, 2003.

Ladin, Joy. "Ours for the Making: Trans Lit, Trans Poetics." *Lambda Literary*, December 2011, https://lambdaliterary.org/2011/12/ours-for-the-making-trans -lit-trans-poetics/.

—— . "'What I Assume You Shall Assume': Democracy, the First Leaves of Grass, and the Future of American Poetry." *The Poetry of Walt Whitman: New Critical Perspectives*, edited by Kanwar Dinesh Singh, Atlantic Publishers and Distributors, 2009, pp. 14–31.

Lauridsen, Inger Thorup, and Per Dalgard. *The Beat Generation and the Russian New Wave*. Ardis, 1990.

Lazarus, Emma. *Emma Lazarus: Selected Poems*, edited by John Hollander, Library of America, 2005.

Lehman, David. *The Last Avant-Garde: The Making of the New School of Poets*. Anchor, 1999.

Lerner, Ben. "On Disliking Poetry." *London Review of Books*, vol. 37, no. 12, June 2015, pp. 42–43.

—— . *10:04*. Picador, 2015.

Levi, Jan Heller, editor. *A Muriel Rukeyser Reader*. W. W. Norton & Company, 1995.

Levine, Herbert. "The Voice We Need Now: Whitman at 200." Tikkun, May 2019, www.tikkun.org/the-voice-we-need-now-whitman-at-200/.

Levinson, Julian. *Exiles on Main Street: Jewish American Writers and American Literary Culture*. Indiana UP, 2008.

—— . "The Seventh Angel Woke Me: Adah Isaacs Menken and the Return of the Israelite Prophecy." *Studies in American Jewish Literature*, vol. 33, no. 1, 2014, pp. 147–165.

Li, Xilao. "Whitman and Ethnicity." *Walt Whitman of Mickle Street*, edited by Geoffrey M. Sill, U of Tennessee P, 1995, pp. 122–109.

Lundquist, Sarah. "The Fifth Point of a Star: Barbara Guest and the New York 'School' of Poets." *Women's Studies*, vol. 30, no. 1, 2001, pp. 11–41.

Lyons, Bonnie. "An Interview with Marge Piercy." *Contemporary Literature*, vol. 48, no. 3, 2007, pp. 327–344.

—— . "Marge Piercy, Jewish Poet." *Studies in American Jewish Literature*, vol. 27, 2008, pp. 34–39.

MacPhail, Scott. "Lyric Nationalism: Whitman, American Studies, and the New Criticism." *Texas Studies in Literature and Language*, vol. 22, no. 1, 2002, pp. 133–160.

Malkoff, Karl. "The Self in the Modern World: Karl Shapiro's Jewish Poems." *Contemporary American-Jewish Literature*, edited by Irving Malin, Indiana UP,

1973, pp. 213–228.

Martin, Robert K., editor. *The Continuing Presence of Walt Whitman: The Life After the Life.* U of Iowa P, 1992.

Martin, Wendy, and Annalisa Zox-Weaver. "Adrienne Rich: The Poet of Witness." *The Cambridge Companion to American Poets*, edited by Mark Richardson, Cambridge UP, 2015, 409–424.

Menken, Adah Isaacs. "Myself." *Jewish American Literature: A Norton Anthology*, edited by Jules Chametsky, John Felstiner, Hilene Flanzbaum, and Kathryn Hellerstein, W. W. Norton & Company, 2001, pp. 90–91.

———. "Swimming Against the Current." *Sunday Mercury*, 1860, p. 1.

Middlebrook, Diane. "Making Visible the Common World: Walt Whitman and Feminist Poetry." *Kenyon Review*, vol. 2, no. 4, 1980, pp. 14–27.

Miller, James E., Jr. *The American Quest for Supreme Fiction: Whitman's Legacy in the Personal Epic.* U of Chicago P, 1979.

———. "Karl Shapiro in Nebraska." *Seriously Meeting Karl Shapiro*, edited by Sue B. Walker, Negative Capability Press, 1993, pp. 45–47.

———. "Whitman's Multitudinous Poetic Progeny: Particular and Puzzling Instances." *Whitman: The Centennial Essays*, edited by Ed Folsom, U of Iowa P, 1994, pp. 185–200.

Miller, James E., Jr., Karl Shapiro, and Bernice Slote, editors. *Start with the Sun: Studies in the Whitman Tradition*, U of Nebraska P, 1960.

Miller, Louis. *Lider fun bukh: "Bletlekh groz."* Yiddish Cooperative Book League of the Yiddish International Workers Order, 1940.

Miller, Matt. "Getting the Joke in 'Of Being Numerous': George Oppen as Heir to Walt Whitman's Public Poetics." *Resources for American Literary Study*, vol. 37, 2014, pp. 153–180.

———. "Makings of Americans: Whitman and Stein's Poetics of Inclusion." *Arizona Quarterly*, vol. 65, no. 3, 2009, pp. 39–59.

Miller, Stephen P. "Relentlessly Going On and On: How Jews Remade Modern Poetry Without Even Trying." *Radical Poetics and Secular Jewish Culture*, edited by Stephen P. Miller and Daniel Morris, U of Alabama P, 2010, pp. 343–353.

Miller, Stephen P., and Daniel Morris, editors. *Radical Poetics and Secular Jewish Culture*, U of Alabama P, 2010.

Minot, Leslie A. "'Kodak as You Go': The Photographic Metaphor in the Work of Muriel Rukeyser." *"How Shall We Tell Each Other of the Poet?": The Life and Writing of Muriel Rukeyser*, edited by Anne F. Herzog and Janet E. Kaufman, St. Martin's Press, 1999, pp. 264–276.

Mishler, Peter. "In Conversation with Jorie Graham." Literary Hub, February 2018, https://lithub.com/in-conversation-with-jorie-graham/.

184 WORKS CITED

Mitchell, Felicia. "Marge Piercy." *Dictionary of Literary Biography: American Poets Since WWII*, edited by R. S. Gwynn, Gale Group, 1992, pp. 248–253.

Moore, Deborah Dash, and Andrew Bush. "Mitzvah, Gender, and Reconstructionist Judaism." *Women Remaking American Judaism*, edited by Riv-Ellen Prell, Wayne State UP, 2007, pp. 135–152.

Mort, Jo-Ann. "The Poetry of Muriel Rukeyser." *Jewish Quarterly*, vol. 28, no. 4, 1980–1981, pp. 20–21.

Nadler, Steven. "Baruch Spinoza." *Stanford Encyclopedia of Philosophy*, https://plato .stanford.edu/entries/spinoza/.

Norich, Anita. "Jewish Literatures and Cultures: Context and Intertext." *Jewish Literatures and Cultures: Context and Intertext*, edited by Anita Norich and Yaron Z. Eliav, Brown Judaic Studies, 2008, pp. 1–8.

Norich, Anita, and Yaron Z. Eliav, editors. *Jewish Literatures and Cultures: Context and Intertext*. Brown Judaic Studies, 2008.

November, Yehoshua. "Foreword." *101 Jewish Poems for the Third Millennium*, edited by Matthew E. Silverman and Nancy Naomi Carlson, Ashland Poetry Press, 2021, xi–xv.

O'Hara, Frank. "Another Word on Kenneth Koch." *Poetry Magazine*, vol. 85, no. 6, 1955, pp. 349–351.

Omer-Sherman, Ranen. *Diaspora and Zionism in Jewish American Literature*. Brandeis UP, 2002.

———. "Emma Lazarus, Jewish American Poetics, and the Challenge of Modernity." *Legacy*, vol. 19, no. 2, 2002, pp. 170–191.

Oostdijk, Diederik. "Someplace Called *Poetry*: Karl Shapiro, *Poetry* Magazine and Post-War American Poetry." *English Studies*, vol. 4, 2000, pp. 346–357.

The Open Siddur Project. "Nishmat Kol Hai," translated by Rabbi Zalman Schachter-Shalomi, https://opensiddur.org/prayers/solilunar/shabbat/shabbat-shaharit /nishmat-kol-hai-interpretive-translation-by-zalman-schachter-shalomi/.

Oppen, George. *Collected Poems of George Oppen*. New Directions, 1975.

Ostriker, Alicia Suskin. "Beyond Confession: The Poetics of Postmodern Witness." *American Poetry Review*, vol. 30, no. 2, 2001, pp. 35–39.

———. "Blake, Ginsberg, Madness, and the Prophet as Shaman." *William Blake and the Moderns*, edited by Robert J. Bertholf and Annette S. Levitt, SUNY P, 1982, pp. 111–134.

———. *The Crack in Everything*. U of Pittsburgh P, 1996.

———. "Foreword." *"How Shall We Tell Each Other of the Poet?": The Life and Writing of Muriel Rukeyser*, edited by Anne F. Herzog and Janet E. Kaufman, St. Martin's Press, 1999, pp. xiii–xiv.

———. "Loving Walt Whitman and the Problem of America." *Dancing at the Devil's Party: Essays on Poetry, Politics, and the Erotic*, U of Michigan P, 2000, pp. 21–37.

———. *The Mother/Child Papers*. Beacon Press, 1980.

———. *The Nakedness of the Fathers: Biblical Visions and Revisions*. Rutgers UP, 1997.

———. *No Heaven*. U of Pittsburgh P, 2005.

———. "The Poet as Jew: 'Howl' Revisited." *Dancing at the Devil's Party: Essays on Poetry, Politics, and the Erotic*, U of Michigan P, 2000, pp. 102–123.

———. "Reflection on Jewish Identity: Entering the Tents." *Feminist Studies*, vol. 15, no. 3, 1989, pp. 541–547.

———. "Secular and Sacred: Returning (to) the Repressed." *Radical Poetics and Secular Jewish Culture*, edited by Stephen P. Miller and Daniel Morris, U of Alabama P, 2010, pp. 184–198.

———. *Stealing the Language: The Emergence of Women's Poetry in America*. Beacon Press, 1987.

———. *Waiting for the Light*. U of Pittsburgh P, 2017.

Pacernick, Gary, editor. *Meaning and Memory: Interviews with Fourteen Jewish Poets*. Ohio State UP, 2001.

Parmar, Nissa. *Multicultural Poetics: Re-visioning the American Canon*. SUNY P, 2018.

Pelton, Theodore. "Kenneth Koch's Poetics of Pleasure." *The Scene of My Selves: New Work on New School Poets*, edited by Terence Diggory and Stephen P. Miller, National Poetry Foundation, 2001, pp. 327–344.

Perlman, Jim, Ed Folsom, and Dan Campion, editors. *Walt Whitman: The Measure of His Song*, 2nd ed., Holy Cow! Press, 2014.

Phillips, Robert S., editor. "Karl Shapiro." *The Madness of Art: Interviews with Poets and Writers*, Syracuse UP, 2003, pp. 48–73.

Piercy, Marge. *The Art of Blessing the Day: Poems with a Jewish Theme*. Knopf, 2000.

———. *Circles on the Water: Selected Poems of Marge Piercy*. Knopf, 1982.

———. *He, She, and It*. Fawcett, 1993.

———. "How I Came to Whitman and Found Myself." *Massachusetts Review*, vol. 33, no. 1, 1992, pp. 98–100.

———. *Made in Detroit: Poems*. Knopf, 2015.

———. *On the Way Out, Turn Off the Light: Poems*. Knopf, 2020.

———. *Sex Wars*. William Morrow, 2005.

———. *Sleeping with Cats: A Memoir*. Harper Perennial, 2002.

———. *Woman on the Edge of Time*. Fawcett, 1985.

Pinsker, Sanford. "Walt Whitman and Our Multicultural America." *Virginia Quarterly Review*, vol. 4, 1999, pp. 716–722.

———. "Weeping and Wailing: The Jewish Songs of Gerald Stern." *Studies in American Jewish Literature*, vol. 9, no. 2, 1990, pp. 186–196.

186 WORKS CITED

Poetry Foundation. "Charles Reznikoff," www.poetryfoundation.org/poets/charles
-reznikoff.

———. "Introduction to the New York School of Poets," www.poetryfoundation
.org/collections/147565/an-introduction-to-the-new-york-school-of-poets.

Porter, Lavelle. "Should Walt Whitman Be #Cancelled? Black America Talks Back to
'The Good Gray Poet' at 200." *JSTOR Daily*, Apr. 17, 2019, https://daily.jstor.org
/should-walt-whitman-be-cancelled/.

Pound, Ezra. "A Pact." *Selected Poems of Ezra Pound*, New Directions, 1957, p. 27.

———. "What I Feel About Walt Whitman." Poets.org, June 15, 2010, https://poets
.org/text/what-i-feel-about-walt-whitman.

Prager, Leonard. "Walt Whitman in Yiddish." *Walt Whitman Quarterly Review*, vol.
1, 1983, pp. 22–35.

Price, Kenneth M. *To Walt Whitman, America*. U of North Carolina P, 2004.

Price, Kenneth M., and Stefan Schöberlein, editors. *The Oxford Handbook of Walt
Whitman*. Oxford UP, forthcoming.

Quayum, M. A. "Transcendentalism and Bellow's 'Henderson the Rain King.'"
Studies in American Jewish Literature, vol. 14, 1995, pp. 46–57.

Rahv, Philip. "Paleface and Redskin." *Image and Idea: Twenty Essays on Literary
Themes*, New Directions, 1957, pp. 1–6.

Rakosi, Carl. *The Collected Poems of Carl Rakosi*. National Poetry Foundation, 1986.

Ray, David. "Charles Reznikoff." *Contemporary Poets*, edited by Rosalie Murphy, St.
James Press, 1970, pp. 913–915.

Raz, Yosefa. "Untuning Walt Whitman's Prophetic Voice." *Walt Whitman Quarterly
Review*, vol. 36, no. 1, 2018, pp. 1–26.

Rehm, Maggie. "'Try Telling Yourself / You Are Not Accountable': Adrienne Rich as
Citizen Poet." *Women's Studies*, vol. 46, no. 7, 2017, pp. 684–703.

Reznikoff, Charles. *The Complete Poems of Charles Reznikoff: 1918–1975*, edited by
Seamus Cooney, Black Sparrow Press, 1989.

Rich, Adrienne. "Beginners." *Kenyon Review*, vol. 15, no. 3, 1993, pp. 12–19.

———. *Collected Poems: 1950–2012*. W. W. Norton & Company, 2016.

———. "Compulsory Heterosexuality and Lesbian Existence." *Adrienne Rich's
Poetry and Prose*, edited by Barbara Charlesworth Gelpi and Albert Gelpi, W. W.
Norton & Company, 1993, pp. 203–224.

———. "The Genesis of 'Yom Kippur 1984.'" *Adrienne Rich's Poetry and Prose*, edited
by Barbara Charlesworth Gelpi and Albert Gelpi, W. W. Norton & Company,
1993, pp. 252–258.

———. "Motherhood and Daughterhood." *Essential Essays: Culture, Politics, and the
Art of Poetry*, edited by Sandra M. Gilbert, W. W. Norton & Company, 2018, pp.
107–148.

WORKS CITED   187

———. "On Karl Shapiro's *The Bourgeois Poet*." *The Contemporary Poet as Artist and Critic*, edited by Anthony Ostroff, Little, Brown and Company, 1964, pp. 192–194.

———. "Split at the Root: An Essay on Jewish Identity." *Adrienne Rich's Poetry and Prose*, edited by Barbara Charlesworth Gelpi and Albert Gelpi, W. W. Norton & Company, 1993, pp. 224–238.

———. "When We Dead Awaken: Writing as Re-Vision." *Adrienne Rich's Poetry and Prose*, edited by Barbara Charlesworth Gelpi and Albert Gelpi, W. W. Norton & Company, 1993, pp. 166–177.

Rosenfeld, Morris. "Walt Whitman (America's Great Poet)." *Jewish American Literature: A Norton Anthology*, edited by Jules Chametsky, John Felstiner, Hilene Flanzbaum, and Kathryn Hellerstein, W. W. Norton & Company, 2001, pp. 136–137.

Rosenthal, Macha L. *The New Poets: American and British Poetry Since World War II.* Oxford UP, 1967.

Rothenberg, Jerome. *New Selected Poems: 1970–1985.* New Directions, 1986.

———. *Pre-faces & Other Writings.* New Directions, 1981.

Rubenstein, Rachel. "Going Native, Becoming Modern: American Indians, Walt Whitman, and the Yiddish Poet." *American Quarterly*, vol. 58, no. 2, 2006, pp. 431–453.

Rubin, Louis D. "Karl Shapiro 1913–2000: He Took His Stands." *Sewanee Review*, vol. 109, no. 1, 2001, pp. 108–119.

———. "The Poet in Eclipse." *Sewanee Review*, vol. 99, no. 4, 1991, pp. 554–556.

Rukeyser, Muriel. *The Collected Poems of Muriel Rukeyser*, edited by Anne F. Herzog and Janet E. Kaufman, U of Pittsburgh P, 2005.

———. "Craft Interview with Muriel Rukeyser." *The Poet's Craft: Interviews from the New York Quarterly*, edited by William Packard, Doubleday & Co., 1974, pp. 153–176.

———. "The Education of a Poet." *The Writer on Her Work*, edited by Janet Sternberg, W. W. Norton & Company, 2000, pp. 217–230.

———. *The Life of Poetry.* 2nd ed., Kraus Reprint Co., 1968.

———. *Out of Silence: Selected Poems*, edited by Kate Daniels, Northwestern UP, 1994.

———. "Under Forty: A Symposium on American Literature and the Younger Generation of American Jews." *Contemporary Jewish Record*, vol. 7, no. 1, 1944, pp. 4–9.

———. *Willard Gibbs.* Doubleday, Doran & Company, 1942.

Sandburg, Carl. "1916: Sandburg Anoints Pound." *Poetry*, 1916, pp. 249–257, www .poetryfoundation.org/poetrymagazine/articles/59005/the-work-of-ezra-pound.

Schneiderman, Josh. "The New York School, the Mainstream, and the Avant-Garde." *Contemporary Literature*, vol. 57, no. 3, 2016, pp. 346–378.

188   WORKS CITED

Scholem, Gershom G. "Reflections on the Possibility of Jewish Mysticism in Our Time." *Ariel*, vol. 26, 1970, pp. 43–52.

Schumacher, Michael. *Dharma Lion: A Biography of Allen Ginsberg*. U of Minnesota P, 2016.

———, editor. *Iron Curtain Journals: January–May 1965*. U of Minnesota P, 2018.

Schuster, Joshua. "Looking at Louis Zukofsky's Poetics Through Spinozist Glasses." *Radical Poetics and Secular Jewish Culture*, edited by Daniel Morris and Stephen P. Miller, U of Alabama P, 2009, pp. 127–150.

Schwartz, I. J. "Kentucky." Translated by Gertrude W. Dubrovsky. *Jewish American Literature: A Norton Anthology*, edited by Jules Chametsky, John Felstiner, Hilene Flanzbaum, and Kathryn Hellerstein, W. W. Norton & Company, 2001, pp. 225–226.

Sentilles, Renee M. "Identity, Speculation and History: Adah Isaacs Menken as a Case Study." *History & Memory*, vol. 18, no. 1, 2006, pp. 120–151.

Sexton, Anne. *Anne Sexton: A Self-Portrait in Letters*. Ecco, 2004.

Shapiro, Karl J. "The American-Jewish-Writer." *MELUS*, vol. 3, no. 2, 1976, pp. 6–9.

———. *Collected Poems*. Random House, 1978.

———. "Cosmic Consciousness." *Start with the Sun: Studies in the Whitman Tradition*, edited by James E. Miller, Jr., Karl Shapiro, and Bernice Slote, U of Nebraska P, 1960, pp. 29–42.

———. *Essay on Rime*. Random House, 1945.

———. "The First White Aboriginal." *The Poetry Wreck: Selected Essays (1950–1970)*, Random House, 1975, pp. 156–174.

———. "Is Poetry an American Art?" *College English*, vol. 25, no. 6, 1964, pp. 395–405.

———. "Notes on Raising a Poet." *Seriously Meeting Karl Shapiro*, edited by Sue B. Walker, Negative Capability Press, 1993, pp. 109–130.

———. *Poems of a Jew*. Random House, 1958.

———. *The Poetry Wreck: Selected Essays (1950–1970)*. Random House, 1975.

———. "T. S. Eliot: The Death of Literary Judgement." *In Defense of Ignorance*, Vintage Books, 1960, pp. 35–60.

———. "The Three Hockey Games of T. S. Eliot." *Antioch Review*, vol. 22, no. 3, 1962, pp. 284–286.

Shreiber, Maeera Y. "The End of Exile: Jewish Identity and Its Diasporic Poetics." *PMLA*, vol. 113, no. 2, 1998, pp. 273–287.

———. "Jewish American Poetry." *The Cambridge Companion to Jewish American Literature*, edited by Hana Wirth-Nesher and Michael P. Kramer, Cambridge UP, 2003, pp. 149–169.

———. *Singing in a Strange Land: A Jewish American Poetics*. Stanford UP, 2007.

—. "'Where Are We Moored?': Adrienne Rich, Women's Mourning, and the Limits of Lament." *Dwelling in Possibility: Women Poets and Critics on Poetry*, edited by Yopie Prins and Maeera Y. Shreiber, Cornell UP, 1997, pp. 301–317.

Shulman, Robert. *The Power of Political Art*. U of North Carolina P, 2000.

Siedlecki, Peter A. "Gerald Stern's Mediation of the I and the I." *World, Self, Poem: Essays on Contemporary Poetry from the "Jubilation of Poets,"* edited by Leonard M. Trawick, Kent State UP, 1990, pp. 110–119.

Simon, Linda. "Reznikoff: The Poet as Witness." *Charles Reznikoff: Man and Poet*, edited by Milton Hindus, National Poetry Foundation, 1984, pp. 233–250.

Skoog, Ed, and Ben Lerner. "A Pint on the House: A One-Question Interview with Ed Skoog and Ben Lerner." Edited by Matthew Dickman, *The Honest Pint*, vol. 22, 2014.

Slavitt, David R. "Karl (Jay) Shapiro." *Contemporary Jewish-American Dramatists and Poets*, edited by Joel Shatsky and Michael Taub, Greenwood Press, 1999, pp. 554–559.

Slotkin, Richard. "The Contextual Symbol: Karl Shapiro's Image of 'The Jew.'" *American Quarterly*, vol. 18, no. 2, 1966, pp. 220–226.

Smith, Martha Nell. "Introduction: Alicia Ostriker Thumbtacking Her Theses to the Bulletin Board." *Everywoman Her Own Theology: On the Poetry of Alicia Suskin Ostriker*, edited by Martha Nell Smith and Julie R. Enszer, U of Michigan P, 2018, pp. 1–7.

Smith, Martha Nell, and Julie R. Enszer, editors. *Everywoman Her Own Theology: On the Poetry of Alicia Suskin Ostriker*. U of Michigan P, 2018.

Somerville, Jane. *Making the Light Come: The Poetry of Gerald Stern*. Wayne State UP, 1990.

Sova, Reagan M. *Wildcat Dreams in the Death Light*. First to Knock, 2022.

Spurr, David. "Kenneth Koch's 'Serious Moment.'" *The Scene of My Selves: New Work on New School Poets*, edited by Terence Diggory and Stephen P. Miller, National Poetry Foundation, 2001, pp. 345–356.

Stern, Gerald. "Ginsberg and I." *What I Can't Bear Losing: Notes from a Life*, Trinity UP, 2009, pp. 265–290.

—. "Hot Dog." *Odd Mercy*, W. W. Norton & Company, 1997, pp. 67–112.

—. "Sundays." *What I Can't Bear Losing: Notes from a Life*, Trinity UP, 2009, pp. 1–16.

—. *This Time: New and Selected Poems*. W. W. Norton & Company, 1999.

—. "What I Have to Defend, What I Can't Bear Losing." *What I Can't Bear Losing: Notes from a Life*, Trinity UP, 2009, pp. 303–319.

Sternburg, Janet, and Alan Ziegler. "A Conversation with Charles Reznikoff." *Montemora*, vol. 2, 1976, pp. 113–121.

Stevenson, Anne, and Michael Farley. "Charles Reznikoff and His Tradition." *Charles*

Reznikoff: Man and Poet, edited by Milton Hindus, National Poetry Foundation, 1984, pp. 177–185.

Svonkin, Craig. "Manishevitz and Sake, the Kaddish and Sutras: Allen Ginsberg's Spiritual Self-Othering." *College Literature*, vol. 37, no. 4, 2010, pp. 166–193.

Tapscott, Stephen. *American Beauty: William Carlos Williams and the Modernist Whitman*. Columbia UP, 1984.

Terris, Virginia R. "Muriel Rukeyser." *Contemporary Literary Criticism*, edited by Jean C. Stine, Gale, 1984, pp. 410–412.

Trilling, Leonard. *Speaking of Literature and Society*. Oxford UP, 1982.

Tuerk, Richard. "Michael Gold on Walt Whitman." *Walt Whitman Quarterly Review*, vol. 3, 1985, pp. 16–23.

Turpin, Zachary. "Yearning to Breathe Free: Emma Lazarus's Queer Innovations." *J19*, vol. 4, no. 2, 2016, pp. 419–424.

Vogel, Dan. *Emma Lazarus*. Twayne Publishers, 1980.

Wald, Alan. *Exiles from a Future Time: The Forging of the Mid-Twentieth-Century Literary Left*. U of North Carolina P, 2002.

Waldinger, Albert. "Stopping by the Woods: Classic American Poems in Yiddish." *TTR*, vol. 16, no. 2, 2003, pp. 155–174.

Walker, Sue B., editor. *Seriously Meeting Karl Shapiro*. Negative Capability Press, 1993.

Walt Whitman Archive. Edited by Matt Cohen, Ed Folsom, and Kenneth M. Price, https://whitmanarchive.org.

——. "Review of *Leaves of Grass*, 1855." Feb. 18, 1856, https://whitmanarchive.org /criticism/reviews/lg1855/anc.00019.html.

Wechsler, Shoshana. "A Ma(t)ter of Fact and Vision: The Objectivity Question and Muriel Rukeyser's 'The Book of the Dead.'" *"How Shall We Tell Each Other of the Poet?": The Life and Writing of Muriel Rukeyser*, edited by Anne F. Herzog and Janet E. Kaufman, St. Martin's Press, 1999, pp. 226–240.

Whitman, Walt. "Doings at the Synagogue." *The Journalism*, vol. 1, edited by Herbert Bergman and Peter Lang, 1998, pp. 83–84.

——. *Leaves of Grass*. Thayer and Eldridge (1860–1861). Available at the Walt Whitman Archive, https://whitmanarchive.org/published/LG/1860/whole.html.

——. *Leaves of Grass*. David McKay (1891–1892). Available at the Walt Whitman Archive, https://whitmanarchive.org/published/LG/1891/whole.html.

——. *Whitman: Poetry and Prose*, edited by Justin Kaplan, Library of America, 1996.

Williams, Amy. "Alicia Ostriker." *Dictionary of Literary Biography: American Poets Since World War II*, edited by R. S. Gwynn, Gale, 1992, pp. 239–242.

Williams, C. K. *Misgivings: My Mother, My Father, Myself*. Farrar, Straus and Giroux, 2000.

———. *On Whitman*. Princeton UP, 2010.

Williams, William Carlos. "An Essay on *Leaves of Grass*." *Leaves of Grass: One Hundred Years After*, edited by Milton Hindus, Stanford UP, 1955, pp. 22–31.

———. "Introduction to 'Howl.'" *Allen Ginsberg: Collected Poems 1947–1997*, Penguin Books, 1987, pp. 819–820.

———. Preface. *Selected Essays of William Carlos Williams*. New Directions, 1954.

Wirth-Nesher, Hana. *Call It English: The Languages of Jewish American Literature*. Princeton UP, 2005.

———. "Defining the Indefinable: What Is Jewish Literature?" *What Is Jewish Literature?*, edited by Hana Wirth-Nesher, Jewish Publication Society, 1994, pp. 3–12.

Wirth-Nesher, Hana, and Michael P. Kramer, editors. "Introduction: Jewish American Literatures in the Making." *The Cambridge Companion to Jewish American Literature*, Cambridge UP, 2003, pp. 1–11.

Wolosky, Shira. "What Do Jews Stand For? Muriel Rukeyser's Ethics of Identity." *Nashim*, vol. 19, 2010, pp. 199–226.

Zierler, Wendy. "In Search of a Feminist Reading of the Akedah." *Nashim*, vol. 9, 2005, pp. 10–26.

Zukofsky, Louis. "Sincerity and Objectification: With Special Reference to the Work of Charles Reznikoff." *Poetry*, vol. 37, 1931, pp. 272–285.

INDEX

"A Backward Glance O'er Travel'd Roads" (Whitman), 7

"A Broadway Pageant" (Whitman), 158n29

"A Compassionate People" (Reznikoff), 25, 35–37

"A Pact" (Pound), 33–34

"A Supermarket in California" (Ginsberg), 27

"A Walker in the City" (Ostriker), 120, 125, 171n28

"After Whitman & Reznikoff" (Ginsberg), 28, 96–97

"Akiba" poems (Rukeyser), 27, 80, 85–88

Alexie, Sherman, 12–13

Alkalay-Gut, Karen, 6

Allen, Gay Wilson, 12

America, per Whitman: critiques of, 12–13, 115–116, 117–118, 124–125, 127–130; as democratic and progressive, 20–21, 88, 115–116, 125–126, 160n13; ethnocentrism of, 12–13, 115–116

"An Atlas of the Difficult World" (Rich), 112, 114, 169n12, 170n18

"An Essay on *Leaves of Grass*" (Williams), 34

anaphora, 27, 36–37, 72–73, 91, 118, 128

antisemitism: experience of, 42–43, 69, 168n10, 172n39; exploration in poetry, 104–105, 168n10; of High Modernists, 59, 100–101, 155n4, 166n38, 173n1

assimilation, 19–20, 81, 104–105, 110, 157n18, 164n20

"Aunt Jennifer's Tigers" (Rich), 168n6

"Autobiography: Hollywood" (Reznikoff), 41–42

"Autobiography: New York" (Reznikoff), 39–41

"Beat! Beat! Drums!" (Whitman), 172n36

Beit Simchat Torah congregation, 142

Ben-Oni, Rosebud, 150n12

Ben-Porat, Ziva, 151n21

Bernstein, Charles, 5, 141; "Solidarity Is the Name We Give to What We Cannot Hold," 141

194 INDEX

Biale, David, 110

Bible: imagery of, 164n28; as poetic subject, 43–46, 72–73

Bible, influence of: on Ginsberg, 91; on Menken, 153n30; on Ostriker, 29; on Piercy, 30; on Rich, 112, 115, 118–119; on Rukeyser, 85–88, 163n13, 163n17; on Whitman, 10, 38

Blake, William, 129

Bloom, Harold, 23

body, celebration of: in Ginsberg's work, 27, 97; in Koch's work, 74; in Piercy's work, 133, 136; in Rakosi's work, 35; in Rukeyser's work, 79, 86–88, 162n11; as Whitmanian theme, 27, 74, 95, 97, 133, 136, 162n11, 167n52, 170n23

Bollingen Prize controversy, 59

Breslin, James, 34

Burt, Stephanie, 6

"By the Waters of Babylon" (Lazarus), 16–17, 153n34, 153n35

Carruth, Hayden, 55

cities, as poetic subject, 19, 22. *See also* New York School; Objectivists; in Ginsberg's work, 97–98; in Ostriker's work, 125–127; in Reznikoff's work, 39–43; in Rich's work, 116–118, 169n16; in Stern's work, 102–106

Conrad, CA, 110

contradictions: of Jewish American existence, 72–73, 157n18, 157n19; of Whitman, 18, 32–33, 63–65, 124–125, 141, 150n13

"Cosmic Consciousness" (Shapiro), 61

critics, Jewish American, 21–23

Crosby Street Synagogue, 149n4

"Crossing Brooklyn Ferry" (Whitman), 49, 82

death: in Ostriker's work, 128–130; in Reznikoff's work, 37, 49; in Rich's work, 118; in Rukeyser's work, 82–83, 86, 164n19, 164n24; in Stern's work, 104; in Whitman's work, 37, 63–64, 167n51, 167n52

Di Yunge, 18

Dickinson, Emily, 114, 169n13

"Diving into the Wreck" (Rich), 112, 164n22

"Doings at the Synagogue" (Whitman), 1–2

"Drug Store" (Shapiro), 159n3

Drum-Taps (Whitman), 30

"Dry Hours: A Golden Shovel Exercise" (Ostriker), 30, 125, 127–128, 171n30

DuPlessis, Rachel Blau, 11

"Early History of a Writer" (Reznikoff), 25, 32, 33, 37–39, 42–43

"Easter" (O'Hara), 161n20

Eberly, David, 68

"Elegy Before the War" (Ostriker), 30, 128–130, 172n36

Eliot, T. S., 9, 23, 26, 58–60, 70, 100, 139–140, 173n1

Emerson, Ralph Waldo, 9, 14–15, 151n18; "The Poet," 9

Erickson, Peter, 116

Erkkila, Betsy, 11

Feldman, Irving: "The Pripet Marshes," 157n17

Fiedler, Leslie, 22, 23

"Fix" (Ostriker), 171n25

Flanzbaum, Hilene, 55, 59

Folsom, Ed, 12, 48–49, 84, 150n6

Fredman, Stephen, 34–35

"Fresh Air" (Koch), 26, 54, 66, 70–72

Galchinsky, Michael, 110

"Gauley Bridge" (Rukeyser), 84

"Ghazal: America the Beautiful" (Ostriker), 125

Ginsberg, Allen, 27; deep engagement with Whitman, 3, 77–78, 89–99, 149n2, 154n46, 165n34; engagement with High Modernism, 90, 92–94, 165n36, 165n37, 166n39; engagement with Reznikoff and Objectivism, 90, 94–99, 159n31, 166n41; engagement with Williams, 165n36, 165n37; as Jewish American poet, 89–90, 165n32, 165n35; other influences on, 89; poetics of witnessing, 27–28, 77–78, 90, 94–99, 166n42; responses to, 54, 129, 165n30; "A Supermarket in California," 27; "After Whitman & Reznikoff," 28, 96–97; "Howl," 27, 54, 166n42; "Improvisation in Beijing," 28, 93; "Kaddish," 27, 166n42; "Waking in New York," 28, 97–98; "War Profit Litany," 92–93; "Yiddishe Kopf," 28, 90–92, 165n31

God, conceptions of, 43–46, 135–136

Gold, Michael, 21–22; *Jews Without Money*, 22; "Ode to Walt Whitman," 22

Goldman, Emma, 21

Graham, Jorie, 4–5

grass, 42–43, 50–51, 157n20, 157n21. See also *Leaves of Grass* (Whitman); nature

Grünzweig, Walter, 11

Halpern, Rob, 5, 6, 150n13

Harshav, Barbara, 19

Harshav, Benjamin, 19

Heller, Michael: "Sag Harbor, Whitman,

As If an Ode," 5

Herzog, Anne F., 82

Heschel, Susannah, 110

Hindus, Milton, 40, 44

Hirsch, Edward: "Whitman Leaves the Boardwalk," 150n9

Hogue, Cynthia, 119–120

holiness, vii, 2–3, 43–46, 122, 134, 136, 151n20. *See also* God, conceptions of; secularism

Holocaust: specific references to, 35–37, 63, 157n17, 160n11, 166n47, 167n48; as theme in Jewish American poetry, 13, 24, 28, 62, 102, 130

"Hot Dog" (Stern), 28, 99, 102–106, 167n53

"How I Came to Walt Whitman and Found Myself" (Piercy), 130

"Howl" (Ginsberg), 27, 54, 166n42

Hughes, Langston: "I, Too," 126

humor, 54, 58, 64–65, 67–68, 71, 73, 91, 101, 123, 161n26, 166n46

"I Am an Atheist Who Says His Prayers" (Shapiro), 64–65

"I Saw in Louisiana a Live-Oak Growing" (Whitman), 127

"I, Too" (Hughes), 126

identity, Jewish American. *See* individual poets: complications for women, 113–115, 122–123, 168n9; contradictions of, 72–73, 157n18, 157n19; different strands of, 80–81, 163n14; dualism of, 110–111, 164n20; as immigrant identity, 39–43; navigating with Whitman, 51–52, 106–111, 140; Yiddish language and, 7, 9, 17–21, 24, 102, 104–105, 154n42

identity, transgender, 150n11

196 INDEX

"Idyl" (Lazarus), 153n36

Imagists, 25, 34

"Improvisation in Beijing" (Ginsberg), 28, 93

"In the Jewish Synagogue at Newport" (Lazarus), 16

intertextuality, 11, 151n21

"Jerusalem the Golden" (Reznikoff), 44, 46

Jewish people, 1–3, 39–43, 62–65, 69, 149n3, 150n5

Jewishness, 62–65, 68–69, 72–76, 113–114, 122–123, 168n9, 168n10. *See also* identity, Jewish American

Jews Without Money (Gold), 22

Jordan, June, 12

Judaism: feminist challenges to, 118–119, 122–123, 135; Reconstructionist, 30, 131–132, 134, 151n20, 172n40; Reform, 78, 80

"Kaddish" (Ginsberg), 27, 166n42

Katz, Wendy, 21

Kaufman, Shirley, 6, 87

"Kentucky" (Schwartz), 154n41

Koch, Kenneth, 26; criticism of High Modernism, 26, 54–55, 70–72; embrace of Whitman, 26, 53–55, 66–69, 70–72, 160n13, 160n14; humor of, 160n16, 161n26; Jewish identity of, 66–67, 68–69, 72–76; New York School and, 26, 66–69; reactions to the poetry of, 54, 67–68, 160n16; thoughts on Ginsberg, 54; "Fresh Air," 26, 54, 66, 70–72; "To Jewishness," 26, 69, 72–73; "To Jewishness, Paris, Ambition, Trees, My Heart, and Destiny," 26, 72, 73–76

Kramer, Aaron, 4, 10

Kumin, Maxine, 5, 162n9

Lazarus, Emma, 14–17, 125–126, 153n31, 153n34, 153n35, 153n36, 153n37, 171n29; "By the Waters of Babylon," 16–17, 153n34, 153n35; "Idyl," 153n36; "In the Jewish Synagogue at Newport," 16; "The New Colossus," 14, 16, 17, 125–126, 153n35, 171n29

Leaves of Grass (Whitman), 1–3, 7, 18, 34, 38–39, 149n1, 160n13

Lerner, Ben, 5; *10:04*, 5

"Letter to the Front" (Rukeyser), 82

Levine, Philip, 4

Levinson, Julian, 8–9, 18–19

Leyvik, H.: "To America," 20–21

liturgy, influence of, 30, 74–75, 118, 130, 132–138, 167n49

Lowell, Amy, 34, 155n6

MacPhail, Scott, 110

"Manahatta" (Ostriker), 17, 30, 125–127

"Manhattan, 1975" (Rakosi), 35

"Mannahatta" (Whitman), 16–17, 125–126

Martin, Wendy, 113

"Mearl Blankenship" (Rukeyser), 85

Menken, Adah Isaacs, 8, 13–14, 139, 152n29, 153n30; "Myself," 14

Middlebrook, Diane, 109

Miller, Matt, 8, 35

Miller, Stephen Paul: "Relentlessly Going On and On," 9–10

Modernism, High. *See* Eliot, T. S.; Pound, Ezra; Williams, William Carlos: attitudes regarding Whitman, 33–34, 58–60; Jewish American poets' engagement with,

3, 25–28, 58–60, 139–140; New
York School's criticism of, 66–68;
Objectivists' engagement with, 25, 33,
34–35, 155n8; Whitman as counter to,
23, 59–60, 66–67, 109
Mort, Jo-Ann, 81
"Myself" (Menken), 14

nature: God as or found within, 44–46,
134; as poetic theme: in Koch, 71,
72, 75; in Piercy, 134, 136, 137; in
Reznikoff, 39–43; in Whitman,
39–43, 71, 134
New Criticism, 59–60, 66–68, 70, 80,
110, 140, 162n10, 169n14
New York School, 26, 66–69, 160n15,
161n17
"Nishmat" (Piercy), 30, 133, 135–137,
173n44
November, Yehoshua, 4, 5

Objectivists, 4, 7, 9, 15, 33–35, 94–99, 139,
156n11, 156n12, 158n8
"Ode to Walt Whitman" (Gold), 22
"Of Being Numerous" (Oppen), 35,
158n27
O'Hara, Frank, 26, 67–68; "Easter,"
161n20
Omer-Sherman, Ranen, 8, 47
On the Way Out, Turn Off the Light
(Piercy), 137–138
Oppen, George, 35; "Of Being
Numerous," 35, 158n27
Ostriker, Alicia, 29; engagement with
Whitman, 29–30, 119–130, 171n33,
172n34, 172n36; exploration of Jewish
American identity, 120, 122–123; on
Ginsberg, 89–90, 154n46; influences
on, 121, 171n28; poetic themes and

goals, 119–120, 125–127, 171n25; on
Rukeyser, 162n10; "A Walker in the
City," 120, 125, 171n28; "Dry Hours:
A Golden Shovel Exercise," 30, 125,
127–128, 171n30; "Elegy Before the
War," 30, 128–130, 172n36; "Fix,"
171n25; "Ghazal: America the
Beautiful," 125; "Manahatta," 17, 30,
125–127
"Out of Childhood" (Rukeyser), 169n14
"Out of the Cradle Endlessly Rocking"
(Whitman), 35–37, 153n36
outsiders: within cities, 40–41, 125–127;
dangers of solitude for, 117–118;
Jewish Americans as, 19–21, 39–43,
56–67, 102–106, 113–114, 168n10;
poets as, 12–13, 19–21, 39–43, 56–67,
102–106, 168n10; women as, 113–114,
131–132

Pacernick, Gary, 150n8
"Paleface and Redskin" (Rahv), 22
"Passage to India" (Whitman), 171n33
photography, 48–49, 83–85, 164n22,
164n23, 164n25, 164n26. See also
witness, poet as
Piercy, Marge, 30; explorations of
Jewishness, 30, 130–138, 155n48,
172n39; poetics of, 30, 131–138,
173n42; political activism of, 130,
134–135, 137–138; Reconstructionist
movement and, 30, 131, 133–138;
"How I Came to Walt Whitman and
Found Myself," 130; "Nishmat," 30,
133, 135–137, 173n44; On the Way Out,
Turn Off the Light, 137–138; "Praise
in Spite of It All," 30, 130, 137–138;
The Art of Blessing the Day, 133–137;
"The Art of Blessing the Day," 30, 133,

198   INDEX

134–135; "The Ram's Horn Sounding,"
131; "To Be of Use," 130
"Poem Out of Childhood" (Rukeyser),
78, 164n25
poet: as Jew, 56–57; as outsider, 12–13,
19–21, 39–43, 56–67, 102–106, 168n10;
as prophet, 3, 27–28, 61, 81–83,
117–118; as witness, 27–28, 47–51,
77–78, 83–88, 90, 102–106, 166n42
"Poet" (Shapiro), 57
poetry, Jewish, 4, 9–10
poetry, Jewish American: cadences
of, 10; humor of, 54, 58, 64, 65, 67,
68, 71, 73, 91, 123, 161n26, 166n46;
multiplicity of, 151n15; as political, 81,
119–120, 130, 134–135, 137–138, 163n18,
164n19, 170n20; themes explored
by, 13, 24, 28, 33, 62, 69, 91, 102, 130;
Transcendentalism and, 151n17
poets, Black, 12, 152n26
poets, Jewish, 6, 152n23
poets, Jewish American, 3–8, 23–25, 90,
98, 99, 156n9, 173n2
poets, Native American, 12–13, 152n27
poets, women, 28–30, 108–138, 167n2,
167n3, 168n8, 168n11
poets, Yiddish-language, 7, 9, 17–21
"Poland: Anno 1700" (Reznikoff), 33,
44–46
Porter, Lavelle, 110
Pound, Ezra. See Modernism, High:
antisemitism of, 59, 100–101, 155n4,
166n38; fascism and, 155n4, 166n38;
influence of, 70; Jewish American
poets' engagement with, 3, 23,
26, 34–35, 58–60, 92–94, 139–140,
156n10; Whitman and, 32–34; "A
Pact," 33–34; "What I Feel About
Walt Whitman," 33

"Praise in Spite of It All" (Piercy), 30,
130, 137–138
Price, Kenneth M., 21
prophet, poet as, 3, 27–28, 61, 81–83,
117–118

race and racism: in High Modernism,
100; poets' exploration of, 84, 102,
117, 127–128, 172n39; in Whitman's
work, 110
Rahv, Phillip: "Paleface and Redskin," 22
Rakosi, Carl, 35; "Manhattan, 1975," 35
"Relentlessly Going On and On"
(Miller), 9–10
Reznikoff, Charles, 25; engagement with
history, 156n16; High Modernism
and, 25, 33, 38, 157n18; influence
of Spinoza on, 25; influence on
Ginsberg, 28, 90, 94–99, 166n41;
Objectivism and, 25, 33, 34, 38,
156n11, 158n25, 159n31; as Objectivist
poet-witness, 25, 38, 47–51, 94–95,
158n24, 158n25, 158n26, 158n28,
159n31; response to Whitman, 32–33;
use of litanies and catalogs, 157n17;
as walker of cities, 40, 50–51; "A
Compassionate People," 25, 35–37;
"Autobiography: Hollywood," 41–42;
"Autobiography: New York," 39–41;
"Early History of a Writer," 25, 32,
33, 37–39, 42–43; "Jerusalem the
Golden," 44, 46; "Poland: Anno
1700," 33, 44–46; *Rhythms*, 49;
"Sunday Walks in the Suburbs,"
33, 50–51, 94; "Uriel Accosta," 95;
"Walking in New York," 33, 47–49
Rhythms (Reznikoff), 49
Rich, Adrienne, 29; on Biblical
influences, 115; conflicting identities

of, 113–114, 115; engagement with Rukeyser, 78–79, 109, 114–115, 164n22, 167n2, 169n14; engagement with Whitman, 29, 108, 111–116, 169n12, 169n13, 169n16, 170n18; explorations of Jewish American identity, 108, 113–114, 168n7, 168n9, 168n10; New Criticism and, 169n14; relationship with her parents, 168n7, 168n8, 168n9, 168n10, 168n11; sexual orientation of, 113–114, 168n11; use of Whitmanian poetics, 112, 115, 117, 118–119; "An Atlas of the Difficult World," 112, 114, 169n12, 170n18; "Aunt Jennifer's Tigers," 168n6; "Diving into the Wreck," 112, 164n22; "Tattered Kaddish," 29, 112–113, 118–119, 170n21, 170n22; "The Genesis of 'Yom Kippur 1984,'" 29, 115–116; "Yom Kippur 1984," 29, 112–113, 116–118, 169n14

Rosenfeld, Morris: "Walt Whitman (America's Great Poet)," 19

Roskolenko, Harry, 67

Rothenberg, Jerome, 4, 5, 140–141

Rubenstein, Rachel, 18

Rukeyser, Muriel, 27; Biblical and Jewish influences, 87–88; engagement with Whitman, 77–78, 81–83, 163n13; influence of, 29, 78–79, 108–109, 114–115, 162n9, 162n10, 164n22, 167n2, 169n14; Jewish American identity of, 80–81, 163n14, 163n15, 163n17, 163n18, 164n20, 167n1; Modernism and, 78, 80; photographic gaze of, 83–85, 164n22, 164n23, 164n25, 164n26; poet as prophet or seer, 81–83; poetics of witnessing, 77–78, 85–88, 163n12, 164n26, 164n27; political activism

of, 81, 163n18, 164n19; Rabbi Akiba and, 86; Reform Judaism and, 78, 80; Transcendentalism and, 162n8; "Akiba" poems, 27, 80, 85–88; "Gauley Bridge," 84; "Letter to the Front," 82; "Mearl Blankenship," 85; "Out of Childhood," 169n14; "Poem Out of Childhood," 78, 164n25; "The Book of the Dead," 27, 80, 83–85; "The Disease," 164n24; "The Road," 27, 80, 83–85; "The Witness," 86–88; "Then," 82–83; "To Be a Jew," 164n20; "Under Forty," 27, 81

"Salut au Monde!" (Whitman), 1, 149n3

Sandburg, Carl, 4, 156n9

Schneiderman, Josh, 67

Scholem, Gershom G., vii, 2–3

Schwartz, Demore: "America, America!," 4

Schwartz, I. J.: "Kentucky," 154n41

secularism: as aspect of Jewish American identity, 43–46, 56, 65, 101–102, 122–123, 157n23; as basis for holiness, vii, 2–3, 118–119, 122, 134–138, 151n20

sexuality: explored by Ginsberg, 54, 92; explored by O'Hara, 161n19; explored by Ostriker, 122; explored by Piercy, 131; explored by Rich, 29, 111–114, 117, 168n11; explored by Rukeyser, 162n10; and Whitman, 14, 60, 89, 142, 161n19

Shapiro, Karl Jay, 26; as "American poet," 55–56, 159n2, 159n3; embrace of Whitman, 53–55, 57–58, 60; Ginsberg and, 54; High Modernism and, 26, 54–55, 58–60; on Jewishness and being Jewish, 56, 62–65,

200 INDEX

160n12; as poet outsider, 56–57, 168n10; "Cosmic Consciousness," 61, 160n9; "Drug Store," 159n3; "I Am an Atheist Who Says His Prayers," 64–65; "Poet," 57; "The First White Aboriginal," 26, 57–58, 60–61; "Travelogue for Exiles," 57; "University," 159n6

Shreiber, Maeera Y., 8, 24, 81, 119

Siedlecki, Peter, 103

Slotkin, Richard, 62

"Solidarity Is the Name We Give to What We Cannot Hold" (Bernstein), 141

solitude, 116, 117–118. *See also* outsiders

Somerville, Jane, 99

"Song of Myself" (Whitman): conception of God in, 43–44, 46; as "fresh air" against stifling convention, 71–72; inclusivity of, 118–119, 134, 142; poetic self and voice of, 1, 117, 121–122, 136, 169n12; relationship between speaker and audience, 128–129, 172n34; theme of contradiction in, 18, 64–65; witnessing in, 77

"Song of the Answerer" (Whitman), 1, 149n3

"Song of the Open Road" (Whitman), 83, 85

Spinoza, Baruch, 25, 33, 43–46, 157n22, 157n23

Stern, Gerald, 28; influences on, 99–100, 101, 166n44, 166n45; as Jewish American poet, 99, 101–102, 166n46, 166n47, 167n48, 167n49, 167n50; poetics of witness and, 28, 77–78, 166n44; response to Whitman, 28, 77–78, 99–100, 101, 167n51; thoughts

on the High Modernists, 100–101; "Hot Dog," 28, 99, 102–106, 167n53; "The Day Without the Jews," 167n48; "The Poem of Life," 166n47; "The Sabbath," 167n48

"Sunday Walks in the Suburbs" (Reznikoff), 33, 50–51, 94

Svonkin, Craig, 91

Tapscott, Stephen, 34

"Tattered Kaddish" (Rich), 29, 112–113, 118–119, 170n21, 170n22

The Art of Blessing the Day (Piercy), 133–137

"The Art of Blessing the Day" (Piercy), 30, 133, 134–135

"The Book of the Dead" (Rukeyser), 27, 80, 83–85

"The City Dead-House" (Whitman), 105–106, 167n52

"The Day Without the Jews" (Stern), 167n48

"The Disease" (Rukeyser), 164n24

"The First White Aboriginal" (Shapiro), 26, 57–58, 60–61

"The Genesis of 'Yom Kippur 1984'" (Rich), 29, 115–116

"The New Colossus" (Lazarus), 14, 16, 17, 125–126, 153n35, 171n29

"The Poem of Life" (Stern), 166n47

"The Poet" (Emerson), 9

"The Pripet Marshes" (Feldman), 157n17

"The Ram's Horn Sounding" (Piercy), 131

"The Road" (Rukeyser), 27, 80, 83–85

"The Sabbath" (Stern), 167n48

"The Sleepers" (Whitman), 16–17, 47, 77

"The Witness" (Rukeyser), 86–88

"Then" (Rukeyser), 82–83

"To a Common Prostitute" (Whitman), 105–106
"To America" (Leyvik), 20–21
"To Be a Jew" (Rukeyser), 164n20
"To Be of Use" (Piercy), 130
"To Foreign Lands" (Whitman), 31
"To Jewishness" (Koch), 26, 69, 72–73
"To Jewishness, Paris, Ambition, Trees, My Heart, and Destiny" (Koch), 26, 72, 73–76
Transcendentalists, 9, 14–15, 151n18, 151n19, 162n8
Traubel, Horace, 15, 21
"Travelogue for Exiles" (Shapiro), 57
Trilling, Lionel, 22–23
Tuerk, Richard, 21–22

"Under Forty" (Rukeyser), 27, 81
"University" (Shapiro), 159n6
urban life. *See* cities, as poetic subject
"Uriel Accosta" (Reznikoff), 95

"Waking in New York" (Ginsberg), 28, 97–98
"Walking in New York" (Reznikoff), 33, 47–49
"Walt Whitman (America's Great Poet)" (Morris), 19
"War Profit Litany" (Ginsberg), 92–93
"What I Feel About Walt Whitman" (Pound), 33
"When Lilacs Last in the Dooryard Bloom'd" (Whitman), 116–117
Whitman, Walt: affinities with Spinoza, 43–44, 157n22; as American, 149n2, 168n4; and the Civil War, 124–125, 127–128, 129; contradictions and multiplicities of, 8, 18, 23, 29, 61, 63–65, 124–125, 141, 150n13; empathy of, 28, 47, 92, 105–106, 120, 158n25; interest in photography of, 48–49, 84; as "Jewish," 55, 61–62, 63–65, 101, 143; Lazarus and, 15–16; as "lowbrow," 22, 33–34; notion of death, 37, 167n51, 167n52; as outsider, 12–13, 20–21, 39–43, 101, 103; presence in Black poetry, 12, 152n26; presence in French literature, 11; presence in German literature, 11; presence in Jewish American poetry (overview), 8–11; presence in Native American poetry, 12–13, 152n27; presence in Yiddish-language poetry, 17–21; racial and economic privilege of, 169n13; racism of, 110; secular holiness of, vii, 2–3, 43–46, 61, 151n20; self-publication of, 38; sexuality of, 14, 27, 60, 89, 161n19; and the Transcendentalists, 9, 151n18, 151n19; transnational reception of, 152n23; understandings of God, 43–46; vis-à-vis Modernism and the Modernists, 23, 33–34, 57, 59–60, 66–67; vis-à-vis the Objectivists, 34–35 (*See also* Reznikoff, Charles); women's use of, 120, 131–132; Yiddish translations of, 18, 153n38, 153n39, 153n40, 154n41, 154n42; "A Backward Glance O'er Travel'd Roads," 7; "A Broadway Pageant," 158n29; "Beat! Beat! Drums!," 172n36; "Crossing Brooklyn Ferry," 49, 82; *Drum-Taps*, 30; "I Saw in Louisiana a Live-Oak Growing," 127; *Leaves of Grass*, 1–3, 7, 18, 34, 38–39, 149n1, 160n13; "Mannahatta," 16–17, 125–127; "Out of the Cradle Endlessly Rocking," 35–37, 153n36; "Passage to India,"

171n33; "Salut au Monde!," 1, 149n3; "Song of Myself" (*See also* "Song of Myself"); "Song of the Answerer," 1, 149n3; "Song of the Open Road," 83, 85; "The City Dead-House," 105–106, 167n52; "The Sleepers," 16–17, 47, 77; "To a Common Prostitute," 105–106; "To Foreign Lands," 31; "When Lilacs Last in the Dooryard Bloom'd," 116–117

"Whitman Leaves the Boardwalk" (Hirsch), 150n9

Whitmanian poetics: Biblical cadences of, 10, 38, 140; celebration of the body in, 27, 74, 95, 97, 133, 136, 162n11, 167n52, 170n23; evocations of nature in, 40, 41–43; listing and cataloging, 22, 64–65, 71, 137, 161n27, 169n16, 171n33; liturgical cadences of, 132–133, 135–136; non-fixed verse forms, 37–38; poet as prophet, 61, 82; poet as witness, 27–28, 47–51, 77–78, 83–85, 95, 103; use of anaphora, 27, 36–37, 72; the Whitmanian "I," 14, 64–65, 82, 141, 172n34

Williams, Amy, 120

Williams, C. K., 4, 5, 141–142, 174n3

Williams, William Carlos, 25, 28, 33, 34, 58, 92, 165n36, 165n37; "An Essay on *Leaves of Grass*," 34

Wirth-Nesher, Hana, 140, 154n45

witness, poet as, 27–28, 47–51, 77–78, 83–88, 90, 102–106, 166n42. *See also* photography

witnessing, poetics of: in Ginsberg, 27–28, 77–78, 90, 94–99, 166n42; in Ostriker, 171n25; in Reznikoff, 47–51, 158n24, 158n25, 158n26, 158n28; in Rukeyser, 77–78, 85–88, 163n12, 164n26, 164n27; in Stern, 28, 77–78, 166n44; in Whitman, 27–28, 47–51, 77–78, 83–85, 95, 103

Wolosky, Shira, 81, 87

Yeats, W. B., 26

Yezierska, Anzia, 21

Yiddish, 18, 24, 102–105, 153n38, 153n39, 153n40, 154n41, 154n42. *See also* poets, Yiddish-language

"Yiddishe Kopf" (Ginsberg), 28, 90–92, 165n31

"Yom Kippur 1984" (Rich), 29, 112, 116–118, 169n14

Zox-Weaver, Annalisa, 113

Zukofsky, Louis, 4, 25, 33–35, 139, 156n10, 156n11, 156n13, 157n23

THE IOWA WHITMAN SERIES

*The Afterlives of Specimens: Science,
Mourning, and Whitman's Civil War*
by Lindsay Tuggle

*Conserving Walt Whitman's Fame:
Selections from Horace Traubel's
"Conservator," 1890–1919*
edited by Gary Schmidgall

Constructing the German Walt Whitman
by Walter Grünzweig

*Democratic Vistas: The Original
Edition in Facsimile*
by Walt Whitman, edited by Ed Folsom

*"The Disenthralled Hosts of Freedom":
Party Prophecy in the Antebellum
Editions of* Leaves of Grass
by David Grant

*Every Hour, Every Atom: A
Collection of Walt Whitman's Early
Notebooks and Fragments*
edited by Zachary Turpin
and Matt Miller

The Evolution of Walt Whitman
by Roger Asselineau

*Intimate with Walt: Selections
from Whitman's Conversations
with Horace Traubel, 1888–1892*
edited by Gary Schmidgall

*Leaves of Grass, 1860: The 150th
Anniversary Facsimile Edition*
by Walt Whitman, edited by Jason Stacy

*Life and Adventures of Jack Engle: An
Auto-Biography: A Story of New York at
the Present Time in Which the Reader
Will Find Some Familiar Characters*
by Walt Whitman, introduction
by Zachary Turpin

"The Million Dead, Too, Summ'd Up":
Walt Whitman's Civil War Writings
Introduction and commentary by Ed
Folsom and Christopher Merrill

A Place for Humility: Whitman,
Dickinson, and the Natural World
by Christine Gerhardt

The Pragmatic Whitman:
Reimagining American Democracy
by Stephen John Mack

Selected Letters of Walt Whitman
edited by Edwin Haviland Miller

Song of Myself: With a
Complete Commentary
by Walt Whitman, introduction
and commentary by Ed Folsom
and Christopher Merrill

Supplement to "Walt Whitman:
A Descriptive Bibliography"
by Joel Myerson

"This Mighty Convulsion": Whitman
and Melville Write the Civil War
edited by Christopher Sten
and Tyler Hoffman

Transatlantic Connections:
Whitman U.S., Whitman U.K.
by M. Wynn Thomas

Transnational Modernity and the Italian
Reinvention of Walt Whitman, 1870–1945
by Caterina Bernadini

Visiting Walt: Poems Inspired by the
Life and Work of Walt Whitman
edited by Sheila Coghill
and Thom Tammaro

Walt Whitman: The Centennial Essays
edited by Ed Folsom

Walt Whitman: The
Correspondence, Volume VII
edited by Ted Genoways

Walt Whitman and the Class Struggle
by Andrew Lawson

Walt Whitman and the Earth:
A Study in Ecopoetics
by M. Jimmie Killingsworth

Walt Whitman and the Making
of Jewish American Poetry
by Dara Barnat

Walt Whitman and the World
edited by Gay Wilson
Allen and Ed Folsom

Walt Whitman, Where the
Future Becomes Present
edited by David Haven Blake
and Michael Robertson

Walt Whitman's Reconstruction:
Poetry and Publishing between
Memory and History
by Martin T. Buinicki

Walt Whitman's Selected Journalism
edited by Douglas A. Noverr
and Jason Stacy

Walt Whitman's "Song of Myself":
A Mosaic of Interpretations
by Edwin Haviland Miller

Walt Whitman's Songs of Male
Intimacy and Love: "Live Oak,
with Moss" and "Calamus"
edited by Betsy Erkkila

Whitman & Dickinson: A Colloquy
edited by Éric Athenot and
Cristanne Miller

Whitman among the Bohemians
edited by Joanna Levin
and Edward Whitley

Whitman and the Irish
by Joann P. Krieg

A Whitman Chronology
by Joann P. Krieg

Whitman East and West: New
Contexts for Reading Walt Whitman
edited by Ed Folsom

Whitman Noir: Black America
and the Good Gray Poet
edited by Ivy G. Wilson

The Whitman Revolution:
Sex, Poetry, and Politics
by Betsy Erkkila

Whitman's Drift: Imagining
Literary Distribution
by Matt Cohen